COMMONS WITHOUT TRAGEDY

COMMONS WITHOUT TRAGEDY

Protecting the Environment from Overpopulation — a New Approach

Robert V. Andelson, editor

SHEPHEARD-WALWYN · LONDON
BARNES & NOBLE · SAVAGE · MARYLAND

© 1991 Centre for Incentive Taxation Ltd
177 Vauxhall Bridge Road
London SW1V 1EU

This edition first published 1991
in the United Kingdom by
Shepheard-Walwyn (Publishers) Ltd
26 Charing Cross Road (Suite 34)
London WC2H 0DH

First published in the United States by
Barnes & Noble Books
8705 Bollman Place
Savage, MD 20763

All rights reserved

British Library Cataloguing in Publication Data
Commons without tragedy: The social ecology of
land tenure and democracy.
I. Andelson, R. V.
363.9

ISBN 0-85683-126-3 (UK Edition)

Library of Congress Cataloging-in-Publication Data
Commons without tragedy/Robert V. Andelson, editor
    p.   cm.
ISBN 0-389-20958-9 (U.S.)
1. Environmental policy. I. Andelson. Robert V., 1931-
HC79.E5C612   1991
333.7--dc20

Typeset by Alacrity Phototypesetters
Banwell Castle, Weston-super-Mare
Printed and bound in Great Britain by
BPCC Wheatons Ltd, Exeter

Contents

Preface	vii
1 The Commons and Property Rights: towards a synthesis of demography and ecology ROY DOUGLAS	1
2 Commons Without Tragedy: the congruence of Garrett Hardin and Henry George ROBERT V. ANDELSON	27
3 The Crisis of Transition from the Commons: population explosions, their cause and cure FRED HARRISON	44
4 Post-Communal Land Ownership: poverty and political philosophy DAVID RICHARDS	83
5 Commons and Commonwealths: a new framework for the justification of territorial claims T. NICOLAUS TIDEMAN	109
6 The Remaining Commons: a challenge to equity, efficiency and ecological responsibility ALEXANDRA HARDIE	130
7 The Tragedy of the *Unmanaged* Commons: population and the disguises of Providence GARRETT HARDIN	162
About the Contributors	186
Index	188

TO MY WIFE, BONNY

So, clothed about with perfect love,
The eternal end shall find us one,
Alone above the Night ...
   (*Rupert Brooke*, 'The Call')

Preface

THIS BOOK may be viewed as an indirect outgrowth of the Benjamin Minge Duggar Lecture delivered by Garrett Hardin at Auburn University on the evening of April 17, 1986.* Upon hearing the lecture (which was devoted to a different, although related, theme), I became convinced that I owed it to myself to get better acquainted with Hardin's work, to which I had been hitherto exposed only through a cursory reading of a couple of anthologized extracts.

As a longtime student of the thought of Henry George and proponent of his central thesis, I took it upon myself to defend that thesis from what I understood to be an implicit attack in Hardin's famous essay, 'The Tragedy of the Commons,' which has been reprinted more than 80 times since it first appeared in *Science* in 1968. But as I examined the essay more carefully, especially in the context of Hardin's other writings, I discovered that its message had been misconstrued, not only by myself but by most commentators, and that, with respect to the tenure of land, the differences between Hardin and George are merely verbal whereas their commonalities and congruities are profound.

I developed this discovery into a paper for presentation at the International Henry George Sesquicentennial Conference held at the University of Pennsylvania in the Summer of 1989. Before the conference, I sent a copy of the paper to Professor Hardin to make sure that I had not misrepresented his position. His long and gracious reply did more than confirm my interpretation. It (and further letters from him) contained, I felt, a number of highly stimulating original ideas which, expanded, might form, together

---

* It is a source of deep regret to me that Dr William H. Mason, late associate dean of the College of Science and Mathematics, did not live to see this spin-off from his efforts in arranging for Hardin's visit. I believe that it would have given him pleasure.

with an amended version of my paper, the conceptual nucleus of a provocative and worthwhile volume. Such, I am persuaded, has turned out to be indeed the case.

In his initial letter to me, Hardin remarked: 'I have known ... of Henry George's work for a long time and always thought it a shame that he could not have been born two centuries earlier and laid out the ground rules for the development of the New World.'

The notion of a Georgist program (the heart of which would be a single tax on the rent of land exclusive of improvements) shaping the destiny of the New World, is a tantalizing idea, but it is not a *fantastic* one. Adam Smith identified the rent of land as a uniquely suitable source of public revenue as far back as 1776, and was anticipated in this a half-century earlier by Spinoza. And some of the colonists (most notably William Penn) employed a tax on the rent of land as the instrument with which to finance their communal needs; a policy that was, alas, allowed to lapse.

We can confidently sketch the broad outlines of what society would have been like in the 19th and 20th centuries had this approach been revived and fully implemented. For example, there would have been a more orderly pattern of settlement, rather than the mad scramble to fence off as much territory as a man could appropriate. The economic dislocations — called recessions — that followed the periodic bouts of land speculation, would probably not have occurred. Cities would have organically evolved in a much more compact form, eliminating the sprawl that was to characterize the modern American city. Urban architecture would certainly have assumed, toward the end of this period, a character less intimidating and impersonal and better expressive of human scale. And if we are to accept the postulates of economic theory, we can legitimately hypothesize that the lowest wages would have been higher than those that were to be paid to the factory workers once the western frontier was closed in the 1880s, giving rise to a prosperity that would probably have tempered, if not obviated, the need for the Welfare State in the 20th century.

It is thus evident that Hardin's 'if only/what if' proposition is a useful heuristic device for testing policy. For most peoples in history, such an exercise would be relegated to the realms of academic speculation: rarely do people have the opportunity to witness, let alone intentionally influence, major transformations of social and economic systems, ones that give their names to epochs. However, in the dying years of the second millennium the world has been catapulted into the post-Marxist era. Marxism provided an unsparing and widely-accepted critique of 'capitalism,' but it has now been buried by the weight of reality.

The time is now upon us, then, for Great Ideas to display their wares. These must be subjected to the correct tests by social scientists and by the standards of acceptability required by representative government. We are obliged to hope that people will rationally select appropriate models to meet the challenges of the future. This is a central purpose of our book. The authors confront a major contemporary problem — demographic pressure on the natural environment — to discover whether the theory associated with the name of the premier social philosopher to have been born in the United States, a theory that was attainable in practice but was (despite glimmerings by Jefferson and Franklin) to elude the Founding Fathers, might now be rescued to chart a course that may yet lead, with the dawning of the 21st century, to the effective opening of a broad, new 'commons' for the temperate, rational, and equitable use of humankind.

Finally, a word of thanks to Pat Aller, Julia Bastian and David Redfearn for their editorial assistance in preparing the manuscript.

R. V. A.
June, 1991

1
The Commons and Property Rights: towards a synthesis of demography and ecology

ROY DOUGLAS

FOR MANY YEARS, there has been a running argument about the interrelationship of economic growth, population size, and human living standards. In comparatively recent times, this debate has tended to concentrate on the widespread claim that the world is already — or will soon become — overpopulated. Is this claim correct, and, if so, what can be done to reduce the threat, and by whom?

On these questions, the several contributors to this book are by no means in agreement. Two main currents of opinion may be discerned; those who believe that the problem requires positive and direct intervention by the organs of government, which would necessarily involve some kind of restrictions on the right of citizens to make their own decisions about family size; and those who believe that such intervention is unnecessary, or that it would fail to produce the desired results. People in the second group either believe that the problem has been overstated, or that there are other methods of treatment which would be less objectionable and more effective. They are disposed to think that direct intervention would not only produce objectionable interferences with personal liberty, and doubtless many unforeseen side-effects, but it would also prove counter-productive for the declared object, since it would distract attention from the real cause of the trouble.

Despite this area of disagreement, there is one very important matter on which the contributors are in complete agreement. They all agree that any answer to the population problem must include, whatever else, some serious attention to the problem of what may conveniently be called 'the commons' — that is, those global resources which are not arrogated to particular individuals or states. At present the 'commons' include the open oceans; some of the great rivers; the air; 'space'; and a few patches of dry land, such as parts of Antarctica. Alex Hardie argues that the surviving 'commons' are divisible into what she calls 'Remnant Commons' and 'the Last Commons'. Some of the contributors consider that the 'commons' should be increased beyond their present extent; that natural and locational benefits should accrue to all, and that socially-produced benefits should accrue to the community which produced them. There is unanimity that some kind of guiding principles must be articulated as to what are, or should be, 'commons', and what sort of rights of access there should be to those 'commons'.

Malthus and George

The classic analysis from which the population debate derives is Thomas Malthus's *Essay on Population* (1798; extensively revised 1803), Malthus's argument is familiar enough. Human populations, like all natural populations, tend to increase in what used to be called 'geometrical progression' and is now usually called an exponential manner. To give data which were not available to Malthus, United Nations statistics (which will later be discussed more fully) show that the world population approximately doubled in the 36 years from 1950 and 1986, increasing from just over 2.5 thousand millions to a shade under 5 thousand millions. If human reproduction continues exponentially, then in the 36 years 1986-2022 it will grow to 10 thousand millions, by 2058 it will be 20 thousand millions, by 2094 it will be 40 thousand millions, and so on. The meaning and implications of exponential growth are discussed much more fully in Fred Harrison's article.

From what has been said already, however, it is plain that exponential growth cannot continue indefinitely. Supplies of food and other human requirements can only be increased to a finite extent. In the past, the tendency towards exponential growth has been restrained by such factors as starvation, disease, war and infanticide. Sometimes this restraint has taken the form of a sudden and dramatic reversal of population growth. To cite some familiar examples, failure of the Irish potato crop in the late 1840s caused something like half a million people out of a population of rather more than eight millions to die of starvation and of diseases related to starvation. The 'Black Death' of the 14th Century caused the population of Europe to drop enormously; to say that it killed a quarter of the population is probably an understatement. In the Second World War, something like a quarter of the population of Poland died more or less violent deaths.

Even in Malthus's time, technological improvements were allowing considerable population increases to take place with apparent impunity. The Malthusian argument, however, was that technological and other improvements can only prove of brief benefit to the great bulk of the human race, for they merely encourage further reproduction — or, perhaps, a higher survival-rate among children — and so any benefit is soon soaked up. Small 'aristocracies' may contrive to enjoy a high level of culture as a result of the improvements; but most people will continue to live at a level of base subsistence. The only hope for escaping this gloomy prospect which the 'Malthusians' offered was that people might decide voluntarily to limit their families, in order to counter the tendency for populations to increase.

How far Malthus later qualified the doctrine to which his name has been applied is a matter for scholarly dispute. It has been powerfully argued that two anonymous articles attributed to him, which appeared in the *Edinburgh Review* of 1808 and 1809, showed that he had by that date moved a very long way from 'Malthusian' doctrine, and argued that conditions, at any rate in Ireland, could be improved greatly by the application of proposals which sound very much like a tax on land values, of the kind later advocated by the American philosopher and economist, Henry George.

George enters this book as frequently as Malthus, and it is necessary to digress for a moment to explain who and what he was. Henry George (1839-97) was an American philospher-economist, whose *magnum opus*, *Progress and Poverty*, which has been repeatedly reprinted, attracted enormous attention in the United States, in

Britain, and in some other countries, in the late 19th and early 20th centuries. All of the writers in this book consider that George's work has high contemporary relevance. The essence of George's argument was that land is indispensable for all human activities, and that if some people own land to the exclusion of others, all kinds of distortions and injustices will arise which affect urban and rural communities alike. The most vital measure required to conquer poverty, George argued, is to get the land system right; and he had much to say about how that should be done.

To return to Malthus, many later authors sharply criticised the original 'Malthusian' doctrine. Their argument usually turned largely, on the contention that there were enormous quantities of land (which is merely the economists' word for 'natural resources') potentially available for human use, from which people who wished to develop that land were excluded by oppressive laws. If these laws were changed, and all that land became available, then there would be an immediate increase in living standards of the poorer people, and there would be no question of a 'Malthusian' problem arising for several generations. Whether that problem would eventually recur when populations had expanded into the newly-available land, was a question belonging to a future so remote that practical economists could safely ignore it. In the present book, however, Fred Harrison has dealt with the Malthusian argument in considerable detail in the light both of modern demography and the very cogent 19th century criticisms by Henry George.

In comparatively recent years, the original debate has largely lapsed. In the developed countries of the world, there is abundant evidence that living standards of all classes, but most particularly of the poorer people, have improved enormously, and it is today taken as almost axiomatic by most people living in those countries that their personal living standards will improve greatly during the course of their lifetimes. The same thing is happening in some of the less developed countries, and many people have assumed that it is only a matter of time before it happens everywhere.

This empirical evidence seemed to establish that the Malthusian view, at least in its original form, could be largely discounted. Perhaps there was a 'Malthusian' problem in some of the poorer countries of the world; but a combination of economic reform and the arrival of technological improvements from elsewhere would eventually cause that problem to disappear.

The Environment

Yet a new argument, not identical with the old 'Malthusian' analysis but related to it, has appeared in recent years and has secured wide acceptance. The number of human beings in the world has increased enormously in comparatively recent times. The estimated world population in 1913 was 1,810 millions.[2] By 1945 it had reached 2,326 millions, by 1980 it was 4,917 millions. Thus in the thirty-four years 1913-47 the population multiplied 1.28 fold; in the thirty-three years 1947-80 it multiplied 2.11 fold. These 'population problems' are discussed further in Fred Harrison's essay in the present book. There is every reason for thinking that the number of human beings will continue to increase rapidly for many years to come, whatever action governments, economists, religious teachers and other 'leaders' may take. It is now widely believed that these burgeoning populations will soon reach — and perhaps they have already reached — a level at which they impose an intolerable pressure on natural resources.

In all previous ages — so the argument runs — human numbers were such that the natural environment was able to provide for their needs, like food, shelter and energy, without serious damage. The fact that people frequently lacked those requirements was due to economic, political or moral defects which it lay in human power to rectify. Now there are serious signs that this self-regulating system is breaking down. Not only is the number of human mouths rapidly increasing, but the size of the 'cake' they wish to consume is being reduced, and perhaps its very existence is under threat.

At first, the main form which this argument took was the contention that man is destroying irreplaceable resources. Familiar examples are the rapidly-growing rate of extinction of animal species; the destruction of major environments like the Amazon forest; the depletion of finite resources of fossil fuels; the reduction of food resources through over-fishing. Much of this pressure has been exerted on land which in former times was considered 'marginal'. Some of the pressure on marginal land has been spontaneous, but much has been more or less directed by State authorities, or is at least the indirect result of State land policies. This raises an important question: how far have both demographic and ecological distortions been the product of such policies?

The view that man was trenching on irreplaceable resources was to some extent countered by an appeal to man's technological resourcefulness. If people find that fossil fuels are in short supply at known locations, they will discover new places, like the North Sea, where these materials can be extracted. If all the resources of fossil fuels become exhausted or seriously depleted, then people will turn to other sources of energy, like solar power, or geothermal power, or tidal power, or nuclear power. If people cannot extract enough fish from the sea, they will either turn to other foods or breed the fish they require in special conditions.

The extinction of species may be deplorable to the lover of nature, or to the enthusiast for biological science; but mankind can 'live with' these extinctions. Indeed, Nature herself prescribes extinction:

> ... From scarpèd cliff and quarried stone
> She cries, 'A thousand types have gone;
> I care for nothing, all shall go.'

wrote Tennyson.[3] What is new, or even regrettable, about the destruction of species? That view, at least in its crude form, is fortunately a good deal less popular now than it was a few decades ago, thanks largely to the wonderful television programmes which have brought home to many people the intricacy and beauty of wild life.

What is new, indeed, about the destruction of natural habitats like woodlands and forests? The Weald of south-east England was densely wooded not many centuries ago. Today there are still patches of woodland in the Weald; but is it wholly deplorable that there are now fewer woods in the area than was once the case? Nor is the destruction of woodlands a new phenomenon; it was certainly taking place in Europe in Neolithic times, and the human race has survived the process thus far. The ecologist's answer to that sort of argument is that the rate of destruction in recent times bears no comparison with what was happening in the past.

But man is not only trenching on the environment in order to satisfy his positive requirements. He is also producing great quantities of pollutants which impair the capacity of the wilderness to function as a self-regulating system. Chemicals deriving from industrial and agricultural processes are finding their way into the environment, and particularly into water and air, in ever-increasing quantities.

Some of these chemicals are demonstrably toxic. In a sense, these are the less dangerous effluents, for the damage they do is immediate and obvious, and people are able to make calculated decisions as to what — if anything — they propose to do about them. Sometimes people decide to pay the price of stopping the pollution. After a long series of sulphurous 'smogs', culminating in one incident in 1952 which killed several thousand Londoners, a decision was taken in Britain to ban the burning of coal from which the smog derived. On the other hand, smogs of a chemically different kind, which are produced by the burning of hydrocarbon fuels, and vex towns as far apart as Los Angeles, Tokyo and Athens, are apparently considered preferable to the alternative of greatly restricting the number of motor vehicles. Relatively minor improvements have been introduced to reduce the damage and inconvenience, but people evidently prefer cars with smog to the alternative of fewer cars and no smog.

Often, however, the damaging effects of pollutants are not established for a long time. CFCs (chlorofluorocarbons) are relatively non-toxic chemicals. They had been very widely used for many purposes, including propellants in aerosol sprays, and the freezing mechanism of refrigerators, before it was suspected that they were damaging the ozone layer. It has now been discovered that the overall effect of these chemicals has been to allow solar ultra-violet radiation to penetrate to the earth's surface in greater quantities than hitherto, and that this results in a high incidence of skin cancer, particularly among people with fair skins.

The trouble with this sort of effect is that it can only be demonstrated by the use of statistical techniques. Some people will develop skin cancer, and some will escape it, whether or not there is a 'hole in the ozone layer'. The concept of 'probability', familiar enough to the scientist or medical practitioner, is sometimes difficult to explain to people who have had no mathematical training.

To make matters even more difficult, the risk may be greatest in places geographically remote from the place where pollutants are produced. Most CFCs are produced in the northern hemisphere, while the main damage to the ozone layer deriving from those substances appears, thus far, to have occurred in the southern hemisphere. How does one explain to an Indian whose life expectancy is very low because of poverty, and whose dusky complexion largely protects him from the risk of skin cancer, that he should cease producing CFCs which at the moment appear to be doing the greatest damage in Australia? This is even more difficult when he strongly suspects that if his own country ceases the production, others will take it up.

In other cases, the extent of pollution damage remains uncertain to this day. There is still serious argument as to whether the production of carbon dioxide from industrial processes, vehicles and domestic heating is producing global warming through what is usually called the 'greenhouse effect'[4] — and, if so, how extensive that 'greenhouse effect' is likely to be. There have been many occasions in the past where the global climate has warmed up, or cooled down. There is substantial, but not conclusive, evidence that there is today a warming process in operation; but (if this is indeed happening), how does one prove that it is the result of human activities, and not one of those spontaneous developments which have occurred repeatedly in the history of the world, and particularly during the last million years or so?

If, indeed, global warming is taking place, then some of its adverse consequences are predictable, although the likely scale is unknown. It would certainly result in some melting of polar ice-caps, and consequential flooding of low-lying areas. What the 'practical man' wants to know, but nobody can tell him, is how much melting and consequential flooding can be expected in (say) twenty, or fifty, years.

At times, prediction of any kind is impossible in the present state of knowledge. The future climate of Britain is a simple example. At present the country is rather warmer than her latitude would suggest, because of the effect of the Gulf Stream which bathes her western shores with warm water from the south. Global warming might make the British climate warmer; but it could also result in changes in the Gulf Stream which would make the British climate cooler. It is also predictable that global warming would alter the incidence of rainfall; but it is by no means clear how particular places would be affected. Fertile land in some parts of the world would probably become desert; but in other places deserts might become fertile.

Even if it becomes possible to establish and quantify human responsibility for environmental damage — whether through the 'greenhouse effect', ozone destruction or other causes — beyond reasonable doubt, it is likely to take a long time before the necessary adjustments can be made. One aspect of the problem of CFC production control has already been considered. If that is the position with substances which are neither essential nor irreplaceable, and for which many substitutes exist, the resistance to any kind of serious interference with processes which produce carbon dioxide is bound to be very much greater.

All pointers suggest that such problems will multiply. More and more people are demanding more and more technology to satisfy their expectation of rising living standards. Some of that technology will produce damage to the environment: perhaps predictable damage, perhaps unpredictable damage. Some kinds of damage can be stopped, as the effect of London smogs was stopped when it was made illegal to burn coal in urban areas. Other kinds are probably irreversible. Even if people suddenly stopped destroying the Amazon forest, there are strong technical arguments for the view that it would be impossible for forest with its original flora and fauna to reclaim the land which has been lost. But it is proving exceedingly difficult even to protect the Amazon forest from further destruction.

As it is so difficult even to deal with problems like saving the Amazon forests from further destruction, or drastically reducing the emission of CFCs, where the forces resisting policy change would seem to be much weaker than those with an interest in continuing the damage, then how can a problem like global warming be tackled, even on the assumptions (a) that it is taking place at all, (b) that it is occurring on a serious scale, and (c) that it is largely or exclusively due to human activities? How can any government in a developed country which seeks to reduce the use of heating systems and cars expect to overcome the resistance of ordinary citizens who may or may not understand and accept the arguments, but who find it hard to visualise life without those particular conveniences?

There is little point in multiplying examples. Nor is the essential argument affected if some of the examples here considered, or some of the other examples which are widely discussed (like the effect of methane on global warming, or the risks from nuclear waste, or the adverse consequences of acid rain on the forests of Europe, or the various damaging effects of agrochemicals), should prove to be false alarms, based on a misunderstanding of facts, or even deliberate misrepresentation by people with axes to grind. All evidence shows that problems deriving both from direct human pressure on natural resources, and from the effect of human effluent of one kind or other on the environment, are becoming increasingly numerous, increasingly intractable, and increasingly harmful in their consequences both for man and for other forms of life. Human beings are certainly trenching deeply into what Alex Hardie in her article calls 'the last commons'.

'The Commons'

The gloomy empirical evidence that man is rapidly destroying the environment which is essential for his own well-being has been reinforced by philosophical argument, set out with great clarity by the American biologist Garrett Hardin in an important paper entitled *The Tragedy of the Commons*[5], and since developed and refined in other places, including this present book. As Hardin willingly admits, it is by no means a new argument, but was advanced with a similar example as far back as 1833.[6] Hardin's argument, in its original form, runs rather like this. Imagine a large common, on which many herdsmen have the right each to graze an unlimited number of cattle. For a long time this grazing does little or no harm to the pasture, for the numbers of herdsmen, or the numbers of cattle per herdsman, or both, are kept down by various agencies such as disease or war. Then, for some reason, these agencies of control are removed, or their effect is reduced. In a fairly short time, the cattle grazing on the common reach such numbers that any additions to those numbers seriously damage the pasture.

This poses the individual herdsman with a striking dilemma. He knows that by setting another beast to the pasture he will increase his personal wealth. He also knows that he will diminish the value of the pasture, as a result of which he, as well as the other herdsmen, will lose. However, the loss which he will make from the diminished value of the pasture will be much less than the gain he will make by grazing the extra beast. Even if he resists the temptation to increase his own wealth by such selfish behaviour, he knows that others will not show similar restraint, and the productivity of the pasture per beast will be reduced. He must therefore graze more beasts not merely in the hope of a better living, but in order to secure the same standards as he has enjoyed in the past. So every herdsman working the common will increase his herd as much as possible, even though every one of them realises that he will personally be worse off than if they had all refrained from grazing the extra cattle.

The Commons Today

Experience of the modern world emphasises the relevance of that thesis. Suppose, for the sake of argument, that the 'greenhouse' view is proved to be correct. Every factory owner, every car owner, stands to lose if the world becomes too hot as a consequence of the 'greenhouse effect'. Yet all of these people have an interest in generating their own little puffs of carbon dioxide which produce this effect. To move on to more certain ground, everyone who munches a hamburger produced from cattle which grazed on an area which was once Amazon forest stands to lose if the Amazon forest disappears; but each one calculates that his personal loss from not eating the hamburger will be greater than his personal loss from the disappearance of that tiny sliver of forest which was needed to make the hamburger. Everyone who squirts an aerosol spray containing CFC propellants is marginally more at risk of skin cancer in consequence; but he calculates that the risk will be so slight that it does not compare with the convenience of spraying paint on his car. An appeal to 'enlightened self-interest' will not stop the 'greenhouse effect', or save the Amazon forest, or preserve the ozone layer. If the various threatened natural assets are to be preserved at all, this can only be done by the 'herdsmen' getting together and somehow or other limiting their hitherto unlimited rights of 'pasture'. Hardin's 'common' is not only being overgrazed, it is being contaminated as well.

The increasingly acute character of the various problems which have been discussed derives partly from man's growing technological skill and partly from the rapidly-increasing number of human beings. It may or may not be true that — given time — the world could accommodate without mishap both the developing technology and a human population much greater than the present. Unfortunately, all evidence suggests that the necessary time will not be vouchsafed. Nobody can confidently predict what will 'give' to precipitate disaster. It could be some problem already identified. It is just as likely to be a problem of which people today are almost, or quite, unaware. It may even be something to do with the very nature of man himself, and this suggestion is raised by Robert Ornstein and Paul Ehrlich, *New World, New Mind*[7]. Will a creature whose essential physical and mental attributes are those of a late-Palaeolithic hunter/gatherer be able to go on coping with an environment which becomes rapidly more remote from the one in which he was evolved? The one thing that can be said with confidence is that if human numbers and human technology continue to develop at their present rate for more than a very few decades, some major calamity is inescapable.

So what is to be done? Do real herdsmen in the real world act in the way suggested in the original articles? Study suggests that they do not leave it to chance whether their commons will be overgrazed, but make very stringent rules which determine how many beasts each one may graze. Any one who has read — for example — English manorial records will be familiar with the disposition of commoners to insist that nobody should exceed the limits allocated to him, and their determination to punish anyone transgressing the rules. This fact may provide some important clues about possible ways in which one may treat both the technological question and the population question.

For the technological question, it is possible to state certain general principles which need to be applied, even though the practical application of those principles will prove exceedingly difficult. Few people would dispute that the organs of government have the right to control emissions into the environment, or to protect endangered species, or to establish nature reserves, although there is sometimes a good deal of argument about priorities, and about the best ways of producing the effects desired. The problems are so acute that most people would probably be willing to accept considerable infringements to their personal liberty if these were required in order to solve them. To that point it will be necessary to return later; but it may also be necessary to curtail the authority of the nation-state itself.

The Nation-State

Many people consider that the nation-state possesses a kind of moral authority which, in the last analysis, overrides all other matters. All governments, even 'libertarian' governments, have a disposition to encourage that point of view, although it is difficult to see on what moral principle it is based. Nicolaus Tideman's chapter in the present book provides a striking example where even Henry George advances what (on one view at least) looks rather like special pleading for the 'right' of fellow-Californians to monopolise territory which they had fairly recently filched from others.

Yet it would be difficult to discover any fundamental principle which would carry conviction today on which this view of the absolute authority of the state is based. The Amazon forest is not exclusively the concern of Brazil, for its destruction will represent a great loss to the whole of mankind, and perhaps produce secular climatic changes throughout the world. It is difficult to see why Britain has any more moral title to burn minerals whose products fall as acid rain and wreck the woodlands of other countries than a private individual has to make a bonfire of rubber tyres which injures the comfort and health of his neighbor. If it is proved that CFCs, or 'greenhouse gases', produce adverse effects on a large part of the world, then ways must be found of persuading — or, in the last analysis, of compelling — recalcitrant states to conform to the general interest of the world.

The risks inherent in the idea of a nation-state's monopoly over its own resources have recently been brought out with great clarity. The ultimate origin of the Gulf War of 1991 may be summed up rather like this. Kuwait was for centuries a patch of more or less desert of little importance to anybody except its few inhabitants. Then oil was discovered. The country's rulers became fabulously rich from oil revenues, and they had the good political sense to see that the ordinary people of Kuwait attained standards of affluence well ahead of most western countries. The Iraqi government, however, was jealous of this great wealth and seized it. The American government, with some assistance from others, sought to reverse that action, first by the brief (some might say perfunctory) use of sanctions, and then by war. The whole problem derives, in the last analysis, from the very dubious assumption that some nation-state, be it Kuwait or Iraq, has the moral title to wealth which it did not create.

Tideman brings the reader to consider closely some of the principles which underlie, or should underlie, the assumed 'rights' of governments or nations. His suggestions about Lockean notions whose application might 'solve' problems like those of Northern Ireland or the Middle East may strike the reader as naïve and difficult to apply, but the essential Tideman argument that it is vital to get back to fundamental philosophical principles is impressive. How far particular devices will work in particular cases in order to persuade governments to abandon their fatuous claims to absolute sovereignty over particular pieces of the earth, and whether these devices will produce harmful side-effects, are important questions of practical politics, but do not touch the inherent morality of the problem.

Morally, the natural resources of the world belong equally to all human beings, wherever they live. Some people would go even further, and add that they are not exclusively the right of human beings; that, in a sense, man is the trustee for all living things. The logic of all this is that there is an urgent need for everybody to start working out a system not of national but of world ownership of land resources. The surviving 'commons' are a good place to start, for — by definition — they are places in which nobody has an established interest; but eventually it will be necessary to internationalise all land everywhere.

Alex Hardie considers the problem from a different angle. She discusses the way in which law relating to 'commons' evolved in actual societies, and goes on to examine at considerable depth the principles which apply, and which should apply, to relevant aspects of international law. Unfortunately, the 'commons', so far from being extended, are being rapidly 'enclosed'. In comparatively recent years, the concept of 'territorial waters' has changed radically. The old three-mile limit was developed essentially to secure adequate naval defence of a coastline. Today many countries assert much wider limits, essentially in order to claim minerals which lie under the Continental Shelf, and particularly hydrocarbons. There are now signs that territorial claims over oceans are being pushed much further, in order to grant monopolies for the exploitation of mineral nodules on the floor of the abyss[8].

Population: the Problem

The 'technological' question is difficult enough, and compels people to accept some very unwelcome conclusions. The 'population' question, however, is more difficult still. An argument frequently heard today runs rather like this. People have a tendency to multiply to a point where either their demands on the environment, or their effusions into the environment, produce major damage. In the past, that tendency was held back by disease, war and so on. Now people know much more about the prevention and cure of disease, while the risks associated with major war are so enormous that people are less and less inclined to accept the tolerant view of von Clausewitz that it is merely 'political action with the admixture of other means'.[9] Thus these agencies of control are ceasing to apply. The world is approaching a point where there will be so many people that the 'common' on which they rely will be gravely depleted, even though they limit the numbers of technological 'cattle' they choose to graze. If this state of affairs is to be averted, the argument seems to run, then draconian measures will be required to limit human fecundity.

In the present book, Robert V. Andelson seems to accept that view without reserve, and pushes its conclusions to their limit. Andelson is an academic philosopher, who has long been a staunch advocate of freedom in almost every sense of the word, and has been a particularly eager supporter of the libertarian economics and social philosophy of Henry George. However, as early as 1971 he took public issue with the notion that state interference with human procreation is in all cases the violation of a right.[10] Although he has never accepted the view that overpopulation is the fundamental cause of poverty, ecological concerns have led him to regard it, nonetheless, as a compelling problem of the utmost gravity. His position in this respect has been partly shaped by Hardin, and in some ways he out-Hardins Hardin. He goes so far as to declare mandatory population control to be 'the only long-run safeguard against possible environmental doom', declaring that it 'presents a threat only to sentimental and conventional notions of rights and freedom'. Strong words indeed for a libertarian!

Andelson's assertion poses several questions, of which two come immediately to mind. First, has it been established that there are no other 'long-run certainties against environmental doom'? Second, even if that should be the case, has it been established that mandatory population control would provide that certainty? Although there is considerable argument for the view that we are advancing towards 'doom', yet it does not seem to have been proved, by Andelson or anybody else, that mandatory population control on the scale required is even possible, still less that it will provide certain escape from 'doom'.

It is necessary to look closely at the population problem from several different aspects. Those advocating population control sometimes seem to assume that human beings, left to their own devices, will produce about as many progeny as is biologically possible. In some societies, this is doubtless true. In those societies, 'May you have many sons!' is a blessing, for many sons mean many hands to till the family fields, and many children to care for the parents in their old age. People in early-Victorian Britain, echoing the Psalms, spoke of a large family as a 'quiverful' for similar reasons. Children could be put to work at an early age, and an extra pair of hands would soon bring in more money than an extra mouth consumed. But is it correct to assume that this philoprogenitive enthusiasm still operates generally in human societies?

As far as non-human species are concerned, Hardin's statement that 'in the absence of "environmental resistance", exponential reproduction is the innate result of all healthy living' is broadly correct. Mankind, however, differs from all other living organisms in two important respects. Human beings are the only creatures which understand the relationship between sexual activity and reproduction; while people living in the more developed societies are able to pursue sexual activity without reproduction supervening.

The Commons and Property Rights 17

It is instructive to compare the rate of population increase in different parts of the world at different times. Again the thirty-four years 1913-47 and the thirty-three years 1947-80 are useful for the comparison.[11] In the first period, the rate of increase in most of the continents fell within the fairly narrow range of 16% (Europe) to 40% (Africa). The only exceptions were Oceania (57%) and North America (89%), both of which were relatively empty places into which large-scale immigration was taking place. The world-wide mean of 28% growth over thirty-four years was perhaps worrying for people who extrapolated those figures into the remote future, but it was not generally considered alarming; indeed, European countries tended to be more concerned about future population declines than about population increases.

The pattern in 1947-80 has been radically different, and it is clear that the relatively peaceful character of the period by comparison with the earlier one is not the principal explanation. Only in North America (22% increase) and Europe (30% increase) has the rate of population growth kept within the 'normal' 1913-47 range. Oceania has experienced 2.08-fold growth, which may be explained largely by immigration. Elsewhere, the growth has been attributable overwhelmingly to multiplication of the indigenous population, which has ranged from Asia, which has the same growth as Oceania though for very different reasons, through the 2.55-fold increase in Africa to a staggering 3.50-fold in Latin America. If the world rate of population growth had been the same in the second period as in the first, then the 1980 world population would have been a shade under 3,000 millions instead of almost 5,000 millions.

More recent figures bring out the problem even more sharply, but they also point to a possible solution. In Europe (including the USSR), and in countries like the United States, population growth is being kept within bounds. In no European country, with the trivial exceptions of Andorra and Albania, has the annual population growth for 1980-86 reached the 1.2% level of China, and in most of those countries, it was far below that figure. In a number of countries, including the United Kingdom and both sides of Germany, there has actually been a marginal decline in population. Of course, any population increase of any size at all may be a matter of concern; but the experience of Europeans and North Americans bears little comparison with several African countries, where the annual growth rate is over 3%, and in some cases over 4%.

Nor do the strictures of the Catholic Church against contraception appear to have had a great effect on population growth. The overwhelmingly Catholic Republic of Ireland, where the views of the Church about contraception are reinforced by legislation, has had astonishingly stable numbers over a long period; 2,972 thousands in 1926; 2,961 thousands in 1951; 2,978 thousands in 1971. Perhaps the Irish tradition of emigration explains this stability to a certain extent; but no similar argument can explain the slight decline in population of mainly Catholic Hungary in 1980-86. Either Catholics in those countries ignore what their priests tell them, or they find acceptable ways of controlling natural fecundity.

The fundamental difference between what might be called the 'Atlantic' countries on one hand and the poor nations of the world on the other is the circumstances in which babies are brought into existence. On the whole, people in the Atlantic countries have children because they want the company of children, and not because the children follow as an unintended consequence of sexual activity, or because they are sought as an economic benefit for their parents. There is also a high degree of sexual equality in Atlantic countries. Women are not the passive instruments of the sexual desires, or calculations of economic interest, which come from men. Women are able, if they wish, to use contraceptive techniques of their own, without permission from, or even the knowledge of, their male partners.

None of these conditions applies in those countries where population growth is alarmingly high. Fred Harrison provides some striking illustrations of how this operates, and of its close connection with primary poverty and the land problem. Mechanical and chemical contraception are much too expensive for most people in such countries, and are sometimes unobtainable — although Alex Hardie suggests that this difficulty may occasionally be circumvented. In conditions where life is short and precarious, sexual abstinence is highly unlikely. The women are much more likely to adopt a purely passive rôle than in the Atlantic countries. Furthermore, there is often still a powerful economic interest in having a large family. It is also important to remember that there are cultural as well as economic aspects to family size — a matter discussed in considerable detail by Fred Harrison.

In the 'advanced' countries, when living standards began to rise, the first result was a substantial population increase, because of the dramatic reduction in infant and child mortality. In the next phase, 'Atlantic values' were adopted, and the population increased much less rapidly.

At first sight, this argument seems to carry the comforting implication that the poor countries will follow the same pattern, and everything will somehow come out right in the end. Unfortunately, this conclusion is by no means certain. Hardin discusses what is known as the 'demographic transition' — that is, the change within a society from high fertility and high death-rate to low fertility and low death-rate. This certainly operated in European countries in the 19th and 20th centuries; but Hardin asks whether it is operating in the poorer countries today, and his answers are not very comforting.

For one thing, the population growth in some, at any rate, of the poor countries seems mainly attributable, not to a rise in general living standards, but to improved medical knowledge, and living standards may even have declined in certain cases. One, perhaps ambiguous, quotation in Hardin's essay suggests that in Central Africa there has been a further complication, and fertility has risen at the same time. Even if these arguments can be overcome, and the view is accepted that — given time — everything should right itself, it is by no means certain that enough time will be given; and one is reminded of Maynard Keynes's aphorism that, 'in the long run we are all dead'. Thus there is serious doubt whether the 'demographic transition' will occur at all, and even more doubt whether it will occur in time to avert 'doom'.

Hardin raises another worrying consideration. Is there a kind of inverted eugenics in operation? Are there modern societies tending to breed selectively from individuals whom, by all ordinary tests, one would regard as 'unfit'? There is a common argument in Atlantic countries that 'welfare' provisions encourage irresponsible procreation. 'Responsible' people produce no more children than they can reasonably expect to care for from their own resources of money, time and love. 'Irresponsible' people become pregnant, or make others pregnant, to produce casual sexual gratification, without thinking much about such matters, or else anticipating that the state (i.e. the taxpayer) will provide at least the financial requirements. 'Irresponsibility' may be the result of unfortunate experiences in early life; but in some cases it may be linked to heritable, or partly heritable, characteristics like low intelligence.

Population Control

These points suggest to Hardin and Andelson that some kind of mandatory population control may be the answer. Leaving aside the fundamental question whether mandatory population control is desirable, it is worth asking whether the available evidence suggests that it would be effective.

In the past, governments have frequently attempted to control population numbers. In most cases, what they have sought was an *increase* in population, usually for reasons of a political character associated with notions of national aggrandisement. In very recent times, the disposition of governments has more commonly been to encourage, or to enforce, stability or reduction in population. But has it worked?

In the 1980s, the two most famous, and perhaps the most extreme, cases of countries which sought to restrict population growth were India and China. Yet in the period 1980-86, the latest figures available at the time of writing, the annual population growth of those two countries was 2.1% and 1.2% respectively. These figures, from countries which have positively discouraged reproduction, may be contrasted with the annual population growth rate of only 0.7% in Ceausescu's Romania — the most blatant example of a country which at that date still positively encouraged population growth, and which also interfered seriously with the liberty of the subject in order to enforce the government's population policy. Such figures are in no way conclusive, and may perhaps be interpreted in different ways, but they do not suggest that state policies in either direction produce much effect. Certainly they imply that state policies offer no prospect whatever of saving mankind from 'doom'.

We are therefore let out of the extremely difficult problem of considering the morality of mandatory population controls, and a range of almost equally difficult problems about how to apply them.

Who should decide to enforce the controls, and on what criteria? Should the controls be legal constraints, such as punishing people who violate the rules or rewarding people who follow them? Or should the controls be physical, like compulsory vasectomy in males and a corresponding operation on the Fallopian tubes in females? Should the controls be universal, or should they be selective — permitting people with certain characteristics to have more children than others? Must the program be organised on a world-wide scale — and, if so, what happens if some national governments are unable, or unwilling, to cooperate? These problems are so difficult, and so fraught with religious, moral, emotional and political overtones, that it is difficult to escape a certain sense of relief that they are unlikely to arise.

There are, however, other ways of controlling populations besides compelling reluctant citizens to act against their wishes. At present, the countries with enormous 'natural' population growth rates (i.e. not growth rates attributable to immigration), are nearly all very poor. Those countries seek economic and other kinds of aid from the richer countries. It does not seem unreasonable for the richer countries to make it a *sine qua non* for such aid that the recipients should permit, and positively encourage, contraception. The aim of the policy would not be to compel any couple objecting to contraception to cast aside their religious or moral scruples, but rather to give everyone the option of using it if they wish. At the same time, welfare schemes may be devised and subsidised for those countries in order to remove any remaining financial incentive for large families.

Brazil

Turning to another aspect of the 'overpopulation' argument, which is worrying many people today, the environmental damage which human populations are producing is the result not only of a lot of people existing in certain countries, but also of their exact location within those countries. A very important example is referred to by Andelson in his present essay, and discussed by him more fully elsewhere.[12]

Striking evidence exists to show that encroachments on the

Amazon forest are not the necessary consequence of Brazil's growing population, but are

> 'directly attributable to the fact that the Amazon basin is the only part of Brazil where free or cheap land is available, and this, in turn, is attributable to the fact that nearly four-fifths of Brazil's arable acreage is covered by sprawling *latifundos*, half of which are held by speculators who produce nothing. Were the artificial scarcity of available land in the rest of Brazil corrected, as the Georgist remedy would unquestionably do, pressure on the Amazon basin would obviously cease'.

If this statement is true — and there seems every reason for thinking that in essentials it is true — then it becomes a matter of high importance and urgency that other countries should apply every possible pressure on Brazil to enforce land reform.

One must not be naïve about the meaning of the word 'Brazil' in this context. To say that 'Brazil' should be subjected to pressure is not to say that ordinary Brazilians should be pressurised. It is rather to say that the national government which functions in the interest of the tiny minority which controls the *latifundos* should be coerced into giving the vast majority of Brazilians freedom of access to land.

If this principle applies in the particularly famous example of the Amazon forest, it seems very likely that close investigation would show similar conditions applying to others of the world's commons which are currently threatened with destruction, and that similar remedies might be applied. This point is emphasised by David Richards.

So perhaps the reader is being impelled towards a view taking something from both the environmentalists and the libertarians. The environmentalists are right in pointing out the global damage which is being wrought, and the urgent need for drastic action to avert 'doom'. The libertarians, however, are right in suggesting that the best hope of doing so lies in adding to the sum of human freedom, not in detracting from it. There is little reason for thinking that measures like mandatory population control are possible in sophisticated societies, still less that they would produce much overall effect on population even if they could be applied. What does seem to offer some prospect of helping the situation, however, is allowing people to do what their governments are currently stopping them from doing. *Let* people have knowledge of contraception, and *let* them obtain contraceptives. Much more important, *let* people have access to land like the Brazilian *latifundios,* from which at present they are held back. The present author's guess is that not many Brazilians would choose to hack down Amazon forest if they had free access to decent farmland. By all means impose whatever restrictions may seem necessary to preserve land which has ecological importance, but allow people to use the remainder, whether this suits the profits of land speculators or not.

History and Economics

Other contributors to this book cast important light on different aspects of the problem. David Richards is impressed by the idea that, in the historical development of many countries, the ancient notion of land as something *publici juris* gave way to the notion of land as something freely alienable by its occupant. Thus the occupant became an owner, and land came to be treated essentially like chattels. From this change of view about the nature of land sprang an enormous amount of subsequent misery.

From the economic side of Richards's analysis, it emerges that various attempts by governments and supernational authorities to dish out favors to apparently deserving causes, without getting down to the basic question of why everything is screwed up, are all foredoomed to costly failure. Government interference with the life of the citizen is frequently counter-productive, and has even more frequently generated unintended side-effects which are as bad as the original disease. Any attempt to deal with the present plundering of the world's 'commons' without understanding the conditions precedent which made it possible for people to plunder them, is likely to prove unavailing.

This is an exceedingly important message, and it is one which is very widely ignored today, not least by people with impeccable academic credentials. It is very tempting to take some particular phenomenon in isolation, and bend every effort towards dealing with that phenomenon, without understanding the wider context into which it fits. In the comparatively recent past, very disparate kinds of social and economic phenomena have been selected for special treatment; unemployment, inflation, communism, 'urban sprawl', militarism in particular countries ... the list is endless. These attempts to give special treatment without considering the wider context have, without exception, either failed to achieve the object desired, or else have generated other and unforeseen dislocations elsewhere. There is not the slightest reason for believing that an attempt to deal with the 'population problem' or the 'environmental problem' in isolation will prove one whit more successful.

The Land Problem

Both of these problems are related at their roots to the land problem. The expression 'land problem' is here used in its widest possible sense, to mean the whole question who should be allowed to use any kind of natural resources anywhere, and on what terms. Whether certain habitats should be protected from human activity is an aspect of the land problem. Whether sanctions should be applied to prevent people hunting endangered species to extinction is an aspect of the land problem. Whether limits should be set on emissions of carbon dioxide into the atmosphere, or the production of chemicals which endanger the environment, is an aspect of the land problem. The answers which people give to such questions are likely to depend on the views they hold about the nature of land. If they see land as something over which a particular landowner has absolute moral rights they will give one kind of answer; if they see land as something which belongs morally to the whole of mankind, they will give a different kind of answer.

The population problem is also related to the land problem, although the association is more indirect. The connecting link for the purposes of the present study is poverty. Few, if any, relatively rich societies are today increasing at a rate which poses a serious global threat for the foreseeable future. Their technology may be a threat to the earth; their population increase is not. By contrast, the very poor societies are mostly increasing at a rate which does pose a global threat. It is difficult to escape the conclusion that rapid increases in population in modern societies are promoted by poverty, and frequently generate further poverty as a result.

The root of poverty, most particularly in those societies whose population is increasing so rapidly, is land — or rather landlessness.

The *latifundos* which are the primary cause of the poverty of so many Brazilians, are not unique. In most, if not all, of those countries where poverty and population growth are most acute, essentially similar conditions obtain. The great bulk of the population is excluded from access to land: not because that land is of ecological or aesthetic importance, but because it suits the landowner that other people should be so excluded.

Thus the problems of environmental damage and overpopulation alike are seen to be aspects of the land problem. All authors in this book agree that it is essential to articulate a 'theory of the commons' which would form a guide to part, at least, of any solution to the population problem. It is surely significant that Hardin, who played a major part in originating the modern debate, wrote originally about the 'Tragedy of the Commons', but in the present book prefers to discuss 'The Tragedy of the *Unmanaged* Commons'.

The present work is not designed to develop to the full the question how the 'commons' should be managed, but to lay down certain guiding principles which may help towards such a solution. Because no human being has made land, no person and no nation has a better title to land than any other; but those who have made improvements to land have a right to the value of the improvements which they have made. The community may justly impose whatever restrictions seem fit as to the use of land; and it is a matter of the highest urgency that it should consider what restrictions are now necessary for saving irreplaceable species, habitats and other resources, and for preserving the earth from further irreparable damage. As several authors acknowledge, the 'community' which does this must be something much more than the nation-state. All authors recognise an essential difference not of degree but of kind between the 'commons' which no human being has made, and to which no human being has a better title than any other, and those products of human effort which belong by right to the person who exerted that effort. Land reform based on such principles does not provide a guarantee of escape from 'doom', but it is an essential precondition for escape.

NOTES

1. M. A. MacDowell, 'Malthus and George on the Irish Question', *American Journal of Economics and Sociology*, vol. 36, no. 4 (Oct 1977), pp. 401-416.
2. These and other population figures in this essay are based on statistics in the League of Nations Statistical Year Book 1926, and the United Nations Statistical Year Books, especially 1948 and 1985-86.
3. *In Memoriam*, canto LVI.
4. For an interesting presentation of the 'alternative view' that the 'greenhouse effect' is, at best, unproved, see program transcript, *The Greenhouse Conspiracy*, London &c: Channel 4 Television, 1990.
5. Garrett Hardin, 'The Tragedy of the Commons', *Science*, vol. 162 (1968), pp. 1243-1248.
6. William Forster Lloyd, *Two lectures on the checks to population*, 1833; New York: Augustus M. Kelley, 1968.
7. Robert Ornstein and Paul Ehrlich, *New World, New Mind*, London: Methuen, 1989.
8. See, for example, *Financial Times*, 24.x.1985, 25.iv.1986; *Observer*, 8.i.1989, etc.
9. '... politischen Verkehrs mit Einmischung anderer Mittel.' Karl von Clausewitz, *Vom Kriege*, 1952 edn., p. 888, cited in *The Concise Oxford Dictionary of Quotations* (1964, second edn., Oxford &c, 1990).
10. R. V. Andelson, *Imputed Rights: An Essay in Christian Social Theory*, Athens, Ga.; University of Georgia Press, 1971, pp. 112-113.
11. See also Note 2. To make figures easily comparable, 'Europe' includes the Russian Empire/Soviet Union, and 'North America' excludes Mexico and places south thereof, which are included in 'Latin America'.
12. R. V. Andelson, *Commons Without Tragedy* p. 32, and the article there cited, 'Brazil's land reform is caught in a violent cross-fire', *Christian Science Monitor*, 7.v.1987, p. 11. See also his forthcoming book (with J. M. Dawsey), *From Wasteland to Promised Land: Liberation Theology for a Post-Marxist World*, London and Maryknoll, N.Y.: Shepheard-Walwyn and Orbis, in press, chapter 8.

2
Commons Without Tragedy: the congruence of Garrett Hardin and Henry George

ROBERT V. ANDELSON

As PROFESSOR James R. Busey pithily observes: 'What may be true in economic thought may not necessarily be true when turned into unthinking dogma about other spheres of human life.'[1] In Book II of *Progress and Poverty,* Henry George irrefutably demonstrated that widespread, chronic want is the result of social maladjustment, not of any inherent tendency of population increase to outstrip the ability of Nature to sustain it. He argued that, by permitting greater specialization, population growth actually enhances each individual's potential to produce wealth.

In his day, as in our own, some of the most sparsely populated nations were among the poorest, whereas some of the most densely populated had the highest standards of living. Moreover, the presence or absence of natural resources seems to have far less bearing upon living standards than do the institutional structures of a society. Bolivia, with only 16 persons per square mile and an abundance of valuable mineral deposits, has the second lowest per capita income in South America. (Guyana, which is even more sparsely populated, has the lowest.) Japan, with 844 persons per square mile and scarcely any natural resources worth mentioning, and Singapore with 11,910 (!) persons per square mile and even fewer natural resources, have among the highest per capita incomes in Asia — exceeded only by Nauru and Brunei. When George wrote *Progress and Poverty,* world population stood at 1.5 billion; today it is more than 5 billion; we are told that in 32 years it will reach 8 billion. In Busey's words:

> Could there be a limit beyond which democratic or stable government would be impossible? Or some point where either the destruction of the protective ozone shield or a stifling greenhouse effect due to pollutants might be the results of density of population? Or a time when there are so many billions of people that no amount of resources or acceptable energy sources could supply their needs? Or a point of density so great that it would induce the psychological breakdown of a large part of humanity?[2]

George identified land monopoly as the fundamental social maladjustment responsible for poverty, discounting (rightly, for his time) the spectre of overpopulation. But impoverishment need not be narrowly economic in the sense of insufficient food, clothing, shelter, or access to medical care and educational advantages. To be bereft of the chance to breathe clean air, or drink pure water, or eat food that is not adulterated or contaminated, is also to be impoverished. To be crowded on all sides by human masses in a setting of asphalt and concrete, brick and glass, relieved only by occasional plastic, is also to be impoverished. Never to see unspoiled forests or animals in the wild; never to wade in a stream free of sewage, or to swim in a lake not choked with trash, is also to be impoverished. No doubt, with proper land arrangements and the application of advanced technology, the earth could support, after a fashion, a vastly greater population well into the distant future. But when account is taken of the quality of life, and of the environmental degradation that significant increase in population would inevitably entail, the issue assumes a far more ominous perspective.

The fact is that land monopoly engenders artificial overpopulation, whereas overpopulation exacerbates the ills of land monopoly. The population problem and the land problem are *both* serious and real; neither should be used as an excuse to avoid recognition of the other.

In Henry George's day, Malthusianism was the great red herring that diverted attention from the most fundamental cause of poverty. The fallacious mathematical methodology of Malthus' *Essay On Population* was utterly demolished by George in *Progress and Poverty,* but he was "beating a dead horse," as it had been abandoned by Malthus himself, as well as rejected by John Stuart Mill and other proto-Neo-Malthusians. George's treatment of their more sophisticated position, while generally convincing, is marred by overstatement, and amounts to denying the population problem altogether, except insofar as it might obtain in such special isolated instances as Pitcairn Island. In the course of this treatment, he permitted himself deliverances that are truly awesome in their extravagance, most notably the assertion that 'the earth could maintain a thousand billions of people as easily as a thousand millions.'[3]

For this he may be forgiven in view of the obscurantist and callous fatalism that Malthusianism characteristically engendered. Yet Malthus himself was neither obscurantist nor callous, but a conscientious truth-seeker and a humane reformer. It may come as a surprise to many, and was, I'm sure, not known to George, but Malthus had, in fact, proposed a single tax on land values as a remedy for Irish poverty.[4] Nor was Mill in any sense a complacent defender of the *status quo*. His recommendation that future land-value increments be socialized may have seemed to George a half-way measure, and does not go as far as I myself would wish, but it surely pointed in the right direction. I do not claim to be conversant with all or even most of the current literature on overpopulation, but of the major figures who have called attention to this evil in our time, I am not aware of a single one who sees it as a comprehensive and sufficient explanation for involuntary poverty, or who seeks to use it as a rationalization for neglecting efforts toward a better distribution of natural opportunity.

At any rate, if the Georgist perspective is to have any credibility among environmentalists, it will need to incorporate a recognition that the planet's 'carrying capacity' is finite, and that, however much that capacity may be extended by technological progress or by the freeing-up of natural opportunity, its limits, in terms of the integrity of both global and regional ecosystems, may be a great deal closer than adherents to that perspective have typically assumed. The Georgist outlook has always been sensitive to duty to future generations, as evidenced in its emphasis upon the conservation of non-renewable resources. That sensitivity must now be focused also upon the need to keep those generations from swamping the environment.

I shall probably be accused of being alarmist. While I realize that the scientific community is not unanimous as to the precise magnitude or imminence of the ecological ills portended by exploding population, there is broad consensus that at the very least the prospect of such ills is not to be dismissed as nugatory. To do nothing in the hope of some technological miracle would be to court disaster. Mandatory population control, the only long-run safeguard against possible environmental doom, presents a threat only to sentimental and conventional notions of rights and freedoms. The movement to abolish slavery was once considered an assault on vested rights; and efforts to collect for society a greater share of the site-values it creates, are today considered, in all too many quarters, an assault on individual freedom. Self-interest and prejudice must not be permitted to place at risk the condition and perhaps even the very survival of the essential joint-heritage of the human race.

Implicit in this is a necessary repudiation of the assumption that indiscriminate breeding is an absolute right regardless of the burdens that it imposes by default upon society. This statement may seem odd coming from someone who considers himself a libertarian, but libertarianism is not libertinism, and rights that trench upon the rights of others are no rights at all. There is, indeed, a lengthy paragraph, too often ignored, in the fifth chapter of Mill's *On Liberty,* in which he argues forcefully that the biological ability to procreate does not confer on its possessors the right to saddle society with the support of children for whom they are unable or unwilling to make decent provision.* Contemporary Georgism must face this proposition squarely, while continuing to affirm that society does not have the right to maintain institutional arrangements which render it impossible for competent and industrious people to make decent provision for children.

I don't want to oversimplify the ecological issue. If we were to get a handle on population growth, and if access to natural opportunity were open on fair terms to all, there would still be much to be done in

---

*'Americans paid nearly $20 billion in 1988 in public funding to support families begun with a birth to a teenager, says the Center for Population Options in Washington, D.C. Its recent study notes that the average child born to a teen mother in 1988 will wind up costing taxpayers nearly $16,500 by the year 2008, when the child reaches 20. For families receiving public assistance after a teen birth, the cost to taxpayers over 20 years will exceed $49,000 for each family.' *Birmingham News* (Alabama), Nov. 5, 1989, p. 8E.

the way of stemming ruinous habits of consumption that deplete resources, foul the atmosphere, and create mountains of unrecyclable and sometimes toxic waste. But perhaps I am not being altogether fatuous if I dare to entertain the hope that with fewer (and conceivably more responsible) people, and with prosperity more equitably distributed, public demand might turn away from machine-made mass commodities and built-in obsolescence, in favor of craftsmanship and durability; away from chemically grown and processed junk foods raised and marketed by giant agribusinesses, in favor of wholesome organic foods cultivated with care and pride on much less acreage by those who truly love the earth and nurture it.

What I am trying to convey is that while a solution to the land question such as George proposed may indeed be the most decisive step that could be taken toward the diminution if not the total extirpation of involuntary poverty, nevertheless, although it might hugely ameliorate and considerably postpone damage to the environment, in the last analysis salvation of the environment will require control of population. In the words of John Baden: 'With any positive rate of growth, whether it is only 1 percent a year or even .1 percent a year, a population approaches infinity in a relatively short period of time ... Even a 1 percent growth rate will double a population in a mere human lifetime ... An ever increasing population is clearly inconsistent with the maintenance or improvement of the natural environment.'[5] For most of the world's history, growth rates were kept in balance by Malthusian checks (together with abortion and infanticide), but modern medicine has drastically reduced mortality, especially among infants, while well-meaning aid programs have made famines more likely to result in stunted halflives than in outright deaths.

Genuine solutions to both problems, involving as they do the implementation of reciprocity in freedom (freedom to use nature without doing so at the expense of others, and freedom to procreate without placing unsolicited burdens upon others), fall legitimately within the purview of enforcement by government. As George emphasized, the enforcement of the first solution allows for the removal of impediments to the operation of the market; Kenneth Boulding has suggested an ingenious plan whereby the second solution could also be enforced within a market framework.[6] It is at least arguable that with these two solutions in place, market forces might themselves curb ecologically destructive patterns of consumption.

Nothing I have said in underscoring the ecological necessity for population control should be construed to denigrate the ecological side-benefits of George's remedy for poverty. It is incontrovertible, I think, that the rapidly-increasing destruction of the Amazon rain forest (with its resultant 'greenhouse effect' upon the global ecosystem) is directly attributable to the fact that the Amazon basin is the only part of Brazil where free or cheap land is available, and this, in turn, is attributable to the fact that nearly four-fifths of Brazil's arable acreage is covered by sprawling *latifundios*, half of which are held by speculators who produce nothing.[7] Were the artificial scarcity of available land in the rest of Brazil corrected, as the Georgist remedy would unquestionably do, pressure on the Amazon basin would obviously cease. This is but one example, albeit a dramatic one, of the ecological side-benefits to which I have alluded. But if the Brazilian population continues to increase at its present rate, how long would it be before the margin extended again to Amazonia? The environmental advantages of the Georgist program are certainly substantial, but they cannot be permanent unless coupled with restraints on population growth. Neither should anything that I have said be construed to minimize the possibilities of technology. Rather recently, it seemed as if we had strong indications that cold nuclear fusion would give us an inexpensive and inexhaustible supply of clean power within a decade or two. It appears now that these indications were unduly sanguine, but I have no doubt that it (or something like it) will happen sometime within the next half-century. Yet would an inexpensive and inexhaustible supply of clean power save the rhinoceros hunted for its horn or the elephant slaughtered for its tusks? Would it preserve the redwoods from extinction? Would it protect the dolphins from the drift-nets, or the pyramids from the disintegration caused by tourists? It was Henry George himself who characterized man as 'the only animal whose desires increase as they are fed; the only animal that is never satisfied.'[8] If his numbers be not too great, these insatiable appetites can be accommodated without grave stress to the environment. But the environment is fragile, and its carrying capacity, finite. In our day and age, this is too evident to deny. If Henry George were living now,

I am convinced that he would not deny it.* If those who would advance his cause today refuse to admit it, they are being wilfully blind, and cannot expect to be taken seriously.

* * *

Of the Neo-Malthusian voices emanating from ecologist ranks, one of the most powerful and certainly the most provocative is that of Garrett Hardin.

In the remainder of this chapter, I propose to show that, despite secondary disagreements, Garrett Hardin and Henry George may, in what is most germane to the focus of these explorations, be far closer to each other than might first appear. I propose to show that what they have in common is obscured by a semantic difference — ironically, a difference in the meaning that they attach to the *word* 'common'.

When, in Book VI, chapter 2, of *Progress and Poverty*, George asserted, '*We must make land common property*,' he was guilty of a tactical blunder that hobbled the advance of his proposal from the start. For although he took pains later in his book to clarify this declaration, it has been used by his antagonists with deadly effect to portray him as an advocate of nationalizing land.

Actually, of course, nationalization, with its concomitant collectivization and regimentation, was not at all what George proposed. By 'common property in land,' he intended to signify the effectuation of common rights in land, not (except in instances involving generally-accepted public functions) its collective use. Neither did he intend to signify a common resource to be drawn on individually without concern for social consequences.

The true meaning of the phrase for George is best exhibited in

---

*George, in point of fact, was ecologically far in advance of his time. The following passage from Chapter 3 of *Social Problems* (1883) reads as though it might have come from the pen of some unusually eloquent member of the contemporary 'Green' movement: 'We do not return to the earth what we take from it; each crop that is harvested leaves the soil the poorer. We are cutting down forests which we do not replant; we are shipping abroad, in wheat and cotton and tobacco and meat, or flushing into the sea through the sewers of our great cities, the elements of fertility that have been embedded in the soil by the slow processes of nature, acting for long ages.'

Book VIII, chapter 1. He first speaks there of a lot in the center of San Francisco: 'This lot is not cut up into infinitesimal pieces nor yet is it an unused waste. It is covered with fine buildings, the property of private individuals, that stand there in perfect security. The only difference between this lot and those around it, is that the rent of the one goes into the common school fund, the rent of the other into private pockets.'

He then turns to the Aleutian islets of St. Peter and St. Paul, the breeding places of the fur seal, an animal so wary that the slightest fright causes it to flee its customary haunts forever:

> To prevent the utter destruction of this fishery, without which the islands are of no use to man, it is not only necessary to avoid killing the females and young cubs, but even such noises as the discharge of a pistol or the barking of a dog... Those who can be killed without diminution of future increase are carefully separated and gently driven inland, out of sight and hearing of the herds, where they are dispatched with clubs. To throw such a fishery as this open to whoever chose to go and kill — which would make it to the interest of each party to kill as many as they could at the time without reference to the future — would be utterly to destroy it in a few seasons, as similar fisheries in other countries have been destroyed. But it is not necessary, therefore, to make these islands private property... They have been leased at a rent of $317,500 per year [partly fixed ground rent, partly payment of $2.62½ on each skin, with an annual harvest limited to 100,000 skins], probably not very much less than they could have been sold for at the time of the Alaska purchase. They have already yielded two millions and a half to the national treasury, and they are still, in unimpaired value (for under the careful management of the Alaska Fur Company the seals increase rather than diminish), the common property of the people of the United States.

Although George thus illustrates his principle by means of actual examples involving leaseholds, his prescription envisages an easier and less drastic application than that of confiscating land and letting it out to the highest bidders. Instead, he advocates that land titles be left in private hands, with rent appropriated by means of the existing tax machinery. Commensurate reductions would be made in taxes on improvements and other labor products (culminating ideally in the total abolition of such taxes), and the machinery reduced and simplified accordingly. 'By leaving to landowners a percentage of rent which would probably be much less than the cost and loss involved in attempting to rent lands through State agency, and by making use of this existing machinery, we may, without jar or shock, assert the common right to land by taking rent for public uses.'⁹ But this is simply a practical refinement; the principle remains the same.

In his seminal essay, 'The Tragedy of the Commons,'¹⁰ Hardin focuses on the inherent tendency of individuals, each in the pursuit of his own interests, to overgraze, denude, and use the commons as a cesspool.* That which belongs to everybody in this sense is, indeed, valued and maintained by nobody. The Enclosure Movement ultimately brought an end to the commons in Europe as a basic institution, but not without exacting a baneful price in human misery that might well be termed 'The Tragedy of the Enclosures'.

It makes no difference, really, whether or not Hardin believes that most people are utility or profit maximizers who value their individual goods more than they do social goods. If common property is free to all without restraint, it only takes one such person, once an area's carrying capacity has been reached, to degrade the area. As with persons, so also with nations. The stocks of blue whales are so

---

*A major theme in Hardin's thought is that the genetic stream is also commons. As stewards, we have an obligation to ensure that it is not overloaded or polluted. I do not know whether he anywhere discusses the specifics of how this should be done, other than to say that if it were left to depend upon appeals to conscience, conscience would soon be bred out of the population. My personal opinion is that if measures are to be taken to reduce population size or to keep it static, then there is all the more reason why measures should be taken to upgrade its quality. Once understood that there is no automatic right to procreate, to prevent the transmission of defective genes will not be regarded as a violation of an individual's private and personal life any more than to prevent the transmission of venereal disease is so regarded. Arbitrary value judgments about what constitutes 'superiority' and 'inferiority' need not enter into the picture; the only judgments required would center upon whether prospective offspring would be likely to become public charges — surely a proper and legitimate public concern! The probable production of offspring with severe genetic handicaps would then become an option only for those wealthy enough to put up surety for their support. Since such people are relatively few and tend in our society to be less prolific anyway, to permit them such an option would not significantly hinder the cleansing of the genetic stream.

(I seriously considered deleting this footnote, since I realize that references to 'the cleansing of the genetic stream,' etc., are likely to evoke knee-jerk accusations of 'Nazism' from some readers, and did not wish to undermine the book's credibility. But I decided that to delete it would be to permit Hitler to establish the parameters of responsible discussion. Why should eugenics be off-limits as a topic simply because in his hands it became a brutal and barbaric travesty?)

depleted that the International Whaling Commission recommends the virtual stoppage of whaling, and all but two nations have ceased whaling on the high seas altogether. But Japan and Russia continue to fish for whales aggressively, and the depletion becomes ever more acute. Soon the blue whale may be extinct. Actually, Hardin does not deny the existence of altruism either in individuals or in societies. But his 'conservative policy,' as he calls it, is 'to regard altuism as a marginal motive.'[11] To me, this policy seems only sensible. Archbishop Temple must have been thinking along similar lines when he defined the art of government as 'the art of so ordering life that self-interest prompts what justice demands.'[12]

When I commenced the research for the paper that evolved into this chapter, I set out, with the aid of two British colleagues, David Redfearn and Julia Bastian, to disprove Hardin's thesis. Together, we compiled an impressive list of counter-examples, showing that the historic commons, far from being an unregulated free-for-all, were mostly operated according to agreed-upon rules that ensured a fair distribution of opportunity, spread work evenly throughout the seasons, and generally tended to conserve the soil and other natural resources.[13] These rules worked effectively in England for about a thousand years. It was only after the enclosure of the open fields was well advanced that the common pastures, having been thus divorced in large measure from their traditional employment, became subject to overgrazing and other environmental abuses as the old regulatory machinery fell into abeyance.[14] Vestigial remnants of the historic commons, such as the Swiss alpine village of Törbel, survive and thrive even today.[15] As for the supposed ecologically beneficent effects of 'private' as opposed to 'common' ownership of land, a recent report in the *Financial Times* of London speaks of pollution resulting from the use of chemical fertilizers and pesticides, deterioration of habitats, erosion, loss of topsoil, acidification of rivers, desertification, unsuitable afforestation, etc.[16] But this is not a brief for 'government' ownership (nationalization); there is probably no sizeable body of water in the world more polluted than is the Aral Sea in Soviet Turkestan.

'The Tragedy of the Commons' was first published in 1968, and has been reprinted in numerous collections since that date. Among the more vigorous efforts to rebut it is an article by John Reader which appeared two decades later. 'The true commons,' Reader properly insists, 'was, by definition, an area of mutual benefit and responsibility, managed by those using it in a manner that acknowledged that environmental resources are not unlimited. Access to the commons was restricted by entitlement; use was regulated to ensure that no individual could pursue his own interest to the detriment of others. Far from bringing ruin to all, the true commons functioned to keep its exploitation within sustainable limits, thus providing every commoner with a dependable food supply in the short term, and maintaining the viability of available resources for generations to come.'[17] A more careful analysis of Hardin's essay demonstrates that, like my own compilation of counter-examples, Reader's attack, while factual enough, is utterly beside the point: What Reader calls the 'true commons' is not what Hardin meant by 'the commons' in his essay. The essay presents a hypothetical illustration of a pasture open to all. Each herdsman, seeking as a rational being to maximize his gain, will try to keep as many cattle as possible on the pasture. So long as tribal warfare, poaching, and disease keep the numbers of both man and beast below the carrying capacity of the land, the arrangement may work satisfactorily. But once that capacity is exceeded, 'the inherent logic of the commons generates tragedy,' since the rational herdsman, knowing that without regulation others will pursue their individual interests even if he abstains, adds animal after animal to his herd. 'Each man is locked into a system that compels him to increase his herd without limit — in a world that is limited.'[18] So much for the hypothetical illustration. But one looks in vain in the essay for historical references.

It is true that, in other work, Hardin alludes in passing to the ecological destructiveness of the system of English commons that was replaced as a result of the Enclosure Movement.[19] In this, he may have been historically inaccurate, but this was a mere incidental error, as in neither case was he writing to establish a historical thesis. Hardin uses the term 'commons' to refer, not primarily or necessarily to any actual historical institution, but to what sociologists, following Max Weber, call an *ideal type* — a pure logical construct, in this instance, one of the four discrete politico-economic systems of environmental utilization. The 'system of the commons' is the one in which the environment is utilized by the group with the proceeds going to the individual. It is, practically speaking, a synonym for anarchy.

In a piece entitled 'Ethical Implications of Carrying Capacity,' Hardin discusses an 'excellent report' by Nicholas Wade, which ascribes the advancing desertification of the Sahel largely to (often well-intended) Western interference. Prior to this interference, the Sahelian peoples carried on a way of life that was a remarkably efficient adaptation to their environment, with migrations, routes, the length of time a herd of a given size might spend at a given well, etc., governed by rules worked out by tribal chiefs. But, according to Hardin, the 'old way of treating common property in the Sahel' was not really the system of the commons but rather a kind of informal socialism.[20] It may, of course, be argued that the words 'commons' and 'socialism' are both used by him in idiosyncratic fashion, but an author is entitled to use words any way he chooses so long as he specifies what he is doing, and Hardin cannot in this context be accused of failing to so specify.

'The morality of an act,' says Hardin, *'is a function of the state of the system at the time it is performed.'*[21] In the Old Testament period, 'Be fruitful and multiply' might have been a sound injunction; today, it is in most cases a mandate to behave irresponsibly. For a lone frontiersman to discharge waste into a stream may harm nobody; as population reaches a certain density, such conduct becomes intolerable. 'Property rights must be periodically reexamined in the light of social justice.'[22] In a complex, crowded, changeable environment, statutory law cannot make adequate allowance for particular circumstances, and must therefore be augmented by administrative law. But Hardin admits that administrative law, depending as it does upon decision-making by bureaucrats, is singularly liable to corruption. To it applies with special force the age-old question: *Quis custodiet ipsos custodes?* — 'Who shall watch the watchers themselves?' Hardin draws attention to this difficulty, but does not attempt an answer.

How can exploitation be adjusted to carrying capacity, allowing for particular and changing circumstances, yet avoiding the corruption and caprice of bureaucratic regulators? Inasmuch as we live in an imperfect world inhabited by imperfect beings, a perfect solution to this dilemma does not exist. Yet the program of Henry George, since it calls for a process that is virtually self-regulating, comes as close to being foolproof as anything conceivable. To leave the land in private hands, while appropriating through taxation the greater part of its annual rental value as determined by the market, would assure, not maximum, but optimum, exploitation.

In an illustration concerning the lumber industry, Hardin correctly remarks that 'high taxes on land that is many years away from being timbered encourage cut-and-run.'[23] But they wouldn't have this effect if combined with heavy severance taxes, which encourage conservation while reducing the land's market value. Thus the tax on annual rental value could be set at a high percentage yet still be low enough to induce retention of title, together with non-injurious harvesting schedules and techniques. Although the taxation of land rent is, of course, the method characteristically emphasized by Georgism, a severance tax is simply a different technical application of the same philosophy, adapted to different circumstances but equally amenable to determination by the market.

I make no pretense of familiarity with the whole of Hardin's copious literary output, but the adverse reference to which I just alluded is the only one I have encountered that speaks explicitly of land taxation. Conversely, in *Stalking the Wild Taboo,* one finds a glancing but favourable mention of the graduated income tax.[24] Yet he proposes internalizing pollution costs (and simultaneously discouraging pollution) through taxation[25] — a proposal very much in keeping with the Georgist accent on using the tax mechanism to protect common rights in the environment within an overall framework of private enterprise. And in a book he edited, Jay M. Anderson suggests, quite possibly with his tacit approval, 'the taxation of industry at a rate proportional to used commons.'[26]

But most significant, I think, is an easily overlooked passage in 'The Tragedy of the Commons' in which Hardin, perhaps unwittingly, endorses by implication the essential Georgist concept:

> During the Christmas shopping season [in Leominster, Massachusetts] the parking meters downtown were covered with plastic bags that bore tags reading: 'Do not open until after Christmas. Free parking courtesy of the mayor and city council.' In other words, facing the prospect of an increased demand for already scarce space, the city fathers reinstituted the system of the commons.[27]

By calling this a 'retrogressive act,' Hardin demonstrates his belief that the meters ought to have been left in operation. Now, parking meters exemplify (in specialized form) the public appropriation of land rent; they constitute payment for the privilege of temporarily monopolizing a site — compensation to the members of the community whose opportunity to use the site is extinguished for a given time by the monopoly. The payment, to be sure, is typically only partial. Compensation reflecting the full market value of the temporary monopoly would be at levels comparable to fees charged by commercial parking lots in the vicinity of the meters.

But more than compensation is involved here. If parking meter fees, instead of being used to pay for community services or even for their own collection cost, were buried in the ground, their collection would still be justified in order, as Hardin puts it, 'to keep downtown shoppers temperate in their use of parking space' [28] — i.e., as a means of rendering monopoly temporary and innocuous. So, also, the public appropriation of land rent in its more comprehensive application, by removing any incentive to hoard and speculate in land, would be warranted in terms of social justice and well-being, even if its yield were cast into the sea. For in rectifying distribution, this approach liberates production; in apportioning the wealth-pie fairly, it increases the size of the pie. Instead of being a cruel contest in which the cards are stacked against most players because of gross disparities in bargaining power, the market becomes in practice what capitalist theory alleges it to be — a profoundly cooperative process of voluntary exchange. And all this is accomplished without stressing the environment. Cities, more compact, return to human scale as artificial pressures for expansion outward and upward are removed. The availability of land at prices no longer bloated by speculation, makes profitable agriculture possible without the wholesale use of ecologically harmful chemicals and machinery.

In addition to the 'system of the commons,' which amounts to anarchy, Hardin distinguishes three other discrete systems of environmental utilization: 'socialism,' 'private philanthropy,' and 'private enterprise,'[29]. He tends in general to favour the last, since under it the individual decision-maker and society usually both lose when the carrying capacity of the environment is overloaded, and thus decisions are more apt to be 'operationally responsible.' Yet he concedes that this is not invariably the case, and is no apologist for absolute private ownership of land.[30] Not only does he grant that an owner, seeking rationally to maximize his gains, may under certain conditions behave in an ecologically *irresponsible* fashion[31] (a conclusion set forth in greater detail respectively by Daniel Fife and Colin W. Clark,[32]) but he holds that the Enclosure Acts, even though ecologically desirable, were unjust.[33] 'We must admit,' he asserts moreover, 'that our legal system of private property plus inheritance is unjust — but we put up with it because we are not convinced, at the moment, that anyone has invented a better system.'[34]

Well, someone surnamed George did 'invent' a better system — one that eminently satisfies all of Hardin's criteria, one that secures the advantages of both commons and enclosures with none of the disadvantages of either. For, paradoxical though it may seem, the only way in which the individual may be assured what properly belongs to him is for society to take what properly belongs to it: the Jeffersonian ideal of individualism requires for its realization the socialization of rent. Were rent socialized, population stabilized, the costs of negative externalities internalized, and the returns of private effort privatized, we and our posterity would prosper, at least roughly, according to our deserts, and healing come to our abused and wounded habitat, the earth.

NOTES

1 James L. Busey, 'Dogma and Population', *Intermountain Frontier*, August 5, 1986, p. 4.
2 *Ibid.*
3 Henry George, *Progress and Poverty* (1879; New York: Robert Schalkenbach Foundation, 1962), p. 133.
4 Two reviews published by Malthus anonymously of books by Thomas Newenham, *Edinburgh Review*, July, 1808, pp. 336-355, and April, 1809, pp. 115-170, respectively. See Michael A. MacDowell, 'Malthus and George on Ireland; Some Comments on Similarities, the Single Tax and Others', *The American Journal of Economics and Sociology*, Oct., 1977.

5 John Baden, 'Population, Ethnicity, and Public Goods: The Logic of Interest-Group Strategy' in Garrett Hardin and John Baden, eds., *Managing the Commons* (San Francisco: W. H. Freeman and Co., 1977), pp. 253, 259.
6 Kenneth Boulding, *The Meaning of the 20th Century* (New York: Harper & Row, 1964), p. 135.
7 'Brazil's land reform program is caught in a violent crossfire', *Christian Science Monitor*, May 7, 1987, p. 11.
8 *Progress and Poverty*, p. 134.
9 *Progress and Poverty*, p. 405.
10 Garrett Hardin, 'The Tragedy of the Commons', *Science*, Vol. 162, Dec. 13, 1968, pp. 1243–1248.
11 Hardin, 'An Operational Analysis of "Responsibility"', in Hardin and Baden, eds., *Managing the Commons*, p. 68.
12 William Temple, *Christianity and Social Order* (1942; London: Shepheard-Walwyn, 1976; New York: Seabury, 1977), p. 65.
13 See C. S. and C. S. Orwin, *The Open Fields* (Oxford: Clarendon, 1938), pp. 38–58; and *Laxton: Life in an Open Field Village* (Nottingham: University of Nottingham, Manuscripts Department, Archive Teaching Unit No. 4), Introduction, pp. 12–17, Transcripts and Summaries of Documents, pp. 10–11.
14 W. G. Collins and L. D. Stamp, *The Common Lands of England and Wales* (London: Collins, 1963), pp. 56–60.
15 John Reader, 'Human Ecology: How Land Shapes Society', *New Scientist*, No. 1629 (Sept. 8, 1988), p. 55.
16 Bridget Bloom, 'Erosion threatens Europe's agricultural land', *Financial Times* (London), July 18, 1988, Environment IV. See also Teri Randall, 'Topsoil erosion "silent crisis", threatens farmers', *Chicago Tribune*, rpt. *Birmingham News* (Alabama), July 19, 1989. Randall quotes William Fyfe, geology professor at Western Ontario University: 'At the root of the problem is a rapidly growing world population. Each year, 90 million babies join the more than 5 billion humans already on Earth, yet the total area of farmland available to feed them decreases.'
17 Reader, p. 52.
18 'The Tragedy of the Commons', p. 1244.
19 Hardin, *Exploring New Ethics for Survival* (New York: Viking, 1972), p. 116.
20 Hardin, 'Ethical Implications of Carrying Capacity' and 'An Operational Analysis of "Responsibility"' in Hardin and Baden, eds., *Managing the Commons*, p. 122 and p. 69.
21 'The Tragedy of the Commons', p. 1243.
22 Hardin, *Exploring New Ethics*, p. 127.
23 *Ibid.*, 26.

24 Hardin, *Stalking the Wild Taboo* (Los Altos, CA: William Kaufman, Inc., 1973), p.177.
25 'The Tragedy of the Commons', p.1245; *Exploring New Ethics*, pp.123, 244f.
26 Jay M. Anderson, 'A Model of the Commons' in Hardin and Baden, eds., *Managing the Commons*, p.41.
27 'The Tragedy of the Commons', p.1245.
28 *Ibid.*, p.1247.
29 'An Operational Analysis of "Responsibility"', p.69.
30 *Exploring New Ethics*, pp.125-127.
31 *Ibid.*, pp.125-126.
32 Daniel Fife, 'Killing the Goose' and Colin W. Clark, 'The Economics of Overexploitation' in Hardin and Baden, eds., *Managing the Commons*, pp.76-95.
33 Hardin, 'Denial and Disguise' in *ibid.*, p.46.
34 'The Tragedy of the Commons', p.1247.

3
The Crisis of Transition from the Commons: population explosions, their cause and cure

FRED HARRISON

DEMOGRAPHY is a highly emotive subject. Objectivity tends to be submerged beneath a warren of interlocking prejudices. Until recently, the significance of questions concerning the size and location of populations had been mainly of a political character, usually involving disputes between nation-states. The size of a population had been presented as either inadequate for the purpose of establishing geopolitical supremacy; or as so overwhelming as to threaten the welfare of neighboring communities.

The new awareness of the ecological problems now facing Mother Earth has extended the demographic debate to embrace the destiny of humanity. Because of this global character, we can now anticipate the emergence of the view that an international approach to solutions is the only way to meet the challenge of 'over-population'. The justification for the use of coercive action would be that the survival of the species was at stake. Should this occur, the right of the individual to remain aloof from whatever corrective action is deemed to be appropriate may be disregarded. This prospect makes it all the more imperative that discussions should be placed on a rational footing, so that moral judgments may be made on the basis of the best information.

A new assessment must take the historic facts as the starting point, which means embracing, no matter how summarily, two million years of history for *homo sapiens*. We can then evaluate the foundation hypotheses of demography, which means returning to Thomas Robert Malthus.

Public debate is generally conducted at the two extremes of beliefs about demographic issues. One school of thought views man as a locust who is parasitically living off the land. This neo-Malthusian attitude is colorfully summarised in a statement by Gore Vidal, the American author and social critic, who wrote:

> Think of earth as a living organism that is being attacked by billions of bacteria whose numbers double every 40 years. Either the host dies, or the virus dies, or both die. That seems to be what we are faced with.[1]

At the other extreme is the benign view. The life-forces of nature will not allow one species to pose a fatal threat to earth. A case for this perspective could be developed by employing the insights offered by James Lovelock, an atmospheric scientist who hypothesised that the world is a living organism — Gaia, he calls her, the name that the ancient Greeks gave to earth.[2] In this view, man is one of the millions of interacting species and processes that make up the totality of a living system that includes inorganic matter and the atmosphere above earth.

Lovelock's holistic model enables us to perceive that, at the outset, man's activities, and the demands he made on his ecological niche, must have accommodated the other species and living matter that make up this moveable feast. We would therefore expect that man evolved a formula for sustaining himself through adaptation not only to take account of other predatory species, but to limit his demands on the environment so as not to jeopardise the survival of the breeding population. That has been the case. It took two million years for the human population to reach an estimated 1 billion people in 1830. And yet, 150 years later — a flicker in time — the demographic situation was transformed. Before, man lived in harmony with nature. Now, the image of the locust, a malignant predator on the rich life systems of earth, appears to be legitimate. The number exploded to an estimated 5.3 billion in 1990. Something unique had occurred. Until we know what and why, the prospects of an enlightened debate on policies for dealing with 'over-population' are not good.

Man's survival and his natural habitat cannot be entrusted to chance, but I am not convinced that current perceptions of what constitutes a crisis ought to be approached primarily in terms of demographic pressure. The position advanced here flies in the face of both popular and scholarly assumption that there is a problem of 'over-population' *per se* which invites correction by means of direct controls over procreative activity.

There is an apparent problem. Why is it necessary for 35,000 men, women and children to die every day from hunger when the world has the capacity to feed everyone without destroying the life-support system? This loss of life is needless; it is institutionally driven. The routinization of death as a cultural phenomenon is absent from the anthropological record. If, as I contend, the problem is not specifically one of 'over-population,' do we have to accept the claim that nature is being niggardly? Or have man's social institutions and behavior become unhinged from the verities that guided him through evolutionary history?

To clarify the nature of the problem, the priority task is to identify the turning points in history that were not consistent with the principles of adaptability and sustainability. I argue that these historical junctures are associated with the transition to private ownership of land. I then review the ideological biases in the writings of Thomas Malthus, in which he sought (not completely successfully) to exclude from his analysis the role of property rights in land as a determinant of 'vice and misery'. Finally, I outline the insights offered by Henry George, the 19th century American social reformer, which appear to correct the Malthusian analysis and lead to policies most likely to transform mankind's social and economic — and as a consequence, demographic — destiny.

Social Ecology

Our starting point is the description of a simple model of how an organism sustains itself. The organism can be anything from a cancerous cell to a healthy human being or a species-specific population. Figure 1 illustrates, in an idealised way, the two courses that life can take. Growth Path A represents the normal development, in which there is an initial formative phase of rapid growth before the organism settles down to a period of sustained and comfortable

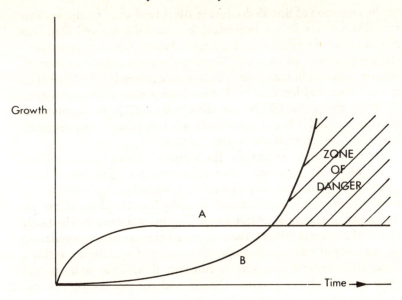

Figure 1

existence. For a human being, the first 20 years are the ones of rapid growth, with the rate slowing down during the teen years. Physical maturity is followed by a relatively stable period of 40 to 50 years, in which the life-force flourishes within what is normally a sustainable environment.

Growth Path B reflects the obverse conditions. The initial growth rate presents the character of a slow period of incubation, followed by an alarmingly rapid development until the growth path assumes an exponential profile. This ever-increasing rate of growth cannot be sustained by the host environment. Cancer follows this path: the time to catch it is during the early period, when the spread of the cells is slow and the damage is limited. By the time the spread has taken off, it is generally too late to contain the damage, which terminates in death for the host organism. In terms of social pathology, the AIDS virus (HIV) fits into this category. The virus started to spread slowly from the 1940s or early 1950s. The world's first recorded victim came to the attention of British doctors in April 1959 when a sailor walked into Manchester Royal Infirmary. He wasted away and died five months later. His doctors, at the time, had no means of classifying the symptoms.[3] For the next 20 years, the virus quietly worked its way through the human population, unrecognised for the killer that it was. Then, suddenly, in 1979, it made its presence felt, and within 10 years about 300,000 people died from AIDS: an exponential growth rate that is out of control and with terminal victims counted by the million, worldwide, within 20 years.

Growth Path A reflects the development of man for two million years. He evolved himself into a niche, multiplying rapidly at first, pushing towards the boundaries that were fixed partly by the endowments of his territory and partly by his own physical, mental and cultural potential. After expanding his numbers to the outer limits of sustainability, he then regulated the size of the population on the basis of homeostasis, achieving a state of equilibrium within a total environment that was in constant flux. That stability was imperative both for social evolution and the preservation of the environment on which man depended for his life.

Mankind's exponential growth rate of the past two centuries is represented by Growth Path B. The rapid rise in the size of the total world population is an unstable one, in terms of the ability of the environment to meet the need for food and natural resources over the alarmingly insignificant time period of the next 20 to 40 years.

The Zone of Danger exists above Growth Path A. Somehow, it is necessary either to curb growth above this level, or alter the parameters of the 'environent' (which consists of both natural and cultural factors) to restore long-run stability. This is not an unrealistic prospect. For in emphasising the sustainability of human behavior in the past, we are not saying that the population growth rate was always a constant one. Man developed from being an instinct-guided species into one that could *use* and enlarge his environment in a controlled way. Through the evolution of culture, man reduced his dependency on the genetic-based mechanisms that guided territorial behavior. In their place, he substituted social customs, some of which were developed into formal sets of rules. Customs that were demographic in character influenced the age of marriage, the size of families, and so on, to balance the desired quality of life with the need to procreate at a rate that ensured survival of the species.

Harmonising with the social dynamics of demography, corresponding rules were developed to regulate the manner in which the environment could be exploited, rules that make up what we now call land tenure systems.

As man progressed from hunter-gatherer to pastoralist, new rules for the use of land were developed to harmonise both social relations between competing groups, and to ensure the continued viability of the ecological niche. Cultural evolution permitted incremental increases in the number of people who could be safely carried within a particular niche. In this earliest phase, living standards were at 'subsistence' level: but we must emphasise that this nonetheless permitted time for the enjoyment of leisure and the accumulation of resources that contributed towards the articulation of increasingly complex systems of knowledge and social rituals.

A major acceleration in numbers occurred with the development of agriculture 10,000 years ago: man could now nurture the soil to produce more food than nature would have made available if left to her own devices. The multiplication of surplus resources to develop ever-grander social institutions was now within man's reach.

Accompanying each of those social revolutions was a parallel articulation of tenurial rules to ensure that the guest population did not abuse its ecological niche. The reverence of nature was expressed through social behavior. Widespread hunger, when this occurred, was caused by climatic change, not malignant social institution.

In each developmental phase, what mattered was man's ability to synchronise his needs and desires with the available resources. He did not abuse his environment: to do so would have been suicidal and contrary to his genetically endowed instinct for survival. To undermine the carrying capacity of the ecological niche was to threaten the population with extermination. That was why it was crucial for man to adopt an appropriate system of land tenure, so that productive exploitation was sympathetically aligned with the available resources. The rules of tenure over land, then, were of primary importance: they were intimately related to the ability of a population to survive if an ever-changing environment in which other species were also competing for existence. The land tenure system was crucial in determining whether a population had acquired the Darwinian capacity to survive over inter-generational timescales. Stability and sustainability were key principles of those systems of land tenure. The conservatism of that stability did not preclude dynamic change and growth: but these were controlled within a framework of adaptation. Thus, the absolute size of the population was not in itself the crucial consideration. What mattered was the ability of the population to achieve stability and work with the grain of the host environment.

Globally the rate of growth of the total human population has now assumed an exponential profile, taking mankind into the Zone of Danger. According to the Washington D.C.-based Population Crisis Committee, if a target of no more than two children for each family was not achieved before the year 2015, the world population would nearly double to 9.1 billion in 2050, but would not stabilise (at 9.3 billion) before the end of the 21st Century (Figure 2). Between now and then, the scope for regional crises is enormous and quite out of keeping with man's history. Why has this happened?

What is characterised as the modern demographic crisis coincided with the emergence of industrial society. This revolution in the mode of production was also accompanied by — but not dependent upon — the transformation of land tenure systems. Some of the dysfunctional elements of demographic behavior have been attributed to the new productive system, but this may be due to an erroneous perception. I believe there has been a serious neglect of the contribution by the new system of land tenure.

The historical paradox is self-evident. The power of the manufacturing process made it possible for Mother Earth to support many more people at ever-higher living standards. Furthermore, there is nothing intrinsic to the industrial system that precludes demographic stability.[4] This is not obviously so for the new land tenure system, the significance of which can only be fully appreciated when compared with traditional systems of land tenure. To summarise the principles of land tenure that pre-dated private ownership, we now need to offer a general theory of land tenure that highlights the general principles that applied through evolutionary timescales.

In tribal-based systems society — not the individual — regulated the use of land. The benefits from land *per se* (as opposed to the fruits

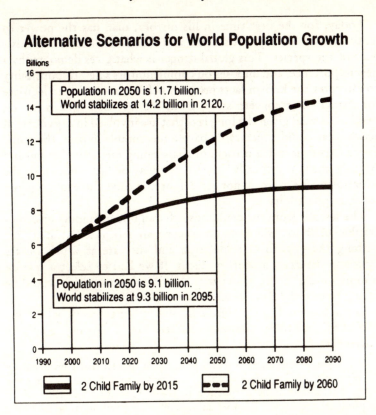

Figure 2

of individual effort) were distributed on a social, not an individual, basis. The right of access was based on the need to *use* land, a right that every member of the population enjoyed as a birthright. The exclusionary powers of private property ownership, which first became socially significant in Britain in the 17th century, were wholly alien to traditional societies. Previously, land was held in common for the benefit of everyone, and not for the privilege of a small class. This communal access to land was a central feature of societies that lived in harmony with nature, societies that homeostatically regulated their population numbers.

Today, for the first time in his history, man has the power to jeopardise his life-support system, and therefore threaten the existence of the species. This global danger is what gives demography a new importance, and imposes on commentators a new responsibility to interpret the known facts properly before proceeding to legislate for change. Our concern stems from the fact that time is not on mankind's side: given the long lags that are involved in any course of action that could conceivably have a measurable impact, the scope for an experimental approach, of abandoning methods that fail and starting anew, is critically limited. We may be near enough to the situation where, if we do not get it right first time, there may not be a second opportunity.

The lessons from the commons offer an understanding of demographic behavior which could lead to an integrated strategy for curbing the growth of population and the rate at which we are inflicting damage on Mother Earth. If we had to select a text to summarise our point of departure for fresh research, it would be fitting to cite the Rev. T.R. Malthus himself.

In the appendix to the third edition of his great work, which was published in 1806, Malthus offered the following emphatic statement:

> It is an utter misconception of my argument to infer that I am an enemy to population. I am only an enemy to vice and misery, and consequently to that unfavourable proportion between population and food which produces these evils. But this unfavourable proportion has no necessary connection with the quantity of absolute population which a country may contain. On the contrary, it is more frequently found in countries which are very thinly peopled, than in those which are populous.[5]

Writing during the early phase of the period that we characterise as the Zone of Danger, Malthus acknowledged that the absolute number of people was not the important consideration. What mattered was the process by which people were rendered hungry and disposed to 'vice'. Paradoxically, however, he also acknowledged — in passing — that the existence of resources was also not the relevant consideration, because the hungriest people lived in relatively land-rich areas. Why, then, the 'vice and misery?' Could it be that the new land tenure system was not working properly in the interests of mankind and Mother Earth? Could it be that the misalignment of land tenure to productive systems and ecological imperatives was such as to create a cultural crisis in which people were degraded to that state which Malthus was wont to label 'vice and misery'?

Culture Crisis: a Hypothesis

Thomas Malthus has attracted venomous attacks ever since his *Essay on the Principle of Population* was published in 1798. This essay was a polemical assault on William Godwin (1756-1836) and the Marquis de Condorcet (1743-94), who had broadcast a vision of social equality and economic prosperity that was anathema to Malthus. To neutralise the prospect of the English being infected by the revolutionary spirit that was then spreading from France, Malthus developed a theory of population that postulated the impossibility of everyone attaining the standard of living to which the revolutionaries aspired.

Having achieved immediate notoriety with the first version of his essay, Malthus then travelled abroad to gather empirical evidence. He published this in the second edition. His mature conclusions, however, were published 30 years later in *A Summary View of the Principle of Population* (1830). An author is entitled to be judged on his final statements, the ones that provide his rounded views after a lifetime's reflections, rather than on his earliest, incomplete hypotheses.[6]

The starting point in our appraisal is with the attempt that Malthus made to integrate his demographic theory with the theory of rent. David Ricardo (1772-1823), whose name is now associated with the theory of rent, devoted the final chapter of his *Principles of Political Economy and Taxation* (1817) to a critique of the Malthusian formulation.[7] In the preface to his book, Ricardo magnanimously acknowledged that Malthus's *Inquiry into the Nature and Progress of Rent* (1815) presented

> the true doctrine of rent; without a knowledge of which, it is impossible to understand the effect of the progress of wealth on profits and wages, or to trace satisfactorily the influence of taxation on different classes of the community ...[8]

There was, however, a theoretical difference between the two economists. The nature of that difference identifies the fatal flaw in Malthus's theory of population.

Malthus explained that the rent of land was the surplus income after paying for all the labor and capital costs of the production. The higher the market price of a product, therefore, and the lower its costs of production, the more the landowner could cream off from the aggregate revenue. Ricardo agreed; but he added a refinement to clarify the process by which the level of rents was determined.

Rent, said Ricardo, was determined at the margin of cultivation. That was the point at which land (working with labor and capital) was able to generate just sufficient income to make it possible to employ labor and capital; there was no surplus to be appropriated by the landowner. People working on the rent-free margins of the economy set the benchmark for wages. Workers engaged on more fertile land could not demand higher wages, because competition in the labor market would hold wages at the level that was being accepted at the margin. Figure 3 illustrates the hypothesis. Wages received by labor on the marginal site (M_1) at time T_1, determine the levels received on intra-marginal sites — those that are more fertile, or where the production costs are lower (as with the locational advantage that entails lower costs of transporting products to market). Ricardo, then, added the spatial dimension to the theory of rent, which, as we shall see, Malthus had failed to recognise as central to the dynamics of demography.

Malthus summarised his integrated theory on page 18 of *An Inquiry into the Nature and Progress of Rent*.

> The accumulation of capital, beyond the means of employing it on land of the greatest natural fertility, and the greatest advantage of situation, must necessarily lower profits; while the tendency of population to increase beyond the means of subsistence must, after a certain time, lower the wages of labor.
>
> The expense of production will thus be diminished, but the value of the produce, that is, the quantity of labor, and of the other products of labor besides corn, which it can command, instead of diminishing, will be increased.
>
> There will be an increasing number of people demanding subsistence, and ready to offer their services in any way in which they can be useful. The exchangeable value of food will therefore be in excess above the cost of production, including in this cost the full profits of the stock

The Crisis of Transition from the Commons

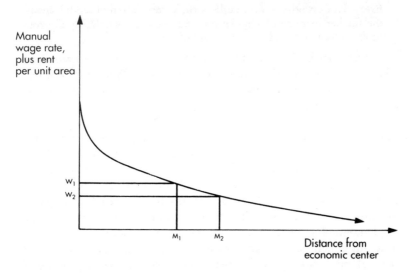

Figure 3

employed upon the land, according to the actual rate of profits at the time being. And this excess is rent.[9]

The Malthusian formulation was a simple one. Among the causes of the rise of rent was 'such an increase of population as will lower the wages of labor.' Ricardo disagreed. 'If wages fell,' he wrote, 'profits, and not rent, would rise.'[10] For dramatic emphasis, he added: 'If the landlord were to forego his whole rent, the labourers would not be in the least benefited.' The beneficiary, he insisted, was the owner of capital. 'Nothing can raise rent, but a demand for new land of an inferior quality ...'[11] Again, referring to Figure 3, we can see what happens when, at time T_2, people move the margin of cultivation outwards (to M_2): subsistence at this point is at a lower level, which through competition leads to a reduction in the general level of wages and leaves an increased surplus for the owners of land.

But although Ricardo insisted that 'If wages fell, profits, and not rent, would rise,' the difference between the two economists on this point was academic. For when it came down to the end result, Ricardo agreed with Malthus.

> Every rise of profits is favourable to the accumulation of capital, and to the further increase of population, and therefore would, in all probability, ultimately lead to an increase of rent.[12]

The difference between them lay in the transmission mechanism by which lower wages led to higher rental income. What they did not disagree over, however, was that — sooner or later — the working poor grew poorer and the idle rich grew richer.

The Malthusian model is a static one, in which the addition of more people competing for jobs leads to lower wages. This seems unexceptionable, in itself, and it would be consistent with the basic economic principles adopted by Malthus if we elaborated his hypothesis to show that more people usually means an extensive sprawl onto less attractive land. Had Malthus incorporated this spatial dimension into his conceptual framework, he might have modified his demographic theory in a way that could have yielded significantly different conclusions about the nature of poverty and the causes of the high population growth rates which existed in the early period of the Industrial Revolution.

Ricardo, while reaching the correct conclusion, did so by a tortuous route: he drew on an early version of the Wage Fund theory (which has since been discredited[13]). Ricardo believed that lower wages, in raising profits, provided capitalists with the extra cash with which to employ more workers. This was a demand-led theory of population. The final outcome, however, in terms of the distribution of income, was the same: an increase in the population meant migration onto less attractive locations, which served to lower wages and raise rents.

But note that Ricardo shared an underlying assumption with Malthus: the rate of population growth would maintain downward pressure on wage levels, despite the increase in productivity which resulted from capital accumulation.

Malthusian checks and balances The three checks on the 'tendency' for population to grow to the limits of the land's capacity to produce food, according to Malthus, were vice, misery and moral restraint. This provides a picture of populations locked into an interaction between individual proclivities and social sentiments, on the one hand, and the environment, in which the supply of land is assumed to play a neutral role, no more than a natural barrier to growth against which populations 'repress' themselves at the level of subsistence.

The Malthusian framework, then, is underpinned by a law of Immiseration. Missing from his analysis was the notion that a general rise in living standards was not inconsistent with stable population growth rates. The absence of this prospect was a logical outcome of his theory. If his equation was correct — more people resulted in lower wages and higher rents — a society in which a minority enjoyed absolute control over the resources of nature would not redistribute income to generate a general improvement in the quality of life.

Yet, paradoxically, Malthus was aware of the way in which culture — specifically, the land tenure system — could distort the supply of land and therefore directly affect population growth rates. He recorded the demographic consequences of variations in the supply of land by citing two examples which happen to illustrate each of our two contrasting paths of growth in Figure 1.

The benign interaction between man and land he illustrated with his example of the freely available land in the United States of America, 'where room and nourishment were the most abundant.[14] The frontier had not been closed, and so the population could expand in response to the supply of land. Culture, in the form of tenurial rights, was not a constraint: for as the speculators enclosed land, so the migrants leapfrogged onto new territory. The high fertility rates, in these circumstances, need not cause anxiety (though we now begin to get a picture of how land was not being used in an optimum way). Man was filling the available space through rapid procreative activity. What mattered was the ability of the population to regulate the birth rate once the supply of new land was exhausted. At that point, in a society whose tenurial system is of a mediating sort, the growth rate should level off on to a stable, long-run trend that could be sustained by the changing proportions of technology and natural resources.

Of a wholly different character, however, was the situation which observers discovered in the Spanish colonies of Central America. Malthus had assumed that the growth of population would be restrained where land tenure limited the supply of land to those who needed it. Much to his astonishment, however, the population was exploding at rates much the same as those to be found in North America. In New Spain,

> almost all the vices in the government of the mother country were introduced into her colonial possessions, *and particularly very unequal distribution of landed property which takes place under the feudal system.* These evils ... necessarily prevent that rapid increase of numbers which the abundance and fertility of the land would admit of.[15]

And yet, noted an astonished Malthus, births exceeded deaths by a large margin. Here was a demographic growth profile of exponential proportions, one that could not be sustained on ecological grounds and which implied a breakdown in those cultural mechanisms that traditionally served to regulate the relationship between man and land.

Cultural crisis and property rights Culture was developed through evolutionary timescales as a facilitator, to better equip *homo sapiens* to adapt to the natural environment. Where rights to land were held in common, the tenurial system was an integrative mechanism for stabilising the absolute number of people, the quality of life they desired, and the ecological imperatives of the niche that they inhabited. The development of private property rights, however, introduced a qualitatively new order. Tenurial rights could now be used to divide man from land; where this occurred, populations had to adapt to a historically unique *milieu*.

Because of the empirical evidence that had recently come to his attention, Malthus had to concede the possibility that land tenure might not be an invariably benevolent mediator between the host environment and the resident population. The awkward feature of the evidence from the Spanish colonies for Malthus's theory of population was the fact that the supply of land was not a constraint to demographic growth. Compared to the United States, 'in abundance and fertility of soil they are indeed superior,' noted Malthus.[16] But people were artificially constricted to the 'evils' of what Malthus chose to tarnish as a feudal system. To sidestep the awkward implications, he sought to distance property rights in the New World (which he characterised as feudal) from those which were even then being used to enclose land and dispossess customary users of access to the commons of the British isles.

The Crisis of Transition from the Commons

And yet it was beyond dispute that something new had been incorporated into society. With the transformation of property rights to land, the population was no longer integrated into a single social system underpinned by a common interest in its territory. Society was now divided between those who owned land — the financially rich and politically powerful — and those who were impoverished by their state of landlessness. Here was a cultural context to ecology. Tenurial rights rather than nature herself arbitrated to determine the supply of resources of nature to the population. If traditional demographic constraints are released, we have *prima facie* evidence of a breakdown in the social system.

The exponential profile of the growth rate, in these circumstances, cannot be sustained indefinitely. The absence of adaptive behavior entails an erosion of either living standards or the environment, or both. There are absolute limits to which a population can exploit either of these courses of action to sustain itself. It can diminish the standard of living until deaths occur for the disadvantaged members of society, and then deplete the rich resources of nature until the existence of the population itself is put at terminal risk. One or a combination of both strategies can be pursued until deaths on a mass scale bring the process to a tragic end. This is the Malthusian nightmare, but it is one which we have arrived at by a route that the reverend himself had failed to systematise into his theory of demography.

Nevertheless, Malthus *was* aware of the fact that land tenure can affect population growth rates. In defending private property rights as the most appropriate for encouraging production and 'to overcome the natural indolence of mankind,'[17] he offered a major concession that has fatal implications for the prescriptions that flow from his theory of population:

> ... yet it is unquestionably true, that the laws of private property, which are the grand stimulants to production, do themselves so limit it as always to make the actual produce of the earth fall very considerably short of the *power* of production. On a system of private property no adequate motive to the extension of cultivation can exist, unless the returns are sufficient not only to pay the wages necessary to keep up the population, which, at the least, must include the support of a wife and two or three children, but also a profit on the capital which has been

employed. This necessarily excludes from cultivation a considerable portion of land, which might be made to bear corn.[18]

Was Malthus being dishonest? He explains the fact of idle land not by reference to the unrequited demands of the landowner (who cannot be paid rent from marginal land), but on the grounds that the laborer would not work on land that did not pay a return on his capital investment. In fact, of course, hungry men will work with their bare hands, so long as land is freely available.

There is little doubt that Malthus had in the back of his mind the exclusionary powers of the landowner. This emerges clearly in the following passage.

> But it must perhaps also be allowed, that, under a system of private property, cultivation is sometimes checked in a degree, and at a period, not required by the interest of society. And this is particularly liable to happen when the original divisions of land have been extremely unequal, and the laws have not given sufficient facility to a better distribution of them.[19]

In fact, the *degree* of maldistribution, which Malthus cites in an effort to soften the responsibility of private ownership *per se*, is irrelevant. What matters, for the purpose of administering an efficient system of land tenure, is the enforceable right to exclude others, irrespective of their need of access to under-used land, whether of an acre or a plantation-sized tract.

Despite his damaging concession that private property rights are used to deny people access to life-giving land, however, Malthus would not make any substantive concessions on private property rights. He justified these as akin to natural rights.

> ... the laws of nature dictate to man the establishment of property, and the absolute necessity of some power in the society capable of protecting it. So strongly have the laws of nature spoken this language to mankind...
>
> Allowing, then, distinctly, that the right of property is the creature of positive law, yet this law is so early and so imperiously forced on the attention of mankind, that, if it cannot be called a natural law, it must be considered as the most natural as well as the most necessary of all positive laws...[20]

If this argument shows an intransigence of mind, nonetheless his analysis of the economic consequences of private property in land was important. Malthus explained that landowners influenced the level of activity in the economy not only through their propensity to favor what we would today call conspicuous consumption, but also because their under-consumption of manufactured goods, 'if not fully compensated by a great desire for personal attendance, *which it never is*, would infallibly occasion a premature slackness in the demand for labour and produce, a premature fall of profits, and a premature check to cultivation.'[21] Malthus was conceding that the distribution of income occasioned by property rights was such as to create a level of demand that fell short of full employment. This was an embryonic theory of business cycles that anticipated the analysis of American social reformer Henry George.

Given these fruitful macro-economic observations, based on a lifetime's reflections, why did Malthus fail to reformulate his theory of population? He stuck to the end with the Law of Immiseration, in which the burden of responsibility fell on the shoulders of the individual. Malthus also retained the notion that poverty, expressed in low wages, led to a diminution in the rate of growth of population.

> ... in every country with which we are acquainted where the yearly earnings of the labouring classes are not sufficient to bring up in health the largest families, it may be safely said, that population is actually checked by the difficulty of procuring the means of subsistence.[22]

This generalised observation offered comfort to Malthus, in that it justified low wages as a necessary condition for stabilising the growth of population. Alas, it was refuted by his own evidence of the explosive growth rates in Spanish America.

Enclosures and Exclusion

As a chronicler of social trends in the early years of the Industrial Revolution, which happened to coincide with the enclosure movement, Malthus allowed his ideology to compromise the conclusions that he drew from his observations. Even so, he established a partial framework for a vital debate on problems associated with the accelerated growth of population. He employed a restricted classification of the factors that constitute the dynamics of demography, but his descriptive account was sufficiently comprehensive to provide later scholars with the opportunity to refine his conclusions. Among these was Henry George.

George's critique of Malthus stemmed from a passionate anger at the impoverished conditions of the masses, which he traced to the maldistribution of rights to land. The importance of George in this debate lies in the way he illuminated the issues that Malthus identified as problems but failed to resolve. His insights enabled him to articulate a theoretical framework which linked ecological issues with the spatial distribution of human populations and the process of production and income distribution. This was a full century before the environmentalists began to awaken solicitude for the biosphere.[23]

George's thesis was that the private ownership of land unleashed economic behavior that was inconsistent with a balanced social existence. But by neutralising the monopoly power of the landlord (which could be achieved by the capture of the annual rental value of land through the tax system) the following distribution of population would result:

> The destruction of speculative land values would tend to diffuse population where it is too dense and to concentrate it where it is too sparse; to substitute for the tenement house, homes surrounded by gardens, and fully to settle agricultural districts before people were driven far from neighbors to look for land. The people of the cities would thus get more of the pure air and sunshine of the country, the people of the country more of the economies and social life of the city.

This rational spatial arrangement would lead to an improvement in the social and economic welfare of the farmer, which would occur only 'if he and those around him held no more land than they wanted to use.'

Integrated into this qualitative enhancement of social and economic life was an explicit concern for the ecological environment:

> Besides the enormous increase in the productive power of labor which would result from the better distribution of population there would be also a similar economy in the productive power of land. The concentration of population in cities fed by the exhaustive cultivation of large, sparsely populated areas, results in a literal draining into the sea of the elements of fertility. How enormous this waste is may be seen from the calculations that have been made as to the sewage of our cities, and its

practical result is to be seen in the diminishing productiveness of agriculture in large sections. In a great part of the United States we are steadily exhausting our lands.[24]

Here, then, was the first model that recognised the impact of the spatial dispersion of the population, standards of living and methods of production on man's ecological niche. The model yielded demographic conclusions of a character that placed George in conflict with Malthus.

The cultural context of demography Malthus did acknowledge that, in certain circumstances, a fairer distribution of land would benefit 'the interest of society'.[25] Ultimately, however, the literal share-out of land was a self-defeating strategy. Malthus claimed that it would lead to procreation at a rate that would eventually create an economic crisis.

In a modern economy, employing that policy can cause an economic crisis even when the birth rate is static or decreasing (as in France in the years after World War 2). The systematic sharing out of land leads, with the passing of generations, to the fragmentation of holdings to units so small that farmers would be left impoverished if they did not find off-farm employment to supplement their incomes. The post-war Mansholt Plan to pension off farmers and amalgamate tiny holdings in Europe — particularly in France — affirms the reality of this concern.

Henry George solved this distributional problem. People need not be deprived of their land; rather, they ought to pay the economic rent of their tracts to the community. This fiscal pressure would, he was confident, lead to an immediate release of under-used land into the hands of those who needed it. This free market policy would correct the problem identified by Malthus, namely that some owners choose to hold land vacant even while people go begging.

Given this economic reform, would there nonetheless be the need for a social program of intervention to control the growth of population? Malthus argued that it was futile for government to attempt to legislate for birth control. For, he concluded, 'direct legislation cannot do much. Prudence cannot be enforced by laws, without a great violation of natural liberty, and a great risk of producing more evil than good.'[26] If correct, this effectively throws the onus for regulating family sizes back on to the individual; and the failure to restrict procreation in line with one's economic circumstances relieves society from the obligation towards the welfare of the poor. This was, indeed, Malthus's attitude towards social welfare, as we will note below.

The contrasting perspective is represented by Henry George. In his view, the community is responsible for providing the *milieu* within which the individual may flourish and exercise a real choice over his destiny. At the heart of that cultural context was the system of property rights, which — so far as land was concerned (but not man-made capital) — Henry George regarded as subordinate to the equal interests of every member of society.

Malthus recognised the stark moral conflict that challenged his ideology. In defending the unencumbered right of private property in land, he was honest enough to acknowledge the existence of cases in which this right might interfere with the freedom of men to labor for their daily bread. What, then, was society's responsibility towards the dispossessed? The route by which Malthus reached his conclusion was, in his terms, the logical one: the rights of the poor were subordinate to the rights of property.

> The existence of a tendency in mankind to increase, if unchecked, beyond the possibility of an adequate supply of food in a limited territory, must at once determine the question as to the natural right of the poor to full support in a state of society where the law of property is recognized.[27]

For Malthus, the right of property was what differentiated man from 'the rank of brutes.' True, he began this part of his analysis with the claim that property was established to promote the public good, and this did allow for a modification — through, for example, a tax — if that served to achieve the ultimate objective.[28] There was a catch to this concession, however.

> But there is no modification of the law of property, having still for its object the increase of human happiness, which must not be defeated by the concession of a right of full support to all that might be born. It may be safely said, therefore, that the concession of such a right, and a right of property, are absolutely incompatible, and cannot exist together.[29]

Nevertheless, Malthus was willing to hold out the prospect of some relief from suffering, but his concession was conditional: the poor were not to marry and procreate while they were receiving the handouts from the property owners.[30] If there was a risk of this happening, then the welfare support could not be countenanced; for this encouragement to population growth would undermine the wellbeing of society. When it came to a conflict between the rights of the poor and the rights of landed property, the problem had to be settled in favor of property.

Henry George sought to solve this conflict. He would not compromise on every individual's birthright to an equal share of land. That right, in his terms, was God-given. Natural resources were freely provided for the benefit of everyone, and no one man — or class — had a right to deprive future generations of *their* right to enjoy the bountiful fruits of nature. In this, Malthus and George were at odds. But George did not prescribe the forcible appropriation of land for the purpose of redistribution. Land-value taxation was the fiscal device that would bridge the institutionally-created divide between the property owner and the landless laborer. The full capture of economic rent, he argued, in providing the revenue for government, would in turn further liberate the individual by removing the need for taxes on the incomes derived by labor and from capital investments. Thus was guaranteed the right of every citizen to an equal share of the cash value of the resources of nature.

In Malthus, then, we are confronted by the core of the moral dilemma that faced society in the 19th century. Something had to be done about a system that was not functioning at levels of efficiency and equity acceptable to the populace at large. The degree of degradation was unacceptable to the sensibilities of enough people to warrant a progressive political amelioration of this condition. Ultimately, a choice was made which rejected the Malthusian position: the poor would be helped by the transfer of income through the tax system. Malthus could have been in no doubt what that would mean in economic terms: the redistribution of income away from the landowners.

If there was to be a redistribution of income through the tax system, it ought to have seemed sensible to take the money direct from the landowner. Adam Smith had laid the foundations for such a fiscal strategy. A tax on subsistence incomes, he said, would merely be passed on, through higher wages, ultimately to reduce the income that was left to be paid as rent to the landowner.[31]

> Both ground-rents and the ordinary rent of land are a species of revenue which the owner, in many cases, enjoys without any care or attention of his own. Though a part of this revenue should be taken from him in order to defray the expenses of the state, no discouragement will thereby be given to any sort of industry. The annual produce of the land and labour of the society, the real wealth and revenue of the great body of the people, might be the same after such a tax as before. Ground-rents, and the ordinary rent of land, are, therefore, perhaps, the species of revenue which can best bear to have a peculiar tax imposed upon them.[32]

On efficiency grounds alone, it would have made sense to adopt a tax on the annual rental value of land, rather than to capture part of that revenue circuitously, via taxes on other sources of income (which were then passed on as costs of production). For not only was the outcome unavoidable (ultimately, the tax-take would be at the expense of the surplus income that landowners could claim as rent), but this was the economically most efficient policy, in terms of the incentives to those who worked to produce the wealth of the nation.

But the politicians were unwilling to adopt Smith's fiscal prescription. Rather, the industrial societies which were to become the first modern democracies adopted the income tax, which was first introduced in Britain by Pitt the Younger in 1800.[33]

Social Policies

To Malthus we owe a debt for the first systematised study of demography. His lasting influence, however, has been seriously damaging both to the conceptual approach to demography, and for the formulation of policies to deal with socio-economic problems such as generalised poverty. Malthus did more than anyone to ingrain an attitude that colors people's attitudes today. He created the impression that nature was niggardly and that poverty was natural. Where blame was to be assigned, this fell largely on the individual who was presumed to have failed to act prudently. This tapestry of impressions has seriously biased social policy ever since. The starting point for the defence of our assessment begins with the philosophy that attracted Malthus into the public arena in the first place: the French revolutionary vision of a good and equal society.

Among the victims of the revolutionaries was the landowning aristocracy. In Britain, Malthus had noted the blood-letting and his position was manifestly clear: he had 'cast his lot with the landed interests'.[34] Of itself, this does not make a convincing case for postulating that Malthus was seeking to defend landowners as a class. Recall, however, his vigorous opposition to the free trade movement in England in the post-Napoleonic war period. Free trade, argued Malthus, would encourage the manufacturing sector, which was not in the best interests of the lower classes. Another consequence of free trade in corn, one that would not have escaped his attention, was that it would lower consumer prices and therefore the rental income of landowners. But even this piece of biographical history is insufficient to accuse Malthus of bending his theory to accommodate a class interest. We search deeper, by asking three questions.

First, to what extent was the Malthusian philosophy successful in distracting policymakers from a realistic appreciation and amelioration of poverty? Second, did Malthus go out of his way to defend the landed interest? Third, was his theory of population a device for serving these twin goals?

Poverty and Welfare Policy A revealing incident in the history of social welfare in Britain occurred at the turn into the 19th century, when Pitt the Younger declared (in 1796) an intention to improve the level of public support for the poor. In 1800 he explained to the House of Commons that he had changed his mind under the influence, in part, of Malthus.[35]

Had Pitt decided to embark on a rational strategy, he would have adopted Adam Smith's prescription as to the most effective way of raising public revenue — a tax on the annual rental value of land — which would have laid the foundations for an equitable distribution of income. This, in turn, would have eliminated the poverty that stemmed directly from the enclosure of land. The fabric of society would have been transformed, for the conditions would have been established for the emergence of a wholly different set of social institutions at this formative period in history. The distribution of income would have favored the creation of more jobs at higher wages. As a result, for example, employees would not have had to resort to aggressive postures towards employers. The psychology of conflict that was built into industrial relations was the direct result of the state of dependency caused by the original loss of common use rights to land. Poverty wages provided fertile ground for the creation of trades unions and collective action based on the perception of divergent interests.[36]

The moral dilemma created by the existence of poverty amidst plenty remains at the heart of political controversy today. The confusions of policy are perpetuated, however, as evidenced by the administrations of Ronald Reagan and Margaret Thatcher in the 1980s. They sought to tilt the scales away from the provision of welfare for the poor without simultaneously correcting the flaw in the structure of property rights which Malthus — in a very casual way — had conceded was one cause of poverty. Few people in the West are now persuaded that poverty can be eliminated by the incentives allegedly associated with the New Right's advocacy of cuts in public sector spending. We are, then, obliged to return to the two fundamental issues underlined but not satisfactorily analysed by Malthus: the causes of poverty and the rights of property.

The Landed Interest Malthus's attitude towards property is most tellingly disclosed by the manner in which he absolved the landowner of responsibility for poverty. Both empirical observation — that much land was not used, thus preventing people from providing for themselves — and Ricardian theory, equipped Malthus with the means to explain how unemployment and distress could be diminished, if not banished. The solution to poverty that seemingly eluded Malthus can be stated in these terms: if intra-marginal land is not being used fruitfully, a policy that attracted people onto it and *away* from the margin would result in a rise in real living standards. But this also has another consequence: in the shortrun, at any rate, there is a drop in the share of the nation's income that can be appropriated by landowners.

Malthus developed an answer that sought to checkmate the practical logic of this theory. In his *Principles of Political Economy* he strenuously denied there was any such thing as marginal (i.e., rentless) land.[37] All land yielded rent. Evidently if some land was kept vacant this was not because the owners were piqued by the prospect of not receiving an income if they allowed others to earn their bread from it. There was no such thing as 'free' land; for Malthus, the Ricardian margin did not exist. By such reasoning, the landowners received absolution from responsibility for institutionalised poverty.

Theory as ideological device If there was a causal connection between poverty and private property rights in land, how could Malthus confute the charge that the owners of property carried special responsibility? The most effective argument was the one that he deployed as a theory of population: namely, that if wages rose above subsistence level, population would increase and force them down again. Hence the strategic futility of challenging the rights of property in any effort to eradicate poverty.

Malthus did not deny that a better use of land would raise income.

> It is unquestionably true, that in no country of the globe have the government, the distribution of property, and the habits of the people, been such as to call forth, in the most effective manner, the resources of the soil.[38]

He merely denied that this would redound to the benefit of the laboring classes for any length of time, for they would drop the checks on their sexual proclivities and increase the birth rate. Indeed, far from being a blot on history, their under-use of natural resources was a boon for the laboring classes, for 'if the distribution of property and the habits both of the rich and the poor had been the most favourable to the demand for produce and labour, though the amount of food and population would have been prodigiously greater than at present, the means of diminishing the checks to population would unquestionably be less'.[39] Fecundity would turn momentary prosperity into the tragedy of babies that could not be fed by their parents. The under-use of land, we are now led to believe, occasioned by the exclusionary powers of private property, was a providential blessing.

'Over-population': relative to what? We now turn to an examination of the manner in which policy is today bedevilled by the tone of discussion established by Malthus. We will review the problem in terms of an attempt to define over-population, the current validity of which is generally taken for granted.

The concept of over-population has no meaning unless we are provided with a second variable against which to measure the consequences of the absolute number of people. Whenever the concept is employed, implicit in its use is one or two possible variables: the depletion of resources or the level of poverty. The explicit invocation of these considerations does not, of itself, resolve the question of whether there is, or is not, over-population in a particular case; nor are they sufficient to establish over-population on a global scale. What we discover in each case, however, is that the analysis is initially complicated, but then clarified, by the need to analyse the distribution of property rights.

Depletion of natural resources Alarm bells over the ecological consequences of population growth rates were rung by Paul Ehrlich in *The Population Bomb* (1968), who restated them in *The Population Explosion*.[40] Studies such as these have a global approach which makes them difficult to analyse.

> No one yet knows what is the optimum number for the human species. The analytic equipment needed to provide the answer is not yet assembled. Assuming the present per capita use of energy, we can guess that at less than 10,000 million we should still be in a Gaian world. But somewhere beyond this figure, especially if the consumption of energy increases, lies the final choice of permanent enslavement on the prison hulk of the spaceship Earth, or gigadeath to enable the survivors to restore a Gaian world.[41]

The postulates can be examined by turning to the treatment of micro-studies, even though this approach is open to the charge of anecdotalism. For example, Julian Ozanne, a journalist who described the Kisii district of Kenya in the *Financial Times*, suffused his facts with the value judgments that are Malthusian in origin and which cloud the fundamental issues:

> As far as the eye can see, the whole district appears to be bursting at the seams under the sheer weight of its rapid population growth. A plethora of bell-shaped huts spreads across the hilly terrain like a carpet of mushrooms. Almost all the arable land is being cultivated, including steep slopes. Plots are becoming smaller and less economic as the holdings are divided up and bordered by hedges, making the fertile equatorial landscape resemble a cluttered chess board.
> Soil erosion, declining productivity and exhaustion of fertility is

becoming more marked as farmers overwork the land. In Kissi town, the district capital, there is no more available land for urban development, prompting builders and town planners to build upwards several storeys high, a remarkable development for a small rural African town.

The pressure on school places and health clinics is immense and rural unemployment is growing ...

Although Kisii district is Kenya's most populated district, the population explosion is nationwide. The Government believes Kenya's population growth will more than double the work force and put almost unbearable pressure on the environment, job creation, urban centres, land and food supply.[42]

Here we have all the classic ingredients of a Malthusian scare story: visible stresses in both demography and ecology, which Malthus would have regarded as validating his thesis — though he would have been left wondering why the birth rates had not collapsed in the face of these intense pressures.

What the reader is not told, however, is that Kenyans suffer from a serious maldistribution of land, the recognition of which transforms the challenge into a strictly economic one for the policy-makers. In 1972 — nine years after formal political independence from Britain — the distribution of land in Kenya was recorded as severely skewed in favor of the fortunate minority. About 0.1% of the landowners shared land made up of holdings that averaged 714 hectares in size, while 96% of the landowners worked holdings that were on average 3.8 hectares. Put another way, about 1,500 owners occupied 1.1 million hectares, while at the other extreme — on the tribal 'reserves' — 5 million hectares were at the disposal of 1.3 million households.[43] In the ensuing years, the maldistribution was not corrected. But the fact that the growth of population on a finite resource base contributed to the *appearance* of a maldistribution of land does not, of itself, represent a demographic component to the problem; for absent from the system is a mechanism for automatically adjusting the equitable distribution of resources. It is only when the latter condition is met, and yet *per capita* incomes continue to be eroded, that we must acknowledge a specifically demographic problem.

What we see in Kenya is not a demographic problem but a political crisis. Society is not able to balance the distribution of life-supporting resources, so a large number of people are forced to over-exploit their meagre holdings to provide subsistence for their families.

The Paradox of Poverty Low incomes are also sometimes taken as an index of an insupportable number of people. If consumers do not have money they cannot buy food, so they die. According to the World Bank, 1.1 billion people in developing countries are living in poverty. Each person was able to spend less than £4 every week on average; half of that income was spent on food.[44] Such statistics are used to justify the need for a stepped-up campaign for birth control policies, but is this emphasis warranted? Again, global perspectives do not help us to disentangle and evaluate the underlying processes, so we focus on a few examples.

The poorest nation in the western hemisphere is reported to be Guyana, in South America; the wretchedness of her living standard is said now to eclipse that of Haiti, whose levels of poverty are notorious. And yet, 'The country should be rich; it has good soil, ample rain, timber, the world's purest bauxite, and fewer than 700,000 rather well-educated people in an area the size of Britain.'[45] Despite this richness of resources, 'Guyana imported rice last year [1989], could not fill its sugar export quota, and has not run its alumina plant since 1982.' Evidently, the reason for the abject poverty has to be sought not in demographic imperatives but in the institutional arrangements. A similar paradox emerges when we turn to Africa. Malawi, for example, is self-sufficient in food,

> But these statistical claims mean little, said international aid workers, who reported not only extraordinary levels of mortality from child malnutrition but also high levels of stunted growth among those who survive.[46]

A concern with fertility growth rates in Guyana and Malawi would not lead to a resolution of the plight of these populations; unless, of course, we start from the premise that institutional reforms are outside the scope of action. But in that case, further research into the problem of poverty would be without purpose.

Rapid increase in fertility rates Intermingled with considerations of poverty and the exploitation of the natural resource base of a population is the assumption that the problem could be solved if only people would bear fewer babies. Rather than confront the problems of the maldistribution of resources — which is another way

The Crisis of Transition from the Commons 73

of saying that people are being denied the right to work — some governments tend to encourage people to migrate onto the periphery of society. Such has been the case in Brazil. Another example, which highlights the inter-relatedness of economics, ecology and demography, is provided by the Philippines, whose policy strategy aggravates the original problem.

> Next to population pressures, perhaps no other factors foster more degradation than the inequitable distribution of land and the absence of secure land tenure. In an agrarian society, keeping a disproportionate share of land in the hands of a few forces the poorer majority to compete for the limited area left, severely compromising their ability to manage sustainably what land they do have.
>
> In the Philippines, for example, agrarian policy over the last several decades has promoted land resettlement rather than redistribution. The elite retained their holdings while landless peasants were encouraged to move to designated resettlement areas. One such area was in Palawan, the country's largest province. Incoming migrants cleared forest to grow crops, but the land could not long sustain production under the methods they used; weeds invaded, farmers abandoned their fields, and new lands were cleared.
>
> The government had made no provisions to protect the land rights of Palawan's indigenous communities, and so as migrant farmers moved in, the local farmers — who had developed sustainable agricultural practices — were forced to retreat to the interior hills. Their plots on the steep slopes yielded only half as much as their lowland fields had. As a result, fallow periods crucial to restoring the land's fertility were shortened from eight years to two, thereby exhausting the soil and further depressing yields. Similar scenarios have played out in numerous countries where striking inequities in land holdings compound population pressures.[47]

Here, despite a perceptive assessment of the role of land tenure in the impoverishment of people and the degradation of the ecological environment, the author insists on associating 'population pressure' with these social processes, according the demographic dimension a validity which it does not deserve. First things first. The demographic dimension is put into its correct perspective when we apply the Ricardian theory of rent and the Georgist fiscal policy, which resolves the spatial distribution of population by neutralising the monopolistic character of property rights in land. Again, referring to Figure 3, we see that if the grip of the Filipino monopolists on the best of land was loosened, a centripetal effect would be unleashed that would attract people into the centre of society and onto the most fertile land, producing an automatic rise in living standards which (on the basis of European and North American evidence over the past century) would automatically encourage a downward pressure on the growth rate of fertility.

A spatial theory of population It appears, then, that the fundamental problem with which we are grappling is a systemic one: a flaw in the structure of a cultural pillar — the land tenure system — rather than the aggregated failures of many individuals feeding off a finite resource base.

We find, furthermore, that contemporary 'crises' — whether initially approached from an economic, ecological or demographic discipline — are best analysed in terms of the fusion of the Ricardian theory with Georgist policy. According to projections made at the beginning of the 1990s, another 1 billion people would be added to the world's population within 10 years. By 2,025, the population will have increased by 3.17 billion. The United Nations predicts that the total will eventually stabilise at about 11 billion people, but, given present fertility rates, the figure is just as likely to be 14 billion. In terms of our model, given that the reforms necessary to dismantle the global Malthusian trap have not been implemented, this means that billions of people will be marginalised, the rent of land will rise and *per capita* incomes will decline. (For a fuller discussion of this process, see the Appendix.) This is, indeed, a social Law of Immiseration. The few will become richer (they are the ones who own the land) and the poor (who have been dispossessed of their traditional rights of access to the commons) will become poorer.

Malthus would regard this centrifugal effect, this displacement of more people onto poorer soil or less advantageous locations, as inevitable; it isn't. He would, furthermore, regard it as proof of his original hypotheses; it isn't that, either. The forces that are generating this outcome are the direct result of the existing structure of property rights in land, which are not — as Malthus would have us think — so akin to natural rights that they must be left untouched. Whether they are reformed, and the nature of any change, are political issues within the purview of a democratic society.

Birth control policies Nothing that we have said counts against the wisdom of social policies aimed at stabilising the growth of population, a facility for which has been with man from primordial times. The degree of social concern will be dictated by the profiles of the growth rates within individual socio-ecological niches. But if corrective policies of a practical character are to be defined, it is imperative to discover the appropriate relative emphasis between direct influence over parents concerning the number of children they ought to have (assuming this can be determined), and the strengthening of those social institutions that have traditionally helped in the regulation of fertility rates.

Malthus sought to place the burden of responsibility on the individual. To be logically consistent, he had to deny government any significant prospect of success through direct intervention. 'It is to the laws of nature, therefore, and not to the conduct and institutions of man, that we are to attribute the necessity of a strong check on the natural increase of population.'[48]

The social stresses engendered during the 19th century precluded Malthus's view from achieving a dominant influence over policy. The failure to institute substantive reforms to those socio-economic processes during this period led to the articulation of two streams of oppositional thought. These found their most powerful expression the 1880s. One was the socialist philosophy represented by Karl Marx. The other was the free market reforms advocated by Henry George.

With the eclipse of the socialist alternative, the perspectives offered by Henry George now seem to warrant re-examination. On the question of population, he compellingly argued that the account provided by Malthus — the 'instinct of reproduction, in the natural development of society, tends to produce misery and vice'[49] — had to be drastically modified. He claimed that we had to embrace the consequences of 'a third check which comes into play with the elevation of the standard of comfort and the development of the intellect.' To bring that check into action constitutes a challenge to the political process, for 'any danger that human beings may be brought into a world where they cannot be provided for arises not from the ordinances of nature, but from social maladjustments that in the midst of wealth condemn men to want.'[50]

It is towards the clarification of this hypothesis that new research needs to be undertaken, to settle the controversies about the causes of poverty and population explosions that originated with Malthus. In particular, property rights in land require close appraisal. In this new debate on the problems that intimately relate demography and ecology it will not be easy to turn a blind eye to property rights. The public concern with the threat to the environment forces the vexed question of property rights into the heart of discussion. The challenge is to discover the way in which a transformation of property rights may lead to the reconstitution of culture into a stable form consistent both with the needs of humanity and the natural environment.

APPENDIX

Institutional Determinants of the Malthusian Trap

The fundamental 'social maladjustment' which Henry George identified in *Progress and Poverty* was the private appropriation of land rent. Given full private land ownership and a population causing the margin of production to be at M_1 in the graph (below), he argued, in effect, that society had the choice of initiating either of two opposing socio-economic tendencies.

Were the government to capture the rent of land for the equal benefit of all its citizens, it would initiate a virtuous circle in which the growth of incomes outstripped the growth of population. The increased productive power of both labor and land would create a powerful tendency for the margin of production to retreat inwards, towards the centre (i.e., from M_1 to M_3 in the graph). Malthus's own macroeconomic observations concerning savings and investment levels, George's analysis of optimal spatial distribution and Adam Smith's strictures on optimal taxation combine to explain how the Malthusian trap would be undone.

But if society were to allow full private land ownership to continue unabated without the fiscal disciplines of the land-value tax, the vicious circle — the 'natural tendency' perceived by Malthus which resulted in the 'iron law of wages' — would continue to operate. This pushes the margin of production ever outward into remoter areas, onto less fertile or higher-cost (e.g., transportation) land. This establishes the conditions for increasingly unsustainable activity. The concomitant waste of capital (to provide infrastructure on an extensive basis), and natural resources, does nothing for conservation of the environment, either.

In the graph, the wage (plus interest) level W_1, at time T_1, and the future prospects of the unskilled manual worker at the base of the wage structure, are low enough to make a large family appear a surer basis for material security than economic enterprise. The dismal Malthusian mechanism of population growth exceeding the growth of production is therefore triggered, which forces the margin of settlement out to its sustainable limit (M_2) at current productivity levels. In time, and out of desperation, people will even migrate beyond this point to fragile environments where periodic famine and permanent depreciation of 'nature's capital' occur (between M_2 and M_4). Beyond this point, however, mere survival by normal cultural means is not even temporarily possible.

In this dismal situation, capital accumulation which raises *per capita* productivity is insufficient to allow the margin of production to contract to the point at which the wages of the masses are enough to encourage them to change their procreative habits. The Malthusian trap is still closed. The productivity increase ultimately serves only to extend the sustainable margin beyond M_2 (to M_2^1). Wages do not rise, and society is called upon (through the Welfare State, or foreign aid) to ameliorate the impoverished conditions of the displaced families by means of income transfers or charitable donations.

Malthus appears, therefore, to have put his finger on the *proximate* cause of the population crisis within the current institutional setting. Henry George responded to him by pointing to the *underlying* institutional cause.

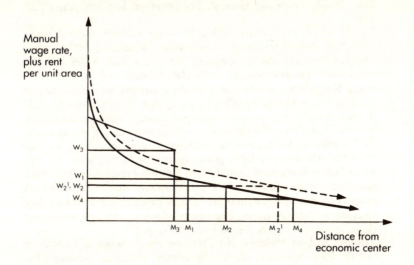

Figure 4

For graphical simplicity, W_1, W_2, etc., include both the absolute wages earned by an unskilled manual worker on a marginal site and the absolute returns to his capital. Competition turns the marginal wage into the going wage for all similar workers throughout the economy; it also equalizes the absolute returns to the same value of capital employed at all locations (interest rates are uniform throughout an economy). Hence, an unskilled manual worker working with the same value of capital produces the same value of output (W_1, W_2, etc.) wherever he works between the centre and the margin of the economy. In addition to the returns to labor and capital there is surplus output, rent, which accrues to the owner of land. The average rent per unit of land along concentric rings surrounding the centre of production tends to diminish with distance from the centre, so cross-sections of the rent in the economy are depicted in the figure by the triangular areas above the wage-plus-interest lines, W_1, W_2, etc. The triangular area above W_3 is drawn to depict how public appropriation of land rent leads to a more efficient use of land, an upward shift of the production curve, and a more even distribution of output between the center and the margin.

NOTES

1. Gore Vidal, 'Gods and Greens', *The Observer*, London, August 27, 1989.
2. J.E. Lovelock, *Gaia: a new look at life on earth*; (1979) page references are to the Oxford University Press paperback edition, 1987.
3. Phil Davison and Sharon Kingman, 'How the first AIDS case was unravelled', *The Independent on Sunday*, London, July 8, 1990.
4. Using Karl Marx's notion that 'capitalism' needed 'an army of surplus workers,' it might be possible to argue that factory owners would benefit from a breakdown in fertility control mechanisms. Marx, however, failed to explain how this could be materialised in a form that would influence behavior in the bedroom. On the other hand, we shall show that there is a perfectly good explanation for the scale of unemployed labor in the early period of the industrial revolution, stemming directly from the enclosure of the commons as a result of Parliamentary support for the new system of land tenure based on private ownership.
5. Quoted in Patricia James, *Population Malthus: His Life and Times* (London: Routledge & Kegan Paul, 1979), p.124.
6. Thomas Robert Malthus, *An Essay on the Principle of Population* (1798). Page references are to the edition edited by Antony Flew (Harmondsworth: Penguin, 1970), which contains *A Summary View*.
7. David Ricardo, *Principles of Political Economy and Taxation* (1817); page references are to the J.R. McCulloch edition London: John Murray, (1888).
8. *Ibid.*, p.5.
9. Quoted by Ricardo, *ibid.*, p.372, n.
10. *Ibid.*, p.251.
11. *Ibid.*
12. *Ibid.*
13. Fred Harrison, 'Longe and Wrightson: Conservative Critics of George's Wage Theory' in R.V. Andelson, *Critics of Henry George* (Rutherford: Farleigh Dickinson University Press, 1979).
14. Malthus, *op. cit.*, p.226.
15. *Ibid.*, p.234, emphasis added.
16. *Ibid.*
17. Malthus, p.245. This is a surprising defence of private property, given his description of private landowners as gentlemen of leisure prone to keeping their land idle for the benefit of blood sports. *Ibid.*, p.246. He did seek to ameliorate the implications of this under-use of land with his claim that private property secures to 'a portion of society' the 'leisure necessary for the progress of the arts and sciences' (*ibid.*). Artists and scientists did not pursue their objectives by leisurely means, of course, Malthus confused them with idle patrons, the rent-appropriating

The Crisis of Transition from the Commons 81

    landowners.
18 *Ibid.*, pp. 245-6.
19 *Ibid.*, p. 246.
20 *Ibid.*, pp. 268, 269.
21 *Ibid.*, pp. 246-7, emphasis added. The demand-side character of this analysis may explain why John Maynard Keynes (1883-1946) was to side with Malthus against Ricardo. Henry George, taking the same facts, explained unemployment by pointing out the obvious: if landowners denied people access to the land they needed to generate their own wages, why seek further for the primary cause of unemployment?
22 *Ibid.*, p. 247.
23 David Richards, 'The Greens and the Tax on Rent' in Richard Noyes, ed., *Now the Synthesis: Capitalism, Socialism & the New Social Contract* (London: Shepheard-Walwyn; New York: Holmes & Meier, 1991).
24 *Progress and Poverty* (1879; centenary edn., New York: Robert Schalkenbach Foundation, 1979), pp. 451-2.
25 Malthus, op. cit., p. 246.
26 *Ibid.*, p. 251.
27 *Ibid.*, p. 268.
28 *Ibid.*, p. 269.
29 *Ibid.*
30 *Ibid.*, p. 270. This condition was presented in terms of the best interests of the laboring classes, whose 'natural tendency' was to 'increase beyond the demand for their labor, or the means of their adequate support, and the effect of this tendency to throw the greatest difficulties in the way of permanently improving their condition.' *Ibid*. Henry George's point was that, with the tax and tenure system favored by Malthus, there was no way the under-class would ever rise above the level of poverty, no matter how strictly they regulated their fertility growth rates.
31 Adam Smith, *The Wealth of Nations* (1776), pp. 394, 400. Page references are to Vol. II of the Edwin Cannan edition (Chicago: Chicago University Press, 1976).
32 *Ibid.*, p. 370.
33 The absurdity of the fiscal structure established by Pitt and his successors was dramatised in 1990 by the Thatcher administration, when it introduced the Poll Tax in England and Wales. The 120 workers on 12 government-owned farms (administered by the Agricultural Development Advisory Service, the commercial arm of the Ministry of Agriculture Fisheries and Food) were given pay rises to offset the new tax, which ranged between £250 and £500, according to locality. A clearer illustration of the worker passing on the tax to his employer — because he cannot bear the burden on his wages — it would be difficult to find.

That the government should incur the costs of clawing back money which it first paid to its employees raises questions of political pathology that are beyond the concerns of this essay. We must, however, point to the economic outcome, which supports Adam Smith's point. Because competition prevented the farms from raising the prices of their produce to offset the tax liability, the result had to be at the expense of the rental income appropriated by the landowner in this case, the government itself.

34   Joseph S. Keiper, Ernest Kurnow, Clifford D. Clark and Harvey H. Segal, *Theory and Measurement of Rent* (Philadelphia: Chilton Co. 1961), p. 30.
35   Antony Flew, 'Introduction', in Malthus, *op. cit.*, p. 12.
36   Newcastle schoolteacher Thomas Spence was one of those who, at the time, accepted the logic of the Smithian tax on the rent of land, and he advocated its adoption. Had the tax been employed as a major plank of government policy, owners would have been obliged to place their sites at the disposal of people who wanted to use them. This would have been unavoidable: how else could they have met their fiscal obligations? Urban settlements would not have sprawled, prime agricultural land would have been conserved, and the capital costs of providing infrastructure would have been reduced. Spence was imprisoned for his impudence. See Fred Harrison, *The Power in the Land*, London: Shepheard-Walwyn, (1983), p. 30.
37   Thomas Malthus, *Principles of Political Economy* (1820), pp. 181-2.
38   Malthus, *op. cit.*, p. 247.
39   *Ibid.*, p. 248.
40   Paul R. Ehrlich and Anne H. Ehrlich, *The Population Explosion* (New York: Simon & Schuster, 1990).
41   Lockelock, *op. cit.*, p. 132.
42   Julian Ozanne, 'Kenya's family planning gospel wins too few converts', *Financial Times*, January 9, 1990.
43   Claude Ake, *A Political Economy of Africa* (London: Longman, 1981), p. 122.
44   World Bank, *World Development Report* (New York: Oxford University Press, 1990).
45   'Poor man's gold rush', *The Economist*, London, May 12, 1990.
46   Jan Perlez, 'Starving Children of Malawi Shatter Leader's Boast of Plenty', *New York Times*, April 3, 1990.
47   Sandra Postel, 'Halting Land Degradation' in Lester Brown et al., *State of the World, 1989* (New York: W. W. Norton, 1989), p. 38.
48   Malthus, *op. cit.*, p. 248.
49   George, *op. cit.*, p. 138.
50   *Ibid.*, p. 139.

4
Post-Communal Land Ownership: poverty and political philosophy
DAVID RICHARDS

I

ABSOLUTE private ownership of land has been traced by one authority back to the worshippers of Baal in Canaan, and hence to the nature-religions of the earliest civilisations. In the ancient Near East respect for individual human life was subordinated to the gratification of capricious, uncompassionate gods of nature — or, more pertinently, autocratic kings who owned and controlled (and alienated) earthly estates on the gods' behalf.

Archer Torrey argues that seafaring, trading Canaanites — the Phoenicians — took Baalistic land laws (without the kingship) from Tyre to north Africa when they established the colony of Carthage. Those land laws were adopted by the Roman Republic after the Punic Wars, spread by the Empire, and eventually revived by the modern western world.[1] Today, they are on the verge of application to every corner of the natural domain — the atmosphere, the ocean beds, Antarctica — through tradable pollution permits, discretionary mining licences and the like.

If Roman land law was indeed determined by the Phoenicians, then cultural evolution took a wrong turning at Carthage. With the defeat of Hannibal, an unhappy social paradigm was about to be imposed upon the world.

Pliny (the Elder) wrote: 'great estates ruined Italy.' (*Latifundia perdidere Italiam.*) Such estates were the inevitable outcome of the Baalistic tradition, as the Old Testament prophets pointed out before and after Phoenician practices swept through Israel under King Ahab (e.g. 1 Samuel 8:14, 20; Micah 6:16 and 2:2; Isaiah 5:8). Their own Yahwistic tradition guaranteed equal land rights through the Mosaic covenant (e.g. Numbers 26:52-56; Leviticus 25:13-34). Herbert Girardet has spelled out the ecological consequences of great estates:

> With latifundia becoming the main agricultural unit throughout the empire, the interest of the citizens in the land became purely commercial. The link between land and people was effectively broken and the long-term interest in its fertility was put aside.[2]

The Sahara desert eventually encroached on the North African breadbasket of Rome. Man's footsteps on the Earth, it is said, are deserts. The first giant footsteps were made by the first civilisation, in the (originally) Fertile Crescent. The Sumerian city-states of the third millennium B.C. appear to have been gradually infused with the spirit of private landownership by western invaders of the same origins as the Canaanites. Absentee landownership was rife in Babylonia in the middle of the first millennium B.C. when it entered its protracted decline into desert dust.[3]

The socially unjust and economically inefficient system of land tenure which the West inherited from Rome is at the source of the population concerns of the late twentieth century. Abuse of the environment may also be traced directly to the arrogant laws by which Mother Earth is permitted to be 'owned' by her offspring.

Malthusian crises and adaptive technological 'revolutions' were an inevitable result of the spread of Roman land laws, which polarized societies in terms of the distribution of income and wealth. Greater productivity was certainly made possible by the emphasis on individual property rights, but economic historians are wrong in their assumption that private ownership was the only tenurial model available for achieving technical progress and higher productivity.

Exclusive proprietorial rights may best be defined in terms of the exclusionary powers of those who own land. Certain consequences flowed from this system. Ironically, this was not the most effective way to maximise the productivity of land. Also, these rights were at the expense of both equity in the distribution of output and of sound environmental practice. The cumulative result of the thrust of these effects was to generate further demands for additional advances in productivity, which necessarily assumed the character of overexploitation of the natural habitat.

There is a considerable body of opinion among demographers that population problems are caused by poverty rather than by irresponsible fecundity — that poverty leads to high birthrates rather than *vice versa*.[4] The main hypothesis to be advanced in this chapter is that large-scale poverty is primarily the result of the adoption of the Roman version of private land ownership. If this is the case then land reform must feature prominently in any program for relieving population pressure on the environment, let alone poverty relief. A sub-theme will be the direct impact that the rules of land tenure have on the environment.

The merits of alternative land tenure systems cannot be judged without an understanding of land economics. Section II, therefore, briefly introduces the concept of land rent and demonstrates the inevitability of normative decisions, implicit or explicit, regarding its distribution. Section III illustrates the significance of such decisions in the context of the current debate on environmental policy. Section IV draws out the links between land tenure, demographic problems and other environmental problems. Section V turns to the poorer nations of the world, specifically Latin America, where these problems are at their most critical. The 'South' is shown to be following a trail that has already been blazed by the 'North'. This point is reinforced with reference to the Indian sub-continent in section VI, which focuses on the process by which the western path of economic growth leads to the growth of poverty. The contrasting results of two different ways of dealing with the land's rent in Southeast Asia are presented in section VII. The case of Africa appears at first sight to conflict with the main hypothesis, and this is the subject of the final section.

II

'Ownership' of land is in fact ownership of a 'bundle of rights and restrictions' governing land. These rights and restrictions vary between land tenure systems. Full ownership involves 'the *greatest possible interest in a thing which a mature system of law recognizes*'[5] and as far as land is concerned it is most closely approximated in a *laissez faire* market economy with land tenure institutions derived from Roman Law. The most distinctive features of land ownership in such an economy are that owners may seek the most profitable use to themselves of their land, without reference to social costs, and retain all the profits.

The profit, or income (actual and imputed), accruing to land was known by the classical economists as 'rent'. Curiously, neoclassical economists have generalised the concept of rent in a way that excludes much of land rent. They apply the term to the excess of the earnings of any factor of production over the minimum earnings necessary to retain it in its present use. Thus they restrict land rent to that part of a site's income in excess of the income it could get in its next best alternative use. They have not, however, changed our understanding of the nature of the income from land. Robert Dorfman summarises it thus:

> Rent is a payment for the use of any nonproducible resource. Land rents are typical, and are the most important kind. Other examples are the high incomes earned by especially talented individuals, the value of television channels, and the values of artificially scarce resources, such as taxicab licences in New York. By definition, the supply of a rentable resource cannot be changed. The supply curve is a vertical line. The price, or rent, is its value to the user in whose hands it is most productive, to whom it has the highest marginal productivity.
>
> Rent is the purest of unearned incomes. One receives it simply by owning something unique, and one need do nothing to obtain it except to drive a hard bargain. Nevertheless it has an economic function: it allocates unique resources to the uses in which their products are most beneficial according to the test of the market. What has no particular economic function is the identification of rent for the resource — which is a genuine social opportunity cost — with income for the resource owner. *Rental income could be entirely taxed away without any ill effects on the operation of the economy.* Instead we sometimes seem to go out of our way to donate rents to various individuals. Examples are giving away television licenses, charging nominal prices for taxicab medallions, and underpricing irrigation water in arid parts of the country. These giveaways are actually deleterious. They create artificial vested interests and generate struggles for gaining access to the rentable resource.[6]

One may quarrel with some of Dorfman's categorisation of rents. All land rents are composed of a payment for the quality of natural resources and/or a payment for their position within the spatial arrangement of human activity. The fact that licenses to occupy congested public spaces are *only* valuable for the second reason does not mean that their economic value is not land rent. The limited range of airwave frequencies available to television companies clearly produces land rent. However, one must commend Dorfman's concise summary of the issues involved.

The right of the land owner to the rent produced by the land does not appear to have the same moral sanction as the right of the worker to the wages produced by labour, or of the owner of physical capital to the interest produced by capital formation. The former right has no economic function, and in the interests of a 'level playing field' (a prerequisite of efficient, let alone equitable, resource allocation) it is arguable that it *should* 'be entirely taxed away' and distributed fairly. What constitutes 'fair' distribution is open to question. The most obviously fair way to distribute rent would be to provide a citizen's dividend. A case can be made, however, on efficiency grounds, for reducing taxes on other sources of income instead, but the degree of fairness achieved depends on the form of the tax reduction, and on the public goods that are provided by the community.

The need to make normative decisions regarding entitlements to land is not denied by orthodox economists. Kelvin Lancaster notes that the distribution of income is a function of the sale of factor services and therefore depends upon the distribution of wealth (by which he means the ownership of land and capital) and labour skills:[7]

> In general then, each distribution of wealth will tend to be associated with a different equilibrium, and with different prices for goods *and* factors, and for a different distribution of income between labor and owners of wealth ... The contribution of the economist is to note that any distribution of income should leave the appropriate *signals* undisturbed, otherwise the economy is not doing as well as it can, at the chosen distribution of income and wealth.[8]

In a democratic society, therefore, it is necessary to make an explicit decision regarding the 'chosen distribution of income and wealth.' Otherwise the decision will be implicit, and arbitrary: it certainly will not be due solely to the economists' beneficient 'invisible hand'.

III

The free market advocate, Martin Wolf, is quite clear about what constitutes a fair distribution of entitlements to land (i.e. the environment). In a *Financial Times* survey of the world economy he addresses the issue of how to allocate the limited pollution absorption capacity of the global atmosphere 'sink'. The World Bank has indicated that 'The developing world, almost 80% of the world's population, is responsible for only 7% of the industrial emission of carbon dioxide', the 'greenhouse' gas which may cause global warming.[9] Wolf notes that 'Any agreement to curb emissions would, therefore, involve the most delicate international negotiations.' The current distribution of the atmosphere's services clearly cannot be embalmed by equal restrictions on the further use of those services. This is not because the richer countries want to 'do the right thing' by the poorer countries, but because only a demonstrably fair system might be accepted by the latter. Wolf must therefore address the question of what *is* a fair system. And he has no difficulty in providing an answer:

> The equitable solution would be to allocate the rights to gas emission, globally, on an equal basis per head. Those emitting more than their share would then have to buy that right, so compensating the less advanced countries for the damage being done to a global 'common', the atmosphere.[10]

In other words, the use of global commons should be rationed. The right to the commons is an equal one, not an earned one. This means that it is not an alienable one.

Logic requires that buying the right to use the commons means renting it, because the fairness of equal allocation per head cannot apply to one moment in time alone. By extension, as all land was originally commons, and the right is inalienable, all land should be rationed. This does not mean that, ideally, all people should use exactly their share, as sometimes implied by some theoreticians of land reform. It does mean that those using more than their share should pay rent to those using less.

Wolf continues:

National emission rights must then be turned into constraints on individual behaviour. An argument for using the price system is that it would be easier to identify whether other countries are cheating. A high price of gasoline is relatively visible, while controls are far more impenetrable to the outsider.

But he has no illusions regarding the practicality of this solution:

All these mechanisms are merely a way of making painful adjustments more efficiently. The pain remains ... Consider, for example, the effects on American society of gasoline at $10 a gallon. It is difficult to believe that politics will permit such changes ...

Those who are currently capturing the economic rent of the atmosphere — that is, enjoying its services without charge — will not easily relinquish their privilege, it is true. On the other hand, resistance is compounded by the perception that higher gasoline prices, or a more general 'carbon tax', would be regressive, taking a higher proportion of the purchasing power of the poor than of the rich. Of course, much would depend on how the increased public revenue was spent. But if the rationing-of-nonproducibles principle enunciated by Wolf was applied within nations, as well as between nations, the equity problem would be automatically solved. Higher fossil fuel prices would then be accompanied by an equal distribution of the associated mineral rents.

The orthodox counter to the argument that the 'polluter pays' principle is regressive is that the revenue raised may be spent in a progressive way. Professor David Pearce — appointed a special adviser to the UK environment secretary in the wake of the Brundtland Report to the United Nations on 'sustainable development' (*Our Common Future*) — has publicly suggested that part of green revenue should be used to offset income and corporation taxes. Alternatively, the UK's Henley Centre for Forecasting has suggested that pensions and child benefits should be targeted for support.[11]

At the international level, there is general agreement that if the less developed nations are to be persuaded not to follow in the footsteps of the more developed nations in the matter of mining natural resources and discharging pollution, then massive financial transfers will be necessary to replace the incomes foregone. Professor Pearce has written:

> ... conservation values in economic terms, can be very large indeed. But big existence values won't mean much to Brazil or Malaysia or Indonesia if they can't be converted into cash. Yet this is exactly what must now happen if the forests are to be saved ... If we all gain from tropical forest conservation we have to retreat rapidly from the stance that it is somehow all their fault and that we should not have to pay.[12]

By funding such 'aid' out of 'green taxes' in the developed countries and relating it to conservation and pollution abatement programmes in developing countries there could be a double gain.[13]

Such pragmatic measures fall far short, however, of the *systematic* solution for combining market efficiency and equity alluded to by Wolf.

IV

History has shown that where land rents are not equally shared, 'aid' programmes, however well designed, tend, by raising private land rents, to benefit large landowners disproportionately, create further indebtedness and vulnerability, force the poorest off the land or on to the worst land, and thus exacerbate the social divisions and poverty they are supposed to alleviate.[14]

Such inequality 'provides the economic rationale for large families and burgeoning populations.'[15] The poor have to look for security and status in children rather than in wealth, and ultimately only have recourse to pawning their environments for sustenance. It is poverty that created the 'population bomb' which inspired the creation of the Green political parties in the 1970s.

Where each person's equal share in that part of production which is contributed by land (rent) rather than by labour or the products of labour is not guaranteed, a scramble for access to it is set in motion. This is also a scramble for monopoly power over part of society's scarce resource base. Inevitably, might is right in such a struggle. Then the initial advantages conferred by land tend to multiply in a cumulatively causal way. Class systems are the outcome, and disinherited, exploitable labour resources — serfs, proletariat — are created.[16]

At later stages of development, as democracy levers open the landownership base by favouring owner-occupation at the expense of landlordism, this struggle transforms into efforts by landowners to intensify the use of their land in order to raise rents and reap capital gains on sale. Over-extension of activity into sub-marginal, ecologically unsuitable areas, accompanied by under-intensive use of many super-marginal areas, such as speculatively held vacant inner city and urban fringe sites, set-aside farm land, and even mono-cropped prairies, are the result. Mason Gaffney writes:

> Spread and sprawl in forestry, cities and agriculture are common results of the dominant force driving American politics, the quest for unearned increments to land value ... Rising population is one factor pushing up land values, but not the strongest. Increased demand per capita is the main factor. These demands include ... spurious demands ... like the demand of government for land to 'bank' and hold idle, and the demand of speculators 'with a view to getting a little something for nothing' [Thorstein Veblen].
>
> Veblen went on to say that farm technology adapts to the Procrustean bed of absentee ownership. Rather than leading, technology lags changes in land-holdings wrought by rural speculative investors. Thus it is not 'society' or 'efficiency' alone that mandate monocultural chemical farming, but also the peculiar needs of absentee speculators holding more land than they can work themselves or with their families. Logic of, by, and for this minority is set up as logic for all.[17]

The counterpart of the centrifugal force spurred by land purchase is the centripetal force created by ownership concentration. Massive agricultural subsidies in the developed world, the political wing of the rural real estate business, have helped hasten the demise of the family farm. For example, between 1982 and 1987 the number of U.S. mid-sized farms declined by 12.5% while the number of larger farms fell by 2%. But the investment returns on farm real estate between 1960 and 1988 exceeded the composite returns of the companies in the Standard & Poors 500 index.[18]

In the European Community the story is the same. 'It is reckoned that 80% of the vast sums spent on farm support in the EC have gone to bigger farmers and to traders rather than to the small farmer,' writes Bridget Bloom, the *Financial Times* agriculture correspondent.[19] In an address to an Oxford Farming Conference, agriculture professor Alan Swinbank noted that instead of competing to produce food as cheaply as possible, British farmers were competing to buy land in an effort to maximise their production and their share of the subsidy largess. This occurred at a time when milk quotas and land set-aside schemes were supposed to reduce food surpluses. Swinbank concluded:

> In consequence, land prices are higher than they would otherwise be. High land prices undoubtedly cause land to be farmed more intensively, and thus lead to greater environmental degradation than would otherwise be the case.[20]

Concentration of land ownership leads to centralisation of settlement. Rural depopulation and urban production of the capital equipment used by large farmers — and of their luxuries and financial services — go hand in hand. In the poorer nations of the world, where the same processes operate, accelerated rural-urban migration is particularly evident — rural sectors being proportionately larger — creating 'many of the real problems of population.' Michael Todaro writes: 'A more rational and efficient spatial *distribution* of national populations thus becomes an alternative, in some countries, to the slowdown of overall population growth.'[21]

In the richer countries of the world, however, it is 'commodity fetishism' which now congests the urban centres, and increases society's pressure on the environment, as production of standard economic goods is piled up in the individual's ceaseless quest for 'positional' advantage. The 'positional economy', consisting of status symbols which cannot be multiplied by increasing production — the *best* locations, the *best* education, etc. — serves the function of the ever-receding carrot on a stick. It entices producers to turn out more and more commodities, not for their own sake, but for the income needed to outbid others for access to 'positional goods'.[22]

Land in general is a positional good, as 'they aren't making it any more', (though its distribution between particular uses may change). The more individual uses are restricted by regulations or congestion, the more positional the sites in that use become. In most developed countries, therefore, it is expected that as incomes rise the ratio of house prices to incomes will not fall, unlike the ratio of, say, automobile prices to incomes. One must produce more and more, literally in order to obtain the space in which to stand still — unless, that is, one already owns it.

In Japan, where the land value of the Tokyo metropolitan area equals the land value of the whole of the USA, the frustrations of the economic squirrel wheel are particularly intense. House prices in the Tokyo area are 8 to 10 times annual incomes. Nobumitsu Kagami, managing director of Nomura Investment Management, has commented that people are beginning to question why they are working. 'Young people are becoming disillusioned and desperate about this. No matter how hard they work there's no way they can acquire what their elders, like me, got simply by being there first. It's an unfair society and people are beginning to see this.'[23]

One of the arguments against introducing road pricing and higher petrol taxes to reduce traffic congestion and pollution is that they would make the automobile 'an even greater status symbol than at present. The motivation to have this status symbol which gobbles up so many of the earth's resources, would be even more pervasive than today.' These are the words of a correspondent to the New Economics Foundation (David Weston, *New Economics*, issue eleven/autumn 1989), who goes on to advocate decentralising society to reduce the need for travel, and banning the internal combustion engine. More fundamentally, however, it would seem that only limitation of society's annual use of primary resources in conjunction with equal rationing can curtail the voracious appetite of the positional economy.

V

It is in the poorer countries of the so-called South that the pressures of economic growth on the carrying capacity of the environment are producing the subsistence crises with which the name of Malthus is associated. It is generally agreed that the population problems of the South are due to the disruptive effects of the import of western cultural norms and health measures. In effect, the North has exported only one arm of the 'demographic transition'. Birth rates have not fallen as fast as death rates. What is not quite so generally accepted is that the North has also exported a decrease in subsistence security for the masses, thus actively discouraging downward adjustment of birth rates.

The rigging of international trade in favour of the early industrialised countries is a standard complaint. The Bengal textile industry was clearly decimated in this way in the nineteenth century. It is generally accepted that agricultural protectionism in industrialised countries is 'doing vast and incalculable damage to the economies of every country in the world,'[24] more especially to the agricultural sectors of less industrialised countries, which are undercut by subsidised food exports. But what is less widely appreciated is the disruptive effect on colonial economies of the imposition of the western system of land tenure. No better trojan horse could have been introduced to undermine their societies, if that had been the aim.

Latin America has the longest history of private landownership imposed by colonising nations. Its *latifundios*, or very large estates, are notorious for devoting large tracts of potential arable land to pasture, or leaving them idle. In Brazil it was calculated in the 1960s that '*total factor productivity* on family farms was twice as high (and, therefore, unit costs twice as low) as on the large *latifundio* tracts of land'.[25] The latter occupied 60% of the farmland, the former 6%. It was at this time that the generals launched 'Operation Amazonia' to 'inundate the Amazon with civilization' and fulfil Brazil's manifest destiny. It also served to relieve the pressure of a large slice of the population that was denied access to the nation's best arable land.

Land resettlement programmes rather than land redistribution have also been the policy choice in other tropical rainforest countries. In the Philippines and Indonesia, the elites have retained their holdings while landless peasants have been encouraged to clear the forest — with the same results: declining crop yields, abandoned land, further migration.[26]

'A major explanation for the relative economic inefficiency of farming the fertile land on the *latifundios*,' writes Todaro, 'is simply that the wealthy landowners often value these holdings not for their potential contributions to national agricultural output, but rather for the considerable power and prestige that they bring.' Referring to the similar *hacienda* system in the densely populated Andes, Michael Redclift elaborates: 'The shortage of land off the estate, and its poor quality, enabled the landlord to attract or coerce labour onto the estate without much difficulty.'[27]

As for liberal attempts to improve the situation, 'one of the net effects of Latin American land reform has probably been an increase in landlessness. Agrarian reform, or the threat of it, stimulated private land sales and helped ensure that landlords divested themselves of their poorest land. Most landlords could be relied upon to modernize the land they retained with generous government assistance.'[28] This often meant expulsion of labour-tenants and the introduction of wage labour — the process of 'proletarianization.'

The developing nations of the present day have one disadvantage which the richer nations did not have when they were developing. As economic growth is pursued in tandem with private land ownership, foreign lands are less available for decanting displaced landless people and for providing cheap imports of raw materials. Great Britain's industrial revolution was accompanied by massive migration to the New World, as well as internal rural-urban migration. The colonisers behaved every bit as rapaciously towards the 'free' commons of the New World as the colonisers of the Amazon jungle are doing today. Thomas Jefferson remarked, 'We can buy an acre of new land cheaper than we can manure an old one.' Little wonder that the earliest settled areas had become abandoned 'sour lands' even before 1800. In 1817 it was estimated that there was as much abandoned land as cultivated land in North Carolina.[29] Westward expansion soon turned buffalo-laden prairies into 'dust bowls'.

It is significant that Thomas Malthus chose this free-for-all pioneer fringe from which to collect his empirical data for the 'natural' increase in human population. To be consistent he should have restricted the 'carrying capacity' component of his model to similar circumstances — that is, of unlimited free land available for the taking. Unregulated commons are, of course, over-used until necessity determines regulation. The question is, what is the best form of regulation?

The United States has evidently not found it. 'The puny fees paid by ranchers to use federal lands fall short of the cost of managing that land ... In 1985, he [President Reagan] signed an executive order setting grazing fees at a rate far below that of private land ... The Bureau of Land Management budget has dropped so low the agency cannot afford to protect that land from abuse ... two-thirds of the [174 million acres of] BLM range land is in unsatisfactory condition.'[30] Clearly, raising the fees to reduce grazing to a sustainable level is the answer, but the vested interests involved have sufficient political power to block such a reform. That explains why land tenure systems the world over are inequitable: they are the tools of the powerful.

The USSR, before *perestroika*, had the same problem as the federal lands of the US, only it had the excuse of fallacious theory on its side. Believing that land had no value because it contained no labour, it could be forgiven for basing its economic development on the exhaustion of its rich natural resource base. But the lesson of reality has been learned: 'As time went on,' President Gorbachev admitted, 'material resources became harder to get and more expensive... So the inertia of extensive development was leading to an economic deadlock and stagnation.'[31] In early 1990, Soviet citizens received for the first time the right to 'own' or lease land in return for land taxes or rents, *though not to buy or sell it*. Perhaps the errors of western land tenure have also been learned?

It was Marxist theory which misled the Soviets. But it was the frontier spirit of rugged individualism which misled the founders of the United States. Additionally, both nations' economic philosophies were moulded by the experience of abundant land for the taking. Significantly, it was only once the pioneer fringe had dashed itself on the Pacific Ocean that Henry George emerged in the US with the message that the Earth's resources are not infinite and should be shared equally: 'Has the first comer at a banquet the right to turn back all the chairs and claim that none of the other guests shall partake of the food provided, except as they make terms with him?' he asked.[32]

But even while there were still free banquets beckoning those who do not wish to make terms, not all could emigrate to take advantage of them. New Jersey had introduced a comprehensive poor law as early as 1774. The land of New England was already being apportioned into private holdings of the minimum practical size, and by 1790 net emigration was taking place. As in Olde England, when the land was enclosed the 'sturdy beggars' appeared on the streets. An increasingly landless population meant that a quarter of New York city's inhabitants was receiving public or private charity in 1817. Contemporaries put the problem down to vice or drink[33] — another example of the importation of erroneous perspectives from the Old World!

VI

Free banquets are no longer available anywhere in the world. The poorer nations of the South are pressing against environmental limits and touching the sensitivities of the North. But the consequent need for nations to come to agreement over sharing the contents of nature's larder actually puts the South in a bargaining position, because the North has hitherto taken the lion's share. For the first time in history the disinherited of the Earth may have a grip on the economically powerful. The political sovereignty of poor nations over land may yet weaken the unshakeable command over the Earth's natural resources upon which the richer nations depend. For the ownership of land of value is the basis of economic power.

'North' and 'South' are convenient primary labels for classifying the rich and poor nations of the world, though it is accepted that they are evocative rather than precise categories. It is also accepted that the divide between rich and poor runs within nations, and within communities, as well as between them. It applies at all geographical levels. It is instructive, however, to replace the labels in this classification, with the labels 'Landowners' and 'Landless', in order to see to what extent they apply. Of course, there are degrees of landownership, and landownership also includes all those, such as professional agents and moneylenders, who have an interest in the rent of land without being titular owners.

In one Southern continent the distinction between Landowner and Landless has already been shown to be powerful for explaining social problems. As Redclift states:

> The exactions of a *rentier* class and the opposition mounted by peasant farmers in Latin America are demonstrated in the social conflicts that have provided a common theme in Andean history and ethnography ... Control over resources in the Andes was determined by the prevailing systems of land tenure, reflecting established and emerging class interests ... The political power of these classes depends upon maintaining the existing pattern of highly unequal land distribution and land uses.[34]

Turning to southern Asia, the renowned development economist Gunnar Myrdal confirms that 'Colonial rule acted as an important catalyst to change, both directly through its effects on property rights and indirectly through its effects on the pace of monetization in the indigenous economy and on the growth of population.'[35]

European land tenure systems of private ownership were imposed, resulting in the

> breakdown of much of the earlier cohesion of village life with its often elaborate, though informal, structure of rights and obligations. The landlord was given unrestricted rights to dispose of the land and to raise the tribute from its customary level to whatever amount he was able to exact. He was usually relieved of the obligation to supply security and public amenities because these functions were taken over by the government. Thus his status was transformed from that of a tribute receiver with responsibilities to the community to that of an absolute owner unencumbered by obligations towards the peasants and the public, other than the payment of land taxes.[36]

It is no coincidence that this also describes the situation in England in the late fifteenth and sixteenth centuries when the Roman view of land was being re-introduced after the Danish and Norman interludes. The first major enclosures created landlessness, accompanied a population explosion, and led to the enactment of the first Poor Law. Just as the land tax was gradually withering away in England during that transformation of property rights, so the landlord in India and Pakistan today is able largely to avoid it. Todaro judges that 'in many respects, therefore, his position of power in the economic, political and social structure of the rural community is analagous to that of the Latin American *patron*. There is a difference in that the former is an absentee owner whereas the latter often lives on his *latifundio*. But the efficiency and productivity implications are the same.' As are — he might have added — the equity implications.

Professor Myrdal's analysis of the process of the impoverishment of the peasantry has two further components. As summarised by Todaro,

> The creation of individual titles to land made possible the rise to power of ... the moneylender. Once private property came into effect, land became a negotiable asset that could be offered by peasants as security for loans ... At the same time, Asian agriculture was being transformed from a subsistence to a commercial orientation, both as a result of rising local demand in new towns and, more importantly, in response to external food demands of colonial European powers ... [So] the peasant's cash needs grew significantly ... Often moneylenders were more interested in

acquiring peasant lands as a result of loan defaults than they were in extracting high rates of interest. By charging exorbitant interest rates or inducing peasants to secure larger credits than they could manage, moneylenders were often able to drive the peasants off their land. They could then reap the profits of land speculation by selling this farmland to rich and acquisitive landlords. Alternatively they often became landlords themselves. At any rate, largely as a consequence of the moneylender's influence, Asian peasant cultivators have seen their economic status deteriorate steadily over time.

The inevitable outcome of these extremes of wealth and poverty, where children provide either status or security, is a third component — rapid population growth. This creates a vicious circle. Cumulative subdivision and fragmentation of holdings reduces their viability until

> production falls below subsistence level and chronic poverty becomes a way of life. Peasants are forced to borrow even more from the moneylender at interest rates ranging from 50 to 200%. Most cannot repay these loans. They are then compelled to sell their land and become tenants with large debts. Because land is scarce they are forced to pay high rents... And because labour is abundant wages are extremely low. Peasants thus get trapped in a vice of chronic poverty from which, in the absence of major rural reconstruction and reform, there is no escape.[37]

A lament from Sir Thomas More's *Utopia*, published in 1516, concerning a matter 'peculiar to you Englishmen alone' (at the time), provides a fitting refrain in India half a millennium later:

> the husbandmen be thrust out of their own, or else either by covin and fraud or by violent oppression they be put besides it, or by wrongs and injuries they be so wearied, that they be compelled to sell all. By one means, therefore, or by other, either by hook or crook, they must needs depart away, poor, silly, wretched souls, men, women, husbands, wives, fatherless children, widows, woeful mothers with their young babes, and their whole household small in substance and much in number, as husbandry requireth many hands.[38]

Looking back a further 3,000 years, the Biblical story of the Israelite Joseph also has a familiar ring. Joseph, the slave-turned-Egyptian prime minister, organised the accumulation of buffer stocks during seven fat years preceding seven lean years. Herbert Girardet recounts the consequences:

When the drought became severe, the Pharaoh was in a position to sell grain to the people of Egypt (and also to tribesmen such as the Israelites), in exchange for silver and gold they had accumulated. When precious metals had run out they had to sell their herds of cattle and sheep in exchange for wheat and barley. Finally, towards the end of the drought, the Egyptians were forced to sell their plots of land to the Pharaoh in exchange for grain. From then on, he and his successors were able to extract land rent from their subjects, thus greatly increasing the political and economic powers of the ruling dynasties.[39]

(This experience no doubt stood the Israelites in good stead when the Mosaic land laws came to be framed. They were designed to prevent the concentration of land ownership — e.g. Leviticus 25.)

One of the items on the British administration's famine-warning check list in India was falling land prices as people sold their last assets to exchange for food. Landowners expanded their estates at such times. Grain prices naturally rose and speculators and hoarders made their fortunes.[40] In the famine in Bangladesh in 1974, 81% of those seeking food relief owned no land or less than half an acre.[41]

The Green Revolution has turned India into a net food exporter. 'But poor Indians are still hungry. 47% of those living in the countryside still own less than 1 acre of land. 22% own none at all.'[42] The World Bank notes that some 90% of the world's billion or so hungry people live and work in rural areas.

The Brandt Report to the United Nations made the mistake of thinking that land reform can only provide 'small relief' for the landless in densely populated countries such as Bangladesh, where 'large holdings account for only 0.2% of the total land', and so recommended instead investment in irrigation and flood control to allow multiple cropping, thus increasing the demand for labour. Redclift contests this argument:

> In Bangladesh rural poverty is not a consequence of simple population pressure, but of the combined forces of accelerated technological change and a social structure rooted in inequality ... [It] is closely linked with the growth of inequality in command over natural resources ... As Clay suggests, 'If the objective is to eliminate poverty rather than alleviate it, there is no satisfactory alternative to assuring the landless a guaranteed share in the income stream from the one basic resource — land'.[43] Such a prescription has advantages that neither rural public works nor grain purchases possess, and it would do more than relieve seasonal fluctuations in poverty.[44]

Claire Whittemore summarises the position succinctly in an Oxfam booklet, *Land for People*, compiled in the light of the experience of Oxfam's field workers:

> The most powerful people in a rural society are those who have control over the most land. So investment in the rural sector inevitably benefits the landholders and the more land they have, the more it benefits them. They are able to use their increased wealth to buy more land and to mechanise. The result is more landless people and fewer jobs.[45]

Whittemore (p. 37) quotes the World Bank as admitting, in relation to loans for 3,000 deep tubewells in Bangladesh, 'In a project such as this where the major result is to increase the productivity of the land, to a large extent the distribution of direct benefits must reflect the existing land ownership pattern.'

An early draft of the Oxfam booklet was used by a lobby group opposing official views at the United Nations Food and Agriculture Organisation's 'World Conference on Agrarian Reform and Rural Development' in Rome in 1979. Whittemore (p. 33) notes that 'The FAO was created to serve the interests of its member governments. It has to present an acceptable, non-political image to all of them... as such it approaches all the problems of hunger, land and food with technical solutions such as improved irrigation and better varieties of seeds.' The Green Revolution was clearly the apogee of the FAO's approach, but

> It can now be seen to be essentially a short term solution, and inadequate even in the short term. The changes which have accompanied it have made it more difficult, if not impossible, to attack the basic problem of land reform and to achieve an equitable and efficient distribution of productive resources. The power of the present landowners has become almost unchallengeable. The failure of the [Indian] Government even to impose a land tax on the beneficiaries of huge public expenditure on irrigation, credit subsidies, subsidised seed, fertilisers, etc, is an indication of their political power and influence.[46]

Gunnar Myrdal would not disagree: 'Almost everywhere governments have made a sham of it,' he writes. 'Secondary reforms — community development, agricultural extension, credit and other co-operatives — have had an easier passage. But in the absence of effective land reform, they have tended to assist the upper strata in the villages and thus actually increase inequality.'[47]

VII

An historical illustration of how fairer sharing of land rent helps to avoid the Malthusian trap of low output growth and high population growth is provided by Matthew Edel, in what has been called 'by far' the best introduction to the political economy of ecology.[48] He compares the economic development of Java and Japan. Both are large islands off the coast of Asia, but the former has greater natural advantages, particularly its rich volcanic soils.

Before colonisation by the Dutch in the seventeenth century, Java had a lower population density and higher rice yields than Japan. The Dutch then enforced the production of cash crops, particularly sugar. By 1830 landowners were obliged to lend one-fifth of their land to the Governor for sugar production, and landless labourers to provide 66 days labour a year for public construction work. The rental surpluses that formerly supported the Sultans and ensured leisure time for the labourers were thus mainly diverted abroad through the introduction of production for export.

After 1870 Dutch corporate plantations took over the cash crops, which now occupied one-third of the irrigated terraces and still enjoyed enforced labour. Within a few decades the growing population was pressing on the limits of land supply. The Dutch government, under its 'ethical system', began diverting resources into maintaining living standards. This averted Malthusian checks, and population growth continued apace. The area under sugar gradually gave way to rice until, by Independence in 1945, there were virtually no sugar plantations left. *Kolonisatie* policy, precursor of the Indonesian Transmigration programme, was also instituted. 'Surplus people' were decanted as coolie labour to plantations in the sparsely populated 'Outer Islands' of the archipelago.[49]

Japan was not colonised in the seventeenth century. Instead, the Tokugawa Shogunate upheld the nation's independence and, in return, staked a claim on the country's surplus production by taxing the peasants. By 1850, rice yields were the same as Java's. In 1868, the Meiji Restoration disposed of the aristocracy. Edel continues:

> Feudal dues that had consisted of a share of the crop were replaced by a fixed land tax levied on the potential yield of fields. This tax allowed landowners to reap all of the benefits of any productivity increases

beyond the presumed initial capacity of their farms. It is generally acknowledged to have contributed greatly to farmers' incentives. At the same time, the government introduced a system of agricultural education, comparable only to the United States' extension service in its scope. This, too, contributed greatly to productivity. Rising productivity allowed the increase in Japanese population to be diverted out of agriculture into industry.[50]

Two pillars of perfect competition — a fairer share-out of land rent and better information — thus initiated Japan's economic 'take-off'.[51] Equipment and fertiliser were produced for agriculture, and rice yields in the mid-twentieth century were double those in Java. Population density, however, was less than half that of Java, as was the rate of population growth.

VIII

If the private ownership of the rent of land were the fundamental cause of demographic and environmental crises, one might expect these phenomena to be least evident in Africa, where western notions of property have been slowest to penetrate communal social structures. In fact, over the last two decades such crises have been more conspicuous there than in any other part of the world. Drought, desertification, and famine have struck in two major episodes, and sub-Saharan Africa is unique in having declining per capita food production. Population growth is the fastest in the world. Does this cast doubt on the preceding argument?

Closer examination of the incidence of famine and environmental degradation suggests not. As one major study points out, 'it is the distribution of population that has gone awry. In many African countries, people are alternatively crowded into overused lands and elsewhere spread too thin.'[52]

Nowhere is this more obvious than in South Africa where the system of apartheid sets aside less than one-seventh of the land for three-quarters of the population. Many have to migrate to shanty towns near the white centres of employment and send home remittances to their families. The *Bantustans*, where the black population has been resettled, are on the poorest soils, are over-crowded, and are suffering soil erosion and falling crop yields.

Ethiopia is Africa's poorest country. 'Its history is littered with records of famine, not least because, until the 1974 revolution, its elite city life rested on one of the most exploitative systems of land tenure in Africa.'[53]

In the Sahel drought of the early 1970s 'what is incontrovertible, is that the structural processes at work in the region over a long period, particularly the growth of large-scale commercial agriculture [notably cotton], forced more of the rural population to make excessive demands of the natural resource base.'[54]

In the Sudanese famine of 1985-6 the same processes were at work. Half the area under cultivation is devoted to cash crops, the other half — mainly marginal, and the sites of the worst famines — is devoted to traditional farming and pasture. The transfer of the best land to commercial farming has mainly taken place since 1970, increasing the vulnerability to famine. Although the earlier Sahel drought had been as bad, it did not produce famine in Sudan. Until the 1960s rural Sudan was largely 'unowned'. Then the government began granting land leases tantamount to ownership to foreign companies, and selling land leases on very favourable terms to ex-government and ex-army officers. In the 1970s, the Unregistered Land Act made all land the property of the state, unless formally registered. Much land traditionally used by peasant farmers and nomads thus passed to mechanised agriculture within a few years. The World Bank funded the clearing of over 5 million acres of nomadic pasture. By 1985, 1.75 million of the previous occupants were now dependent on seasonal work. 'It is here — in the fundamental shift from self-sufficiency ... to a dependent labour force — that we find the root cause of Sudan's crisis in the 1980s', conclude Jon Bennett and Susan George.[55]

The plans of state bureaucrats, new landowners, merchant cartels, and their foreign advisers, however, relied upon the world price of cotton ceasing to follow its long-established downward trend. It did not oblige, and the IMF was called in just as famine was beginning to take hold. Its rescue package removed food and consumer goods subsidies and raised the price of imports by devaluing the currency. Food riots ensued in the capital, Khartoum, and the president was deposed — but grain continued to be exported to the Gulf States.

These examples confirm that at the root of the African tragedy of the last two decades is the corrosive dynamic identified in other continents: private appropriation of land rent. Throughout the 'Free World', a ceaseless quest is being pursued to turn the banquet of nature into inedible gold through the trade in land titles. Those in possession of more land inexorably displace those in possession of less. Landowners accumulate money in the bank; the landless accumulate children on the land. Those at the margins of the world economy pawn the natural wealth of the South in order to accumulate financial wealth for the North. As Anthony Sampson warns in *The Midas Touch,*

> While money can be multiplied, the land remains finite. Unless we can reverse the vicious circle of poverty and degradation, our greed will begin to undermine the real wealth which is the basis of our existence.[56]

Achieving a fairer share-out of the world's land and natural resources is, therefore, the primary environmental problem requiring the attention of professors, politicians, and the mass media. It is the just and efficient way to raise the living standards and self-reliance of the poorest people in the world. It thus addresses the ultimate source of high birth rates. It is the case, however, that the very existence of this issue is largely obscured from sight by controversies surrounding symptoms rather than causes, with policy emphasis on an assortment of cures — birth control policy, environmental regulations, assorted technological 'fixes', and even faster economic growth — rather than prevention.

NOTES

1. Archer Torrey, 'The Land and Biblical Economics', in *Land and Liberty*, (London, July-August, 1979), p. 63.
2. John Seymour and Herbert Girardet, *Far from Paradise: The Story of Man's Impact on the Environment* (London: British Broadcasting Corporation, 1986), pp. 61-62.
3. *Ibid.*, pp. 24-32. See also Georges Roux, *Ancient Iraq*. (2nd ed; London: Penguin Books, 1980), pp. 129, 133, 170, 370, 372 and 379.
4. For example, World Commission on Environment and Development, *Our Common Future* (Oxford: Oxford University Press, 1987), p. 106,

and affirmative statements in Thijs de la Court, *Beyond Brundtland: Green Development in the 1990s* (London and New Jersey: Zed Books Ltd, and New York: New Horizons Press, 1990), p. 32, and Stuart McBurney, *Ecology into Economics Won't Go, or, Life is not a Concept* (Bideford: Green Books, 1990), p. 109.

5 A. M. Honoré, 'Ownership' in A. D. Guest, ed., *Oxford Essays in Jurisprudence* (Oxford: Clarendon Press, 1961), p. 108, his emphasis.

6 Robert Dorfman, *Prices and Markets* (3rd ed; Englewood Cliffs, N.J.: Prentice-Hall, Inc., 1978), pp. 246-7, emphasis added.

7 Kelvin Lancaster, *Modern Economics: Principles and Policy* (Chicago: Rand McNally & Co., 1973), p. 292.

8 *Ibid.*, p. 307 and p. 303.

9 Speech by Barber Conable, World Bank President, reported by Peter Norman in 'Economics Notebook', *Financial Times* (London, October 2, 1989).

10 Martin Wolf, 'The global sink', in *Financial Times Survey*, 'The World Economy' (London *Financial Times*, September 26, 1989), p. XI. See Michael Grubb, *The Greenhouse Effect: Negotiating Targets* (London: Royal Institute of International Affairs, 1989).

11 John Hunt, 'Pleas for green policies fall on stony ground', in *Financial Times* (London, March 3, 1990).

12 David Pearce, 'Options for the forest' in *Guardian* (London, December 8, 1989).

13 Wilfred Beckerman, *Pricing for Pollution* (London: Institute of Economic Affairs, Hobart Paper 66, 2nd ed., 1990), pp. 13-14; Norman Myers, *The Sinking Ark* (Oxford and New York: Pergamon Press, 1979), Ch. 19.

14 See Claire Whittemore, *Land for People: Land Tenure and the Very Poor* (Oxford: Oxfam Public Affairs Unit, 1981).

15 Michael P. Todaro, *Economic Development in the Third World* (4th ed.; New York: Longman, 1989), pp. 224-228. See also references in 2, above.

16 See Richard G. Wilkinson, *Poverty and Progress: An Ecological Model of Economic Development* (London: Methuen, 1973), Ch. 5; Michael Redclift, *Development and the Environmental Crisis: Red or Green Alternatives?* (London, New York: Methuen), Ch. 3.

17 Mason Gaffney, 'Nonpoint Pollution: Tractable Solutions to Intractable Problems' in *Journal of Business Administration*, Vol. 18 — No. 1 and 2 (Vancouver: University of British Columbia, 1988/89), p. 150.

18 Nancy Dunne, 'Subsidies have failed to save the family farmer' in *Financial Times* (London, August 9, 1989).

19 Bridget Bloom, 'Hunger and Utopian Ideas' in *Financial Times* (London, November 23, 1989).

20 Quoted by Nicholas Schoon, 'EC farming subsidies dismissed as "false remedies" to food surpluses' in *The Independent* (London, January 4, 1990).
21 Todaro, *op. cit.*, p. 209.
22 See Fred Hirsch, *The Social Limits to Growth* (London: Routledge and Kegan Paul, 1977).
23 Interviewed by Anthony Sampson, writer and presenter of *The Midas Touch* (Csaky/Antelope Film production for BBC Television South & East, in association with TV Asahi of Japan and Channel 7 of Australia, 1989). For part of the interview, see Anthony Sampson, *The Midas Touch* (London: Hodder & Stoughton, BBC Books, 1989), p. 85.
24 Richard Body, 'Protectionism, Rent and the Dynamics of Agricultural Degradation' in Richard Noyes, ed., *Now the Synthesis* (London and New York: Shepheard-Walwyn and Holmes & Meier, 1991) p. 207.
25 Todaro, *op. cit.*, p. 305.
26 Sandra Postel, 'Halting Land Degradation' in Lester Brown *et al.*, *State of the World 1989* (New York, London: W. W. Norton & Co., 1989), pp. 28-29.
27 Redclift, *op. cit.*, p. 71.
28 Redclift, *op. cit.*, p. 69.
29 Wilkinson, *op. cit.*, Ch. 7.
30 Jack Anderson and Dale Van Atta, 'Grazing Federal Lands to Dust,' in *Washington Post* (Washington, January 28, 1990).
31 Mikhail Gorbachev, *Perestroika* (London: Fontana, 1988), pp. 19-21.
32 Henry George, *Progress and Poverty* (1879; Centenary Edn; New York: Robert Schalkenbach Foundation, 1979), p. 344.
33 Wilkinson, *op. cit.*, Ch. 7.
34 Redclift, *op. cit.*, pp. 70-71, 67.
35 Gunnar Myrdal, *Asian Drama* (New York: Pantheon, 1968), p. 1035.
36 *Ibid.*
37 Todaro, *op. cit.*, pp. 307-308.
38 Thomas More, *Utopia* (1516; London: Heron Books, published by arrangement with J. M. Dent & Sons Ltd, undated), p. 26.
39 Seymour and Girardet, *op cit.*, p. 30.
40 Jon Bennett and Susan George, *The Hunger Machine* (Cambridge, England: Polity Press, 1987), p. 200.
41 Amartyra Sen, *Poverty and Famines; an Essay on Entitlement and Deprivation* (Oxford: Clarendon Press, 1981), p. 144.
42 Bennett and George, *op. cit.*, p. 25.
43 Redclift, *op. cit.*, pp. 74-75.
44 E. J. Clay, 'Seasonal Patterns in Agricultural Employment in Bangladesh' in Chambers, Longhurst and Pacey, *Seasonal Dimensions to Rural Poverty* (London: Frances Pinter, 1981), p. 100.

45 Whittemore, *op. cit.*, p. 29.
46 Whittemore, *op. cit.*, p. 41.
47 Gunnar Myrdal, 'The Need for Radical Domestic Reforms' in his collection of essays, *Against the Stream* (London: Macmillan, 1973).
48 Matthew Edel, *Economies and the Environment* (Englewood Cliffs, N.J.: Prentice-Hall, Inc., 1973). The commendation is in E. K. Hunt and Howard J. Sherman, *Economics: An Introduction to Traditional and Radical Views* (5th ed.; New York: Harper & Row, 1986), p. 573, note 4.
49 Mariel Otten, 'Transmigrasi: From Poverty to Bare Subsistence' in *The Ecologist*, Vol. 16, No 2/3 (Camelford, UK: 1986), p. 71.
50 Edel, *op. cit.*, p. 55.
51 See Fred Harrison, *The Power in the Land* (London: Shepheard-Walwyn, 1983), Ch. 11.
52 Independent Commission on International Humanitarian Issues, *Famine: A Man-Made Disaster?* (London: Pan, 1985), p. 11.
53 *Ibid.*, p. 66.
54 Redclift, *op. cit.*, p. 67.
55 Bennett and George, *op. cit.*, p. 59.
56 Sampson, *op. cit.*, concluding statement of the TV series.

5
Commons and Commonwealths: a new framework for the justification of territorial claims

T. NICOLAUS TIDEMAN

Introduction

THE TRADITIONAL PROBLEM of the commons is the problem of providing for the efficient and equitable use of resources that belong equally to the members of a 'commonwealth' — a community, nation or other social entity. But there is a prior problem of the commons: On what basis can the members of a commonwealth claim that land belongs to them, and not to some other commonwealth?

I argue that customary justifications of the claims to territory and natural resources are inconsistent and promote conflict, while a variation on the ideas of John Locke has the potential to sustain lasting peace. While justifications of claims to territory and natural resources customarily rest on an inconsistent combination of might-makes-right and appeal to history, I argue that such claims ought to be made instead in a framework that recognizes an obligation to take account of the equal claims of all humanity. The claim of a given commonwealth can then be justified by a correspondence between the fraction of the world's population making the claim and the fraction of the world's land (in terms of rental value) being claimed. As is traditional in economics, 'land' is taken here to include exhaustible natural resources as well as territory.

In a world where this neo-Lockean justification of the claims of nations to land prevailed, people would carry with them their claims to proportionate shares of the world's land when they migrated from one commonwealth to another, and would have the option of exercising their claims in new commonwealths of their own creation. The world would therefore have a resemblance to that proposed by Charles Tiebout, where people with similar tastes formed communities that provided the particular public services that they wanted.[1]

Because people could be presumed to have agreed to the rules of the places where they resided, no rules would be forbidden. This would result in a world with many of the libertarian properties advocated by Robert Nozick.[2] Unlike Nozick's framework, the framework advanced here justifies claims only to the use of land, and not to its ownership in perpetuity.

The equal sharing of land makes the framework advanced here similar to the 'Liberalism' proposed by Bruce Ackerman.[3] The principal departures from Ackerman's framework are that Ackerman implicitly envisions a world-wide Liberal polity that sets the rules for inheritance and allocates extra shares of wealth to people with genetic disadvantages. In the framework advanced here, on the other hand, conventions regarding inheritance and provision for people with genetic disadvantages would be matters for more decentralized decisions.

Competition among commonwealths for citizens could be expected to generate an equilibrium in which taxes on land, as advocated by Henry George,[4] were the predominant source of public revenue. But any rules for taxation to which the people of a commonwealth agreed would be permissible.

George argued vigorously against the Malthusian view of population, contending that the fundamental cause of poverty was not an excess of people relative to resources, but rather an inequitable allocation of land.[5] While the traditional position of Georgists has been that the problem of apparent overpopulation would disappear once land was allocated equitably, some contemporary Georgists and Neo-Georgists (e.g., Andelson in this volume) contend that overpopulation would remain an ecological, if not an economic, problem, even if land were equitably distributed. The framework advanced here supports and extends the Georgist resolution of the economic aspect of this issue, while showing how, in principle, its ecological aspect might equitably be addressed.

One of the most novel aspects of the framework advanced here is that it reverses the traditional relationship between the territorial claims of individuals and of nations. While the territorial claims of individuals and of groups smaller than nations are generally justified in part by the claims of nations, in the framework advanced here the territorial claims of nations and other groups are justified by the territorial claims of individuals.

Current Justifications of Territorial Claims

The territorial claims of nations are generally justified currently by one or both of the following arguments:

1. Might makes right.
2. The claims accord with history.

These arguments cannot be expected to provide the basis for lasting peace, either individually or together.

When the territorial claims of nations are justified by the argument that might makes right, only temporary peace is possible. Changing conditions lead potential claimants to think it likely that current boundaries would not prevail in a showdown. If might-makes-right is the justification of claims, then there is no bar in conscience to breaking the peace and provoking a showdown to see whether existing boundaries can be defended. If boundaries can be altered by conflict, then, under might-makes-right, the new boundaries will have the same justification that the old ones had. Conflict itself is not inevitable with every change in power relations; those whose power diminishes sometimes recognize the changed conditions and concede territory. However, disagreements about effective power are resolved only by breaking the peace.

The argument that might makes right is sometimes dressed up in a bit of rhetoric. One example of this is the nineteenth century assertion that it was the 'manifest destiny' of the United States to expand to the Pacific Ocean. Another is the justification of the existence and expansion of the State of Israel based on the assertion that God instructed Joshua to lead the Israelites into that territory. A third is the justification of the hegemony (a form of territorial claim) that Russia has exercised over other countries, based on the assertion that the Russian Communist Party was the sole possessor of infallible understanding of social progress. The characteristic that reveals these as no more than rhetorical variations on might-makes-right is that they convince almost no one outside the nations that use them to justify expansion.

The argument from history requires separate treatment. The simple form of this argument is that the territorial claims of a nation are justified merely because the boundaries are historical. The difficulty with this argument is that virtually everywhere on the planet, one can go only so far back into the past before a war is encountered that changed the boundaries of nations. How is this to be treated? The answer implicit in political rhetoric seems to be that even though there may be no justification for the boundary changes imposed by past wars, the boundaries of the current status quo ought to be preserved and honored nevertheless. The trouble with this argument is that there is no magic to any particular date after which aggression ought to stop. After any seizure of territory those who did the seizing can say 'Let's freeze all boundaries now,' and the suggestion is no better or worse than freezing the previous boundaries. Trying to go back to earlier boundaries does not work either. If the Libyans should get out of Chad, why shouldn't Russia return the Northern Kuriles to Japan, free Latvia, Lithuania and Estonia, and return the portions of Finland and Poland seized in World War II? Why shouldn't America be returned to Native Americans? Why shouldn't Ireland be returned to the descendants of those who controlled it before Cromwell's invasion? Can any claim be justified?

An effort to provide a respectable foundation for most existing territorial claims without endorsing armed seizures has been made by Murray Rothbard. Rothbard's theory is built on the propositions that the transformation of any previously unowned thing provides the basis of a claim of ownership of that thing in perpetuity, and that anything that is stolen should be returned to the person who first transformed it usefully, or to his or her assignee through trade, gift or inheritance. If that person cannot be identified, the thing belongs properly to its present user, unless the present user stole it.[6]

By Rothbard's theory, any Irish family that can identify the land that was taken from its ancestors and assigned to Scottish immigrants centuries ago has a valid claim to that land, while any Irish family without specific knowledge of what land was taken from its ancestors has no such claim. The Israelis who are using land from which identifiable Arab families were driven in 1948 would have an obligation to return the land to those families, while those Israelis who are using land whose pre-independence users (or their heirs) cannot be identified would have valid claims to the land, unless the present users themselves were the ones who drove the previous users away, in which case the land would belong to the first person to dispossess the current user and apply some labor to it. It is bizarre to make the validity of a territorial claim depend on the accident of whether the descendants of the holder of a previous claim can be identified, when we can be confident that virtually all claims can be traced back to forcible dispossessions.

A Lockean Justification of Territorial Claims

A Lockean justification of territorial claims can be built from the famous 'proviso' in the passage in which Locke assigns property in the products of human labor to those who labor:

> The *Labour* of his Body, and the *Work* of his Hands, we may say, are properly his. Whatsoever then he removes out of the State that Nature hath provided, and left it in, he hath mixed his *Labour* with, and joyned to it something that is his own, and thereby makes it his *Property*. It being by him removed from the common state Nature placed it in, hath by this *Labour* something annexed to it, that excludes the common right of other Men. For this *Labour* being the unquestionable Property of the Labourer, no Man but he can have a right to what that is once joyned to, at least where there is enough, and as good left in common for others.[7]

While this statement is primarily a justification of claims to the products of human labor, it also contains the seed of a justification of territorial claims: The use of territorial resources provides the basis of a claim upon those resources, provided that resources of the same value are left for others.

It might seem that no territorial claims could be consistent with Locke's proviso that there be 'enough, and as good left in common for others,' because the future will bring untold generations, and however little each person draws from the stock of what nature offers, the stock will eventually be exhausted. Locke himself appeared to believe that there was enough unclaimed land in America, when he wrote, for everyone to have as much as he or she could use, so that the proviso would not be an operative constraint.[8] Whether or not such a condition was satisfied when Locke wrote, it is clear that it is not satisfied now. And even if there were unclaimed land now, a growing population would eventually claim it all, leaving none for further claimants, so that the very first claim would be inconsistent with Locke's proviso.

It is crucially important that the problem of eventual exhaustion of land to be claimed does not inevitably arise if claims are made not upon the *stock* of land, but rather upon the *flow* of services from land. If each person makes a claim upon the *use* of land, of a value such that all other people alive at that time can make claims of the same value without exceeding what nature offers, then Locke's proviso is satisfied. It may be difficult to know in any particular situation whether or not a claim to the use of land is consistent with the proviso. The problem of making such determinations is taken up later. What is important here is that while the finiteness of land makes *all* claims to the *perpetual possession* of land inconsistent with Locke's proviso, *some* claims to the *use* of land are consistent with it.

For a resource that is not 'used up' by being used (surface rights), if there is so much of the resource that everyone can use as much as he or she desires (if such surface rights currently command no rent), then any and all use of that resource is consistent with Locke's proviso for as long as the absence of rent prevails. But as soon as rent arises, the proviso limits what a person can claim.

Natural resources share with surface rights the quality of being provided by nature, but differ from surface rights in that they are exhaustible. Therefore the application of Lockean principles to natural resources requires separate treatment. If the world is to last indefinitely (or at least until the sun gives out in five billion years or so), then each person's share of these resources is infinitesimal. But to allocate them in such a way is to make them virtually worthless. The value derived from exhaustible natural resources would be maximized, while treating all people in all generations fairly, if the resources were sold to the highest bidders, the proceeds were invested, and a uniform annual dividend were paid to all people, in all nations, in all generations. Any person's claim upon exhaustible natural resources is consistent with Locke's proviso if the value of the claim is no more than a person's dividend under such a rule would be. Locke's proviso thus constrains the claims that people can make upon exhaustible natural resources as well as surface rights, but it does not impose impossible constraints.

In the neo-Lockean world envisioned in the framework advanced here, the claims of commonwealths to land are derived from those of their citizens. In this inversion of the usual relationship between the claims of commonwealths and of citizens, a commonwealth's claim to land is justified if its per capita claim of territory plus exhaustible natural resources is such that every person in every generation could claim as much as any other person without exceeding what nature offers. If a commonwealth's claim to land was found to be excessive, there would be three possible remedies: The commonwealth could reduce the size of its claim, it could recruit additional citizens, or it could pay compensation to people or commonwealths that were claiming less than their shares of land.

The advantage for lasting peace of justifying territorial claims on the basis of their proportionality is that it is then unnecessary to incorporate endorsement of any past injustices into the justification of a commonwealth's territorial claim. Those making a claim can say simply, 'We have to live somewhere, and what we claim is no more than our share.' It is then unnecessary for the sufferers of past dispossessions, or their descendants, to restart the game of might-makes-right to secure their shares of what nature provides.

Claims on People and on the Products of Labor

While the framework advanced here is concerned primarily with justification of claims to land, it is interesting to note that there are attractive and consistent Lockean theories of claims on people and on the products of labour. It is fairly well settled in the West that nations do not have property claims to people, that the only valid claims of property in competent people are those of each competent person over himself or herself. As Locke said,

> Though the Earth and all inferior Creatures be common to all Men, yet

every Man has a *Property* in his own *Person*. This no Body has any Right to but himself.[9]

Our acceptance of Locke's axiom is reflected in the outrage we feel that citizens of some countries are not able to emigrate at will. It may explain why we have never tried to prevent our richest citizens from exiling themselves to tax havens like Monaco. It is noteworthy that as many restrictions as there are on individual freedom, that are ostensibly for the benefit of those restricted (restrictions on the drugs and medical treatments that we can use, restrictions on who we can hire to cut our hair or give us legal advice), no one in the U.S. ever seems to have suggested that people should be prevented for their own good from emigrating to totalitarian countries. This may be a reflection of how strongly we feel that no one has a justified claim to any other person.

Our record on freedom of emigration is not perfect: The effort to prevent men of draft age from leaving the U.S. during the Vietnam war was not consistent with a principle that claims to people can only be made by the people themselves. However, that effort was never whole-hearted.

Locke's theory of claims on the products of human labor is stated in the passage quoted earlier, containing his proviso. It can be summarized by saying that the products of human labor, which consist of labor combined with land, belong to those who produce them, provided that the amount of land embodied in them is not excessive. It might seem that the pervasive taxation of incomes is evidence that Locke's view has been rejected. However, there is another perspective from which our beliefs are consistent with Locke: People cooperate to provide themselves with a variety of goods and services through governments. There is no reason in principle why these services should not be financed by income taxes if that is the method of financing that people in a particular society want. Taxation would be inconsistent with the Lockean principle of ownership of the products of human labor only if people could not escape the taxation by moving. And while there are many calls for international cooperation, so far we have seen very little if any support for a worldwide tax authority that no one could escape. What is needed to make our practices fully consistent with Locke is the opportunity for people, not only to emigrate to any country that will have them, but also to take with them their claims to their shares of land, or to exercise those claims in new commonwealths of their own creation.

This understanding of the justification of territorial claims resolves the dilemma of how a commonwealth can justify excluding from its boundaries some who wish to immigrate. On the one hand, a desire to exclude others so that the commonwealth's citizens can enjoy disproportionate access to land is not honorable. But on the other hand, there are honorable reasons for seeking to exclude some persons. As Henry George said in a letter to William Lloyd Garrison II in 1893,

> To your proposition that the right of the use of the earth is not confined to the inhabitants of the United States, I must cordially assent. But when you seem to think it follows that 'the humblest Chinaman has as much natural right to the use of the earth of California as yourself, and it is your inalienable right to change your residence to any land under the sun,' I must emphatically deny. Are men merely individuals? Is there no such thing as family, nation, race? Is there not a right of association, and the correlative right of exclusion?[10]

Exclusion is honorable when it is possible to say to those who are excluded, 'We have left as much for each of you as we have claimed for ourselves.'

Valuing Claims to Territory

How could it be ascertained whether any particular territorial claim met the test of being no more than anyone else could claim? Four quantities would be needed: The annual rental value of all territory in the world, the population of the world, the annual rental value of the territory being claimed, and the number of people making the claim. From these four numbers it would be a simple matter to calculate whether a claim exceeded what others could claim.

The first of these four numbers, the rental value of all territory in the world, would be by far the most difficult to estimate. If one were to go simply on the basis of acres, the amount available would be about 33.4 billion acres for the six continents other than Antarctica, or about 6.7 acres per person for 5 billion people. By contrast, the US has about 9.4 acres per person. (Without Alaska it would be about 7.9 acres per person.) Of course, territory varies greatly in its unimproved rental value, and it would be necessary to take account of these variations, both in fertility and in locational factors such as access to rivers and seas, in computing world territorial rent.

In providing for the equal sharing of the unimproved rental value of territory, it would be important to exclude the value arising from current and historical urbanization from the calculation of the amount to be shared. This point is illustrated in Figure 1.

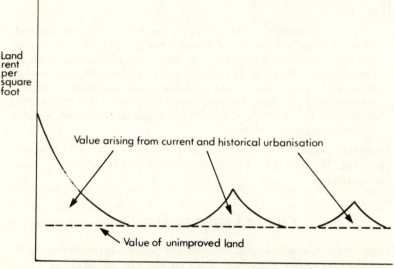

Figure 1

The distinction between the value of unimproved land and the value arising from current and historical urbanization

If all territory were equivalent in its unimproved state, then one could readily make the distinction shown in Figure 1 between the value of unimproved territory and the value arising from current and historical urbanization. The lowest level that rental value reached between cities would represent the value of all unimproved territory. The component of rental value arising from current and historical urbanization would be the product of the labor and capital of current and past generations in a given region. The appropriation of this value in the current generation would properly be determined by the traditional conventions of the region. While the region would be free to allocate this revenue as they chose, one attractive allocation for the bulk of this revenue would be the financing of the local public services that are required to raise urban rents above those of non-urban areas.

Territory, of course, does not have the uniformity presumed in Figure 1. Thus it would be necessary to make adjustment for fertility of soil and for such factors as access to rivers and seas. It would not be possible to achieve perfection in these determinations. It would be necessary to accept such approximations as, 'The land around Marseilles has the same inherent capacity as a port as the land around Barcelona, so France should be charged as much for claiming the land around Marseilles as Spain is charged for the land around Barcelona.'

While it is difficult to make the necessary estimates from the kinds of data that are currently available, there are things that could be done to improve our ability to make these estimates. If societies were prepared to see their boundaries as flexible, then they could state rental prices at which they would be willing to accept marginal changes in their boundaries. In principle, the price per acre for an expansion of boundaries ought to be very close to the price per acre for a contraction. If the value of land at the border was not significantly affected by the development of the society, and if the intrinsic value of the land occupied was reasonably uniform, then the rental value of territory at the border could serve as an estimate of the rental value of territory in the interior.[11]

If a community were willing to subject itself to a very small, insurable risk of dissolution, it could obtain a market determination of the rental value of all the territory it occupied. The community would agree that if a random process yielded a specified outcome with a probability of the order of one in a million, then they would collect on their insurance, remove all of their improvements from the territory, and disband. Before the outcome of the random process was known, they would solicit bids for their territory in the form of annual rental values should they depart, from other potential users. The greatest of these would be the annual rental value of the territory. If just a small, well-dispersed proportion of communities were willing to take such a risk, a reasonable estimate of the rental value of all territory could be made.

These suggested procedures for estimating the rental value of territory are admittedly imprecise. People committed to not claiming more than their shares of land would need to solicit and abide by disinterested expert opinion, and tolerate its imperfection.

It should be noted that there is no need to confine determinants of value to those that are generally regarded as 'economic.' If India and China both wish to claim a part of Ladakh, a desolate region on the Tibetan border, then it would be inconsistent for either one of them to claim both that the territory had an insignificant value and that they had to have it. The value of territory that one nation claims is what that territory would be worth to some other nation (if it had been unimproved), even if there is no way to account for the fact anyone wants it in terms of the customary economic determinants of value. The nation that places the highest value on the territory receives control of the territory, and all other nations receive larger shares of rent as a result.

Valuing Claims to Natural Resources

Natural resources pose greater difficulties in just appropriation than land. Consider the case of oil. The future value of oil depends very greatly on the timing of new technological discoveries. If cheap energy from nuclear fusion or solar power or some other breakthrough is just around the corner, then the best use of oil is to consume it now, when the new technology is not available. On the other hand, if such developments will come far in the future if ever, then we are well advised to conserve oil and use it only where it is extremely valuable.

If oil is privately owned, the owners will have an incentive to attempt to allocate the sale of oil over time in such a way as to maximize its expected value. This suggests the possibility of selling off all natural resources immediately and investing the proceeds for the benefit of all generations, as a way of allocating natural resources efficiently and equitably. The difficulty with this approach is that markets do not provide perfect information about the future value of resources. When the market underestimates the future value of a resource, future generations will be treated unfairly by the sale of their shares of resources at inadequate prices. It is not clear what the best solution to this problem is, but one possibility would be to leave title to resources not yet extracted unassigned, and have those who use exhaustible resources purchase insurance against the possibility of their uses later being shown to be excessive. The seller of insurance would be obliged to pay any losses that emerged later from having used the resources too soon.

Whatever procedure was used to allocate natural resources over time, in a world committed to justifying claims to natural resources by the Lockean proviso, those who extracted natural resources would make payments into an investment fund for future generations, unless they could be confident that the value of what they took did not exceed the value available to others in all generations.

Life in a World with a Proviso Foundation for Claims

In a world where the Lockean proviso was the universally accepted foundation for claims to land, there would be a clearinghouse for compensation for people whose claims were less than their per capita shares. Those whose claims were excessive would pay into a fund, and the fund would pay those whose claims were less than the standard. To reduce transactions costs, people would probably agree to let governments act as their agents. As long as people were free to migrate, it could reasonably be expected that each person would receive the full value of his or her claim even if governments were universally the agents.

Competition among governments for citizens would lead governments to make offers to their current and prospective citizens of the full value of having another citizen, unless citizenship carried with it other privileges that placed costs upon governments, in which case citizens would be receiving part or all of their per capita claims in kind. Thus the sharing of territorial claims leads by a market process to an institution resembling a guaranteed income. People who were otherwise unable to care for themselves would be able to obtain some minimum level of provision for themselves by agreeing to turn over their territorial claims to those who provided for them. Whether such a grant could sustain life without supplements from other sources could only be ascertained after a careful calculation of what the per capita rent would be.

Governments would have relatively little ability to tax the returns to the labour and capital of their citizens, because of competition among governments for citizens. Instead, the source of financing for public activities would be, primarily, the excess of land rents in developed areas above the value of the land in its undeveloped condition. This source would provide sufficient revenue for financing any worthwhile activity, provided that: 1) benefits occur only within the territory of the government financing the activity; 2) marginal-cost charges are used to offset any 'crowding' effects; and 3) the activity is valued as highly by potential beneficiaries who are too far from the activity to benefit from it as by those who are close enough to benefit from it.[12] (In case the need for the third condition is obscure, the idea is that if an activity, say Medieval concerts on Sundays in the park, is valued only by people who live very close to the park, then there will be no unsatisfied demand from elsewhere to bid up rents in the vicinity of the park.)

Another important implication of basing claims to land on the Lockean proviso is that freedom to secede would be not nearly so contested as at present. This is true for three reasons. First, if we are serious about founding our territorial claims on the idea that we are doing no more than others can do, then there has to be some *place* where they can do it. Second, if we compensate others for any excess in our claim, then someone who breaks off a chunk of our territory and takes responsibility for the claim is doing us no harm, as long as there are no lost economies of scale from the public services we provide. Finally, if those who wanted to secede were to emigrate instead, which we could not conscientiously keep them from doing, then our obligations to others for the land we were claiming would rise in proportion to the number of people who left. By taking some land with them, those who left could be doing us a favor.

When the consequences of pollution are internal to a commonwealth, the manner in which the pollution is regulated is an internal matter. When pollution has consequences outside the boundaries of a commonwealth, these must be accounted for in the determination of whether commonwealths are claiming more than their shares of what nature provides. A commonwealth that was a recipient of pollution could take account of the resulting reduction in the rental value of its land in determining whether it was claiming more than its share. The commonwealth that generated the pollution would be obliged to include in its claim upon nature the reduction in the rental value of land elsewhere that resulted from its pollution. Similarly, if one commonwealth undertook activities that raised land rents in a second commonwealth, the first could claim a corresponding credit with the clearinghouse for rent compensation, and the second would be obliged to accept a charge.

It has only recently been realized that the ecological necessity to promote rainfall and limit the carbon dioxide content of the atmosphere may require that vast amounts of land not be developed by humans. This can be taken into account, in a world adhering to the Lockean proviso, either by reaching a general agreement with respect to the land that would not be developed (which would raise the rental value of the remaining land), or by establishing prices to be paid for water evaporation, carbon storage, and other ecological services, so that those who controlled the land would find it in their interest to use the land in the ecologically necessary ways.

It is possible, though not certain, that population growth would be a concern in a world that adhered to the Lockean proviso. Additional people reduce available resources per person, while also making additional economies of scale possible. It is conceivable that people would choose to have more children partly so that their families or their nations could claim larger shares of land in the future. In the absence of economies of scale from a larger population, such behaviour would be destructive for the larger society, because the territory that one society thereby acquired would come from the shares of the other societies. If it could be seen that excessive population growth would result from having all people decide how many children to have purely in terms of advantages and disadvantages to themselves, that would be an indication that 'parenting opportunities' were a limited resource, which we would have an obligation to share fairly, on a world-wide basis. Each commonwealth would then have an obligation either to limit its appropriation of parenting opportunities or else to accumulate enough additional wealth, for appropriation to future generations, that others would not be harmed by its population growth.[13]

While the manner in which each commonwealth regulates its population growth is a matter for the commonwealth itself to decide, it would be inappropriate to diminish the claim of any person to what nature provides on the ground that his or her parents had been too prolific. No one should be held accountable for the actions of his or her parents. And to the extent that a person contributes to a population problem by being alive, we all contribute equally to the problem.

Current Events in a Lockean Proviso World

Some of the most contentious issues of today's world could not arise in a world committed to the Lockean proviso as the foundation of territorial claims, or if they did arise, they would quickly be resolved. Consider the following examples:

The Mideast Crisis: Instead of fighting over who gets to steal the land in the Mideast last, the disputants would bid for it. When it was properly valued, everyone who wanted some could have as much as he or she wanted at the prevailing rental price. The higher the bids went, the greater would be the claims that people elsewhere could make upon land.

Northern Ireland: Instead of defending their claims to territory in Northern Ireland on the grounds that England conquered Ireland fair and square, and it was too long ago anyway, those who wish to live in Northern Ireland while affiliating with England would make their claims on the ground that they have to live somewhere, and are taking no more than their shares of what nature offers.

El Salvador and Nicaragua: Instead of fighting over which factions will be *the* rulers of these countries, the disputants would vie for the allegiance of residents and divide the territory in proportion to the numbers of followers they could attract.

South Africa: The residents would divide themselves into those who did and those who did not want to live under the rule of the present government, and would divide the land of the country accordingly.

Ethnic Tensions in the USSR: The constitution of the Union of Soviet Socialist Republics provides that any Republic may withdraw from the Union, but until recently there was no legislation for implementing such a withdrawal. In setting terms for the withdrawal of a Republic, the Soviet Union could still require that those who withdrew take a share of land that was no more than their share of population. If Armenia wished to control Nagorno-Karabagh and a corridor to Armenia proper, it would be able to bid for the chance to do so. If Azerbaijan wished to exclude Armenians from its territory, it would thereby diminish the amount of territory that it could claim, or else it would incur a recurring obligation to the other Republics for the excessive share of land that it was claiming.

The pattern is clear. International disputes concern claims to land. As long as positions are defended on the basis of history, we will have disagreements about what history is relevant, and we will have a world of injustice and war. We need to base our claims to land on the proportionality of the value of our claims rather than on might-makes-right or on history.

Possible Difficulties of a Proviso World

There are several potential difficulties for a proviso world that can be foreseen. It is worth mentioning them.

Who is a person? To whom will shares of rent be allocated? Do infants count? Fetuses? Gorillas that are able to communicate with us through sign language?[14]

Will there be adequate financing for public goods whose benefits are not determined by location? The most prominent examples of such public goods are redistribution toward those for whom general compassion is felt, the provision of wildlife preserves and other protections for nature, and investments in knowledge. An important subcategory within investments in knowledge is investments in discovering natural resources. All of these public goods would have to be provided by voluntary contributions from either individuals or collectivities. In my view, our ability to see this issue as a potential problem is a reflection of a shared understanding that these causes deserve our support, and that for that reason these causes would be adequately financed by voluntary contributions, much as the United Nations is financed today. Ideally, all societies would recognize their obligations to compensate, in proportion to the benefits they received, those who provided activities with world-wide benefits, even if the activities did not raise land rents.

How the Change Could Occur

Changes in social conventions like the one proposed here always seem impossibly utopian when they are first encountered. Such was the first response to the idea that slavery had to be abolished, that equal political rights had to be accorded to men without property and to women, that the political monopolies of the Communist parties of Eastern Europe had to be ended. And yet all these changes occurred. How does the seemingly impossible happen?

The seemingly impossible happens because the understanding that it must happen becomes a consensus. The process of building such a consensus is tedious, and it is not obvious in advance which proposals for a new consensus will succeed. The combination of moral blindness induced by self-interest, widespread fear of the unforeseeable consequences of any sharp departure from the status quo, and downright knavish genius of those in positions of power often seem to conspire to preclude any reform. And yet the possibility that a reform cannot be attained does not imply that any particular individual should reject that reform. If a proposed reform would be attractive if others accepted it, each person can at least acknowledge this in his or her own mind, and perhaps to friends. One never knows when one's minute contribution will provide the increment that creates a critical mass and starts a self-sustaining chain reaction. It is interesting to note that if everyone who supported a proposal succeeded in convincing one person per month to become a supporter, in a period of 32 months the number of supporters would grow from just one person to over four billion persons.

But before the issue of support becomes relevant, each person must decide whether a proposed reform is even worth evaluating. It is not unreasonable that most of us dismiss most reform ideas we encounter with barely a second thought. What are the chances that

Commons and Commonwealths 127

the idea will deserve our support? We have better uses for our time than to entertain hare-brained schemes. Because the success of a worthwhile proposal for transforming social conventions requires persuading multitudes of people to overcome their natural doubt that the proposal is even worth considering, it is important for the advocates of a proposal to have ways of bringing the coherence of their ideas to the attention of the doubters. In the long struggle to end slavery, one of the early turning points occurred in the mid 1700s, when the Quakers of Pennsylvania voluntarily freed the slaves they had held, amidst growing pressure within their own community. The example of this action made it impossible to deny that freeing slaves was feasible.

Thus it is important that steps toward implementing the framework advanced here can be taken by voluntary individual and community initiative, before everyone agrees on the value of the change. Any person or group can bring his, her or their behaviour into conformity with the proposed norm of equal sharing of land, as a step toward achieving the ideal. For individuals, this would mean estimating the value of the land they use and taking steps to compensate others if the total value was excessive. If only a few people were trying to do this, the most appropriate form of compensation would probably be a contribution to some organization like CARE that provides for people whose claims upon nature are far below the norm. When more people wanted to participate, it would be possible to adjust compensation paid more precisely. Initially, everyone would have to make his or her own estimate of what was owed in compensation. As more people came to participate, it would be worthwhile for someone to undertake systematic research into the best way to estimate one's obligation. Estimates would be published concerning such matters as how much one ought to include in one's obligation for each gallon of gasoline consumed. At a later point, some of the sellers of items like gasoline, with high natural resource components, would guarantee buyers that compensation was already included in the price paid. People would then come to refrain from trading with those who could not provide such guarantees.

People who realized that their holdings of land were excessive would come to see that selling their holdings did not solve the problem, but merely displaced it. Non-profit organizations would be formed for the purpose of holding land titles and the proceeds of sales of natural resources in trust for all humanity. This would be the counterpart of slave owners freeing their slaves rather than selling them, when they realized that slavery was immoral.

As the new understanding spread, a transition would occur from individual to democratic action. Nations would incorporate into their laws the rule that if the nation's use of land exceeded claims consistent with Locke's proviso, then compensation would be paid to people or nations with less than proportionate shares of land. International pressure would be put on all nations to conform to the standard. Once compensation was paid when claims were excessive, nations would have no reason to thwart secessionist movements. They would justify their boundaries not on the basis of history or might-makes-right, but rather on the basis of there being as much and as good left in common for others. Such a convention could provide a basis for sustaining lasting peace.

NOTES

1 Charles M. Tiebout, 'A Pure Theory of Local Expenditures', *Journal of Political Economy* 64 (October 1956), pp. 416-24.
2 Robert Nozick, *Anarchy, State and Utopia* (New York: Basic Books, 1974).
3 Bruce A. Ackerman, *Social Justice in the Liberal State* (New Haven: Yale University Press, 1980).
4 Henry George, *Progress and Poverty* (centennial edition; New York: Robert Schalkenbach Foundation, 1979).
5 *Ibid*, Book II, pp. 89-150.
6 Murray Rothbard, *The Ethics of Liberty* (Atlantic Highlands: Humanities Press, 1982), pp. 56-57.
7 John Locke, *Two Treatises of Government* (Cambridge: Cambridge University Press, 1960), Second Treatise, section 27.
8 *Ibid.*, Second Treatise, section 36.
9 *Ibid.*, Second Treatise, section 27.
10 Quoted in Charles A. Barker, *Henry George* (New York: Oxford University Press, 1955), p. 135.
11 R. V. Andelson remarks (in a letter) that since so much land value accrues from the activities of local communities, each person's share of

global rent might be quite meager. Moreover, poor but resource-rich countries such as Nigeria and Argentina would owe money to rich but resource-poor countries such as Japan and Holland. But this does not invalidate the thesis advanced in this essay. It shows only that correcting for inequalities in the per capita resource endowments of nations would not eliminate inequalities among nations and would not always represent movement in the direction of income equality. International assistance and changes in social structures and government policies would still be needed to promote economic growth.

12 T. Nicolaus Tideman, 'Efficient Local Public Goods without Compulsory Taxes', *Perspectives on Local Public Finance and Public Policy*, 2 (1985) pp. 181-202.

13 In *Social Justice in the Liberal State* (pp. 111-113, 217-221) Bruce Ackerman provides an interesting discussion of the obligation to provide equal shares for future generations, and the acceptability of charging people for having children, provided that other conditions of justice are satisfied.

14 See Francine Patterson and Eugene Linden, *The Education of Koko* (New York: Holt, Rinehart and Winston, 1981).

6
The Remaining Commons: a challenge to equity, efficiency and ecological responsibility

ALEXANDRA HARDIE

SURPRISING as it may seem, the greater part of the Earth's surface, if we count the oceans as well as the land, has not yet passed into the ownership of specific persons, companies, institutions or governments. Much of it has not even been claimed as national territory by governments. This vast expanse comprises the Remaining Commons of the Earth. If we look outwards, Outer Space is also part of the Remaining Commons. Some areas of the Remaining Commons may be taken into specific ownership in the relatively near future. Conventional economists argue that this will be beneficial, since natural resources which belong to no-one are likely to be exploited to destruction.

It may be desirable that property rights should be introduced into the Remaining Commons, but the structure of these property rights is extremely important. The wrong structure will impose restrictions on the freedom of individuals, provoke conflict within nations and between nations, and cause the destruction of resources. Now is the time to think about the correct structure for these property rights.

The stakes are high. As we look around the Earth we find that the rivers, lakes and seas are polluted and filthy, the dry land is despoiled and eroded, the atmosphere is poisoned with noxious substances, ranging from toxic fumes to unseen radiation, which will be lethal, not just for a short while, but for millions of years. Forests are being destroyed, and deserts are expanding. Animal and plant species are being destroyed at record rates; the African elephant is one of the best-known of all animal species, yet it may be extinct in twenty or thirty years from now. The extinction of plant species is less dramatic, but no less significant for human well-being; wild plants can provide new crops, new pesticides, or new drugs. The destruction of the environment has not even allowed the majority of human beings to live in comfort.

The conventional argument is that private property rights are essential to the preservation of the environment, but anyone who looks around England will conclude that, in a country where all land is owned by someone, private property rights have not provided adequate protection for the environment. England has less tree cover than any European country except Eire, soil erosion is a serious problem in the area of East Anglia, many rivers and streams are polluted, and derelict land is wide-spread. Private ownership of land is the rule also in the USA; yet there is soil erosion, derelict land, pollution of streams, lakes and rivers, and destruction of forests. The existence of conventional property rights is not a sufficient condition for the preservation of the environment; it may not be a necessary condition either.

The Remaining Commons present a problem; can property rights be introduced, without imposing injustice or provoking conflict? These commons do, or could, offer a livelihood to people who have not managed to acquire ownership of other natural resources. The freedom of these people would be curtailed if they lost out in the allocation of property rights in the Remaining Commons. In the past, the people who already controlled substantial amounts of private property were the ones who grabbed the largest share of the commons of that era. Yet the Remaining Commons simultaneously present an opportunity; they are a cornucopia of natural resources, which, if properly managed, could offer a decent living to hundreds of millions of people. This is an opportunity which could be seized without loss to any one, since no-one can claim property rights in these commons. A sound system of property rights would allow the equitable, efficient, ecologically-sound utilisation of the Remaining Commons. It would turn an apparent problem into the opportunity of the next millennium.

Finding a solution to the problem of the Remaining Commons requires a systematic approach. There are six questions to consider. Where are these commons? What is the problem? Why is there a problem? Who wants a solution? When is the solution needed? How can the problem be solved?

The first five questions lead on to possible answers to the last question, which is the most important one. The solution is a system of property rights within which utilisation of the Remaining Commons can take place in an efficient, equitable, ecologically sound way.

The Location of the Remaining Commons

The Remaining Commons are of two kinds. First, there are the 'Last Commons' which comprises those regions of the Earth which have not yet been claimed by any nation-state. There are the oceans and the ocean sea-beds beyond territorial limits. There is the atmosphere, except where this has been appropriated as national territory, as in the case of air space over a country. There is Antarctica. Outer Space is also part of the Last Commons. The Last Commons are a reminder of the time when all the Earth was the common possession of mankind, and none of it had passed into the exclusive control of any tribe or nation.

Second, there are parts of the Earth's surface which have been claimed as national territory, but have not been parcelled out as the exclusive private property of any individual, company, institution, or government body. Lands claimed by a particular nation, but not allotted as private property, will be described here as 'Remnant Commons'. These are the remnants left over from the time when the territory occupied by a tribe or nation was regarded as the common property of all its people. These areas are substantial. The Remnant Commons, world-wide, include; jungles and forests; deserts; mountains; rivers and estuaries; sea-shores; the sea-bed adjacent to land; air space over countries.

The behaviour of nation-states with respect to the sea-beds shows what is likely to happen to the Last Commons unless active steps are taken to prevent it. The former three-mile territorial limits were determined by the effective range of shore-mounted cannon. Modern weaponry enables a state to control the sea much further out than this, so that it is realistic for a state to claim territorial rights up to 200 miles from shore. Most states now do this, and thereby substantially increase the natural resources they control. They have turned what was formerly part of the Last Commons into Remnant Commons. The technical developments which made it possible to drill for oil under deep water, and even in stormy seas, led to the allocation of the Continental Shelf to specific nation-states. This allocation was based upon existing national boundaries; a straight line was taken out from each boundary. A trough in the sea bed is usually regarded as the end of a nation's section of the continental shelf, and thus as the boundary of its effective territory. Difficult cases may be settled by negotiation, or by reference to international law courts.

As to Antarctica, it seems that the nations which at present have claims on it, are trying to turn it into Remnant Commons. Argentina arranged for the wife of an Argentine naval officer to be flown to their section of Antarctica, so that she could give birth there. This was to strengthen its claim upon Antarctica, although it is unlikely that it will establish a long-term settlement there, seeing that it has failed to settle Patagonia to any significant extent, even though the climate of Patagonia is relatively mild. In August, 1990, Australia announced that it would not allow any exploitation of minerals in its section of Antarctica; while this is good for conservation, yet it is also a reiteration of territorial claims.[1] Australia is claiming the right to decide how one section of Antarctica should be used.

As far as Outer Space is concerned, the allocation of this into national sectors is, at present, in the realm of science fiction rather than science fact.

Reverting to dry land, even in the densely populated UK, there are still significant areas of commons. There are laws about the use of these commons, which may offer some ideas about how to deal with the Last Commons and with the Remnant Commons.

In the UK, there are now no commons in Scotland; in the Lowlands, the remaining commons were all allocated to specific owners in the 17th Century. The Celtic tradition of common ownership of land by a clan persisted up to the 18th century in the Scottish Highlands, but the laws prevailing in the Lowlands were then imposed there also. In Scotland, the public usually has no legal right of access to privately-owned land, but there may be free access in practice. In England and Wales significant areas of commons remain. Some of them are managed like public parks, and there is free access to them, subject to any regulations which apply. In rural areas, there are commons which are used for agriculture or grazing, as common-land traditionally was used. In England and Wales, commons are owned by someone, even though this may be the local council or central government, or some government body — e.g., the Ministry of Defence. A large area of common-land close to central London can be found at Blackheath. This has been open land for several centuries, yet, as recently as the late 1980s, the persons who owned this land announced that they were investigating the possibility of taking it back into their exclusive private ownership.

English law provides, in detail, for the use of common land. This is a survival from the feudal period, but it should not be despised on that account; all ownership of land in England is ultimately based upon the feudal system of land-holding. Throughout the centuries, a person's right to the land he claimed was dependent upon the ownership of the person he bought it from, or inherited it from, and that person's right was dependent upon the right of the person that he had acquired it from, in an unbroken chain of proven ownership. There are several distinct common rights, such as rights of pasturage, of fishing, of taking brushwood, peat or gravel. There may be restrictions on the type of livestock which can be pastured; it is not permitted to graze a bull in a field through which a footpath runs. Specific common rights are not open to anyone; they are usually linked to the ownership of specific pieces of land in the vicinity. Public footpaths and bridle-paths are open to all.

The system of common land management which operates in England and Wales is based on the English Common Law. Where Roman Law applies, as in continental Europe, there is no common land. However, the general public have access to most of the open land. The British visitor to Greece, or Spain, will find that she or he can walk more freely over land than is the case in Britain. In Italy, shooting is a popular sport, because shooters have access to all open land; the land-owner has no exclusive right to game on his land. This reflects Roman Law, which does not recognise any private property rights in wild animals, birds or fish; these belong not to the land-owner, but to whoever manages to catch or kill them. This is egalitarian, but it harms wild-life, especially in Italy, where it is customary to shoot song-birds. Roman Law also leaves rivers open to access by boat; in contrast, in the UK, land-owners own the rivers running through their land, and may prevent access by boat, or, as with some rivers, charge a fee for access.

In other parts of the world, although a lot of land is owned as private property, there are substantial tracts which are not privately owned. Sometimes they are owned by the government, as in the USA and Canada, but in many countries, some land is not claimed even by the government. In Brazil the law recognises the ownership rights of a person who has cleared land and occupied it for a certain length of time. In practice, influential persons often appropriate land which has been settled by peasant farmers.

Laws about private ownership of land vary among legal systems. Under English Common Law, the land-owner cannot own land as such, but only ownership rights in land. The most complete title to ownership is ownership in 'Fee Simple' which is usually described as 'Freehold Ownership'. The underlying idea is that the sovereign is entitled, as in the feudal system, to dispose of land as he sees fit. If a person owns the freehold of a plot of land, and no rights have been sold off, or acquired by the state, then he holds the land 'Ab Infero ad Superos' (i.e. 'From the Depths to the Heights') which means that he holds whatever lies under his land, and whatever lies on and above it. Several individuals may have ownership rights in the same plot of land; e.g. one person may own the freehold, but another person may have a right of way over the land, and a third person may have acquired the mineral rights. The English Common Law would allow a land-owner to prevent aircraft overflying his land, but statute law has been introduced to allow overflying. In Britain, statute law also makes the state the owner of coal, gas, and oil, although the land-owner retains rights to other minerals. The law of the USA allows outright ownership of land, but land may be acquired by compulsory purchase if the government needs it. Following English practice, the land-owner in the USA owns the mineral rights under his land. In Latin America mineral rights are owned by the state. The way in which the law of a country deals with land and natural resources is important, because it shows one model in practice. Each system has rules for dealing with what might be called 'Occupied Land' (i.e., land which has already passed into private ownership) and also for dealing with other land. The differences in property law found in different countries show that there are several possible models for property law. There is no reason to think that one model is better than the others in all respects.

Identifying the Problem

The problem is that, unless action is taken, the Remaining Commons will be, increasingly, the scene of violent conflict. Conflicts over land occurred in the earliest times recorded and still take place today. Rapid population growth exacerbates strife, or is used as a pretext for it. States disagree about which of them shall control particular natural resources. Disputes occur between groups within states over the ownership of Occupied Land, over the control of the Remnant Commons within a country, or over the allocation of the Remnant Commons to private owners. As other resources run out, progressively greater pressure will be brought to bear upon the Last Commons. Conflict will be inevitable. Some kind of ad hoc 'solution' will arise, but it will not be optimal in terms of equity or efficiency, and it may lead to lasting resentment from the losers. It might also be ecologically unsound, damaging natural resources irretrievably.

Conflict is already occurring in the Remnant Commons. In England, conflict is low-key (i.e. no one has been killed over this issue) but it does occur; the attempt to give the public the right of access to all the commons, has so far, been blocked, as a result of lobbying by land-owners. A demand for boating access to the upper stretches of certain fishing rivers in the North of England has also been opposed; the land-owners include local authorities, and some conservation groups support them, fearing damage to wild-life habitat.

It may be illuminating to see what happened in the past, when the Remnant Commons of those days were parcelled out. In England, the process of introducing exclusive private ownership to what had formerly been commons (i.e., the enclosures of the 18th and 19th centuries) was attended with violence or with the hardship of the dispossessed. Earlier enclosures, during the 16th century, had also led to distress. Much the same happened in Scotland during the Highland Clearances. In Germany, enclosures took place in the early 16th century, during the life-time of Martin Luther. The rulers of Germany introduced Roman Law to Germany, in place of the traditional German Common Law, which was similar to English Common Law. Commons existed in Germany, as in England. But, because Roman Law did not recognise common ownership, this was taken as an opportunity to turn all the existing commons over to exclusive private ownership. The land-lords gained at the expense of the peasants, who were not prepared to accept this. Aroused by other grievances too, the peasants went to war against their rulers in 1625. The rulers won this war, and suppressed the peasants.[2] For three centuries, ordinary people had no part in political life in Germany, so there was no development of the democratic process. The evil consequences of this are apparent up to the present time.

Conflicts about land, especially about the Remnant Commons, occur all over the world. In Canada, where the rights of the indigenous peoples have been respected as compared with other countries in the Americas, a small but significant struggle took place in the late summer of 1990. Oka, a town near Montreal, wanted to take over land for extending a golf-course, but the Mohawk Indians claimed this land as their own. In the conflict, a policeman was killed. The Canadian Government resolved the problem by offering to buy the land. In Brazil, the tropical forests of the Amazon are being destroyed at a record rate. Cleared land can be taken into private ownership as farm-land. There has been much dispute over this cleared land, with wide-spread violence and murder. What is happening in Brazil is that the Remnant Commons are being taken over as privately owned land. It could have been predicted that this process would involve violence, as it has done in the past.

In Asia, too, there is conflict over the tropical forests. The forests are falling to the chain-saw in Malaysia, the Philippines, Indonesia, and India. There is pressure on the forests as a source of timber, both for local use, and for export to the developed countries. Clearance lets local land-owners take former forest-land for themselves. Privately-owned land is the main source of wealth and power in most societies; anyone who can grab part of the Remnant Commons for himself, or herself, has achieved a short cut to these advantages.

In Africa there are disputes over land. Land was a major factor in the conflicts between the indigenous peoples of Africa and the colonial powers. The colonial powers introduced private property in land to areas where land had traditionally been the collective property of the tribe. In Kenya, the Kikuyu strongly resented the acquisition, by British settlers, of traditional tribal lands, even though they themselves were not using the land at the time. White ownership of farmland was, and is, a grievance in Zimbabwe. Land is a serious issue in South Africa.

If we turn to the seas rather than the land, disputes over fisheries occur all over the world; the 'Cod War' between Britain and Iceland led to the exclusion of British fishing boats from their traditional fishing grounds off Iceland. Despite the loss to British fishermen, who received no compensation from the Icelanders, and little from the British government, most observers would probably sympathise with the Icelanders; for fishing is their main way of earning a living. In the Pacific, the use of drift nets has caused disputes between Japan and the various Pacific islands, since it interferes with traditional islander fishing practices. The Falkland Islands have recently demanded an extension of their territorial limits to 200 miles, in order to get the full benefit of their stocks of fish. Most of the Latin American countries extended their territorial limits to 200 miles as far back as the 1940s. Everywhere, fisheries, already suffering from the effects of pollution, are being over-exploited because of growing demand for fish, technical advances in detecting shoals of fish, and government subsidies to fishermen. Pressure builds up on the stocks that are left. British fishermen have suffered from European Community rules, because traditional British fisheries are treated as part of the EC common fisheries, and the quota allocations have been relatively more favourable to French fishermen than to British ones. In 1990, there was conflict over Spanish trawlers fishing in waters that Britain has traditionally claimed as its own.

The UK has gained from the allocation of the sea-beds for oil exploitation. There were some disputes over the North Sea, but these were settled amicably. However, the Scottish Nationalists point out that, on the basis of existing national boundaries, most of the UK's oil belongs to Scotland. Independence for Scotland would probably lead to conflict over this issue.

There has not yet been much conflict over Antarctica, or Outer Space, but no doubt it will occur.

Throughout the world, the pressure is not only on the Remaining Commons; it is felt also by owners of Occupied Land. Land reform is demanded in many parts of Asia, Latin America, and some parts of Africa. Population growth fuels the pressure. Conventional land reform has not proved a panacea for existing ills. Unless the correct measures are employed with respect to the Remnant Commons, controversy over their allocation will cause strife within countries. Unless sound laws are adopted with respect to the Last Commons, their partition will lead to conflict between countries. In view of the injustice, violence, and war which have hitherto been associated with the sharing-out of the Earth, now is the time to think carefully about how to handle the Remaining Commons.

The Reasons Why There Is a Problem

There are three main reasons. The main one is the current size of the human population of the Earth, and its rapid rate of increase. The population of the Earth exceeded 5 billion people by 1990. In 1989, the population growth rate was 1.74% per annum. If this growth rate persisted to the year 2000, world population would exceed 6.3 billion. If the growth rate then fell, to around 1% by the year 2025, world population by that year would be 8.5 billion. But if it increased, to 1.9% from 2000 onwards, total population would be nearly 9.5 billion by the year 2025.[3]

Population forecasts have been wrong in the past. Growth rates may slow down quicker than expected. Natural methods of birth control, which have the advantage of being harmless and costing nothing, may be correctly used.[4] The introduction of even small old age pensions in poor countries would give parents more confidence in the future, and encourage them to limit their families; large families are often a way, not always effective, of insuring against poverty in old age. Generous old age pensions and low birth rates are often found together, as in West Germany. In Latin America, Uruguay stands out from the other countries because of its generous old age pensions; it also has the lowest rate of population increase in that continent. In both India and China sons are preferred to daughters. It is reported that women have selective abortions to avoid having daughters; this practice will limit future population growth. Even so, world population will increase substantially in the next fifty years. For hundreds of millions of people, standards of living are low at present; if standards are to improve, allowing also for the extra people, it will be necessary to use existing natural resources better, or to reduce the pressure on resources for non-essential purposes, or to make use of resources which are under-utilised at present. The third possibility will probably be the one that receives most attention. This leads on to the second reason for the problem; the inefficient use of land.

If resources were properly managed, the use of the Last Commons would not be necessary yet; but this requires efficient use of Occupied Land. It also requires better use of the Remnant Commons. Turning the Remnant Commons into privately-owned land might improve efficiency overall, but it could have disastrous consequences for many people.

It is easy to think that people push into unoccupied areas because their territory is already used to its maximum capacity. In discussions about the Amazon, students, who are, presumably, better informed than the average person, take this for granted. They point out that many people in Brazil are very poor and then go on to argue that this justifies exploitation of the Amazon by the Brazilians. The underlying assumption here is that, when people reach the limit of their resources, they are entitled to move in and exploit under-utilised resources elsewhere. Yet existing national boundaries are taken for granted; no one argues that poverty in Brazil entitles the Brazilian government to take territory from Uruguay, which has a small population relative to its resources.

England is densely populated, yet not all land is used efficiently. Anyone who takes a few train rides will see substantial areas of rural land which are so overgrown with bracken or weeds as to be unsuitable for rough pasture, and extensive areas of urban land, even in London, which are either used for low-grade purposes such as repositories for derelict motor vehicles, or are unused altogether, sometimes over many decades.

There is nothing new about inefficient land use in the British Isles. The 19th century land-reformers offer tomes of detailed evidence to show that agricultural production was less than it could have been, largely because of an unjust system of land tenure. Most of the land was held in huge estates by a small number of landlords. The land was let to tenant-farmers, who employed farm labourers, usually at very low wages. Much land was legally entailed, which meant that the landlord could not sell it, ownership being vested in his infant child, or in a child that he had not yet fathered. Thus his tenants could not buy the land nor could they improve it, as they could not borrow for improvements, because lenders were reluctant to lend to tenants with no legal security of tenure, and rent payments to the landlord took legal priority over interest payments. There was money in Britain for lending, but much of this went abroad. Despite these problems, many tenant-farmers achieved a reasonable degree of prosperity; they may have started with more capital than the typical tenant-farmer, they may have been very hard-working, or have had good landlords. In England, some landlords gave effective security of tenure, and probably many charged less than the market rent. Even so, tenant-farmers often lived in squalid houses, with poor accommodation for their live-stock. Fields remained undrained, although drainage would have improved productivity. Most landlords tried to maintain a higher standard of living than their rent rolls could cover, and they had no spare money for improvements. The situation in Ireland, except for Ulster, was abysmal; the law was biased against the tenant, who could be evicted without cause, and who received no compensation for improvements when he was evicted. Rents were set at the full market level.

Huge estates still exist in Latin America, notably in Brazil and Argentina. These estates cause even worse problems than did the great estates of 18th century England. The land-owner has more land than he can use efficiently himself. He lets some of the spare land to peasant farmers, on terms unfavourable to them, often on a sharecropping basis. Much land is out of use altogether. There is no agricultural improvement; the landowner spends his money on other things, and the tenants have no spare money. These tenants are mainly poor peasant farmers.

There is an answer to the problem of unused, or underused, land.

It is to tax land, and replace most, or all, other taxes with the Land Value Tax (LVT). This would break up big estates, reduce taxes on producers, and encourage efficient use of land in both cities and country. Everywhere in the world, there are powerful political forces making it difficult to introduce this essential reform in the near future. However, the LVT provides an equitable and efficient solution to the problem of the Remaining Commons.

Another reason for the problem of the Remaining Commons is that there is a conflict of uses for them. As well as being a source of raw materials, they are used as a sink for waste products. The oceans are used as a dump; the UK disposes of more than 10% of sewage straight into the sea without treatment. Formerly, it was claimed that viruses in sea water died in a few days; it is now admitted that they can survive for several months. The oceans receive waste oil from ships, and oil spillage is a constant hazard, as the Exxon Valdez disaster in Alaska showed. The oceans receive other waste such as chemical clouds blown out to sea. Increased pressure on the Remaining Commons as a source of raw materials is matched by increased pressure on them as a sink for waste products. It is possible to turn a park into a rubbish tip; or vice versa, as when derelict land is reclaimed for recreational uses. But it is not possible to enjoy a piece of common land both as a park, and as a rubbish tip. The same is true of the oceans. Increasing use of the oceans as a sink will interfere with their use as a source of materials, and as a recreational area. The atmosphere is also used as a sink for waste; as human beings are dependent on the atmosphere even to survive, an objective observer might well be astonished at how easy it is for persons, companies, and governments to pollute it. This pollution causes destruction of the ozone layer, which is essential for human life on Earth; this is very poor 'Planetary Housekeeping'. Some method must be found of reducing pollution of the atmosphere, and of the oceans. Only a concerted international effort will avail. Outer Space is already polluted; the amount of debris is substantial. Some of the debris falls to Earth, where it may cause a disaster, and lead to large insurance claims, but most of it remains in orbit, where it continues to be a hazard to communications satellites. There is no rust, and not much decay, in space.

Greater self-discipline from human beings, the spread of infor-

The Remaining Commons

mation, and the use of the best available technology, are essential for overcoming pollution. Changes in the tax system would help; taxes could be increased on activities harmful to the environment, and reduced on other activities. In the UK, and elsewhere, all sewage should be treated properly. Other changes will be needed too; one interesting proposal is to return drained lands to their original wetland state; the restored wet-lands could then filter out nitrates from the rivers. New technology will reduce waste; it should be possible to burn coal with less pollution. Ensuring that all countries use the best available technology could cut pollution significantly; at present, China produces more pollution from burning coal than France and Germany together. It may be necessary to revert to simpler technology in the West; as compared with water-borne sewage systems, the 'honey cart' method of the Far East does not pollute the oceans.

The Pressure for a Solution in the Near Future

The pressure for a solution to the problem of the Remaining Commons has two aspects; there is the irrational force of population pressure, and the rational force of persons, groups or governments who seek a solution.

It cannot be taken for granted that existing agreements represent a solution to the problem of the Last Commons which is desirable, or even feasible. It will take time to find out what the right solutions are, and time to implement the solutions; there are substantial time lags in reforms of this kind, they need co-operation between countries, regional groupings, and the international bodies. It is not too soon to begin thinking now; to assess proposals already put forward, to suggest other ideas, and to try to weigh up the various possibilities. A good solution for the Last Commons will show how the problem of the Remnant Commons should be solved; therefore, the emphasis here is on the Last Commons.

Finding a Solution

The Solution-Generating Process A solution to the problem is more likely to be found if the correct procedure is used. The aim is to find a sound framework of property rights within which utilisation of the Last Commons can take place.

First, there must be a search for possible solutions. It is important to include solutions even if they seem to be politically difficult, or likely to upset vested interests. Any scheme for dealing with land or natural resources is bound to face these problems. A systematic search would include solutions already put forward, ideas based on a priori reasoning, and schemes adapted from analysis of empirical evidence. The evidence should come from a comprehensive study of methods of dealing with land and natural resources in various parts of the world in the past and the present.

The second step is to establish the decision criteria that are to be used for selecting acceptable solutions. It is necessary to be able to accept or reject solutions, and also to be able to rank order those solutions which are accepted. The criteria should be chosen on rational and consistent grounds, they should be simple to understand and apply, and, once chosen, they should be followed scrupulously.

The third step is to apply the criteria to the solutions proposed. This might be done as a two-stage decision process. Start by screening possible solutions for obvious non-starters. Then, having worked out each remaining solution in detail, analyse these solutions systematically, to accept or reject them, and then to rank the accepted solutions in the preferred order.

The correct approach is that of cost-benefit appraisal. This is the only way of allowing for the major ecological, economic and political implications of making use of the Last Commons.

Cost-benefit appraisal is similar to conventional investment appraisal, where forecasts are made of cash flows, and an investment is accepted only if it yields a positive net present value (i.e., the discounted value of all expected inflows of cash must exceed the cost of the initial investment). The difference is that Cost-Benefit appraisal includes also estimates for, not only all cash benefits, but all social benefits of the project; e.g., if a new transport system will reduce road accidents, an estimate should be made of the value of lives saved. Cost-Benefit appraisal allows for social costs as well as cash costs; e.g., if a project will harm the environment, an estimate is made of this cost. Estimates of social benefits and costs allow for factors which might otherwise be ignored. Benefits and costs should be evaluated in cash terms, because money provides a common measure of value, and investments, however socially desirable, use funds which might buy other things. Once the relevant information is put into cash figures, analysis becomes easier. It is possible to identify trends, and to make forecasts. Political aspects must be considered, both qualitative — e.g., what range of views do governments have on a given topic — and quantitative — e.g., how many countries take a particular view. It is necessary to appreciate the situation as it is, or potentially could be; and not to 'situate the appreciation' (i.e., to engage in wishful thinking, and pretend that things are as the observer would like them to be).

The last step is to consider how the chosen solutions can be implemented. There will be political constraints here, as with other cost-benefit studies. There may be, not one best solution, but several good solutions. It makes sense to try various solutions, so as to find the best one by trial and error. New technology will arise from the challenge of using the Last Commons, and this will determine which solution is the best. Trying out several solutions reduces risk, because it allows for a second chance. Picking one solution because it looks best at the outset could be unwise; if this turned out to be the wrong solution, it might be too late to try one of the other solutions.

The Decision Criteria The decision criteria for evaluating solutions should not be based on ad hoc analysis, or on 'muddling through', but on principles which are plausible in terms of evidence, and logically consistent. The policy-makers can leave companies and institutions to maximise return on their investments; the task of the policy-makers is to establish the 'Rules of the Game'. There might be different sets of rules in different parts of the world, or for different areas of the Last Commons. It is appropriate to talk about 'Rules of the Game' in this context; Henry George explains that

> They [the Physiocrats] were the authors of the motto that in the English use of the phrase 'Laissez Faire' 'Let things alone' has been so emasculated and perverted, but which on their lips was 'Laissez Faire, Laissez Aller' 'Clear the ways and let things alone'. This is said to come from the cry that in Medieval tournaments gave the signal for combat. The English phrase which I take to come closest to the spirit of the French phrase is, 'A fair field and no favour!'.[5]

Thus, laissez-faire implies not the absence of rules, but the presence of fair, impartially-applied, rules.

The rules should reflect a proper understanding of the nature of man, and of the nature of nature, and of the ways in which man interacts with nature, and human beings interact with each other. The crucial fact about nature is that resources are inherently limited, and everything runs down; 'Entropy is Time's Arrow'. To understand nature, freedom is necessary, because a political system that does not respect freedom of speech, of publication, and of association, will limit the acquisition of knowledge. Sir Karl Popper has explained why freedom is necessary; putting the matter simply, no one can be sure of the truth in any field of knowledge, and there is no hope of finding the truth without freedom of enquiry. Experts or governments do not have special access to the truth; there are many cases of experts — and governments — being wrong.

At present, no one has adequate knowledge or experience to deal efficiently with the Last Commons. What is needed is to accept that mistakes will happen, but to arrange matters so that mistakes can be identified early. Even after solutions are implemented, the approach should be like that adopted for new drugs that are brought into use; all reports of unexpected side-effects are reported to a central body. In advance of implementation, possible solutions can be judged both in terms of a priori considerations, and in terms of evidence. The social sciences provide ways of assessing possible solutions. They make it possible to assess solutions in terms of plausibility of assumptions, likely consequences, and consistency with existing knowledge of how human societies work. Moral philosophy offers a guide to ethical aspects. History provides evidence. It records the crimes and follies which have been committed in the past whenever the commons of that period were transferred to private ownership, and thus provides a lesson about what not to do.

Decisions need objectives; decisions relating to the Last Commons are so important that they should be explicitly targeted at a major goal; indeed, what may properly be regarded as the major goal viz. a human society which is ecologically sustainable in the long-term. This objective signals one essential decision criterion; that the solutions chosen should be ecologically sound. For simplicity of reference, this criterion is 'Ecology'.

It is possible, even probable, that a society which is ecologically sound will be unsatisfactory in other ways. Two other criteria must be added; these are the ones used when assessing tax or welfare reforms; they are 'Equity' and 'Efficiency'. Equity means justice and fairness; definitions vary depending on a person's underlying values about political philosophy, but equity must be a criterion, because ethical issues ought not to be ignored. Efficiency is easier to handle; gross inefficiency is easy to identify. Time is wasted, or materials are damaged; shortages occur, or quality is poor. People may agree about issues of efficiency, even when they disagree about equity issues. Ecology, equity, and efficiency are distinct, yet linked.

A given policy might seem efficient in the short run, yet, if it is inequitable, it will not be efficient in the long-run. A policy which looks equitable will not last in the long-run unless it is efficient. Irrespective of whether a policy is equitable in the short-run, efficient in the short-run, or both of these; it will not last in the long-run unless it is ecologically sound. A human society which is sustainable in the long-run must recognise ecology, efficiency and equity*. The symptoms of failure in any of the three criteria are the same as always; poverty, famine, violence, war. Failure to allow for ecology leads to degradation of the environment, which becomes progressively less able to support even the existing population.

At one time, war, although always a negative sum game, enabled some people to gain at the expense of others, by seizing their resources. Under modern conditions, gains are few, and the risks are high. Experience shows that trade is better than war; it gives people access to resources without having to fight. It lets people sell what they make, and buy what they need. Trade weakens the case for war, and undermines the position of the warmongers. Trade requires the recognition of private property rights. Private property rights are also necessary for efficient production; state production is inefficient by comparison. But private property rights can exist without outright ownership of resources. Ownership is not necessary for a person to use resources efficiently. What is necessary is security of tenure; the guarantee that the producer will be able to enjoy the

---

*'Ecology' is a subdivision of 'equity', in the sense that it is intergenerational equity as applied to the natural environment.

benefit of his labours. In the case of the Last Commons, the producer can enjoy security only if there are laws to protect him. Unless the laws are adequate, the potential producer will find other fields for his endeavours. The rule of law must be maintained; good laws are of no value unless they are enforced, and enforced impartially. The producer needs to be confident that he can pursue his activities in peace as long as he obeys the law.

These points must be taken into account when solutions in terms of Equity and Efficiency are being assessed. Allowances must be made for adequate incentives, and for the need to cover all costs. Development of the Last Commons will need new, and expensive, technology. It will present serious risks. Inventors and producers will not incur these costs, and face these risks, unless they can reasonably expect a good return.

To sum up; assessment of possible solutions must be based on the three criteria of equity, efficiency, and ecology.

A Review of the Possible Solutions Each solution proposed should be presented in the form of a model (i.e., a simplified version of the arrangements that would be applied in practice). Models leave out details, but stress the main points of the underlying ideas, so making comparisons easier. In reality, any solution would involve an immense amount of complex legislation.

Models should be assessed in terms of the decision criteria. The three obvious models can be described as; 'Free for All'; 'Common Heritage of Mankind'; and 'Business as Usual'. The emphasis here is on the seabed; if a good solution could be found for this, it could be applied also to Antarctica and Outer Space. Parts of the sea-bed have already been claimed by nation-states, and commercial exploitation is taking place. The deep ocean sea-bed has not yet been claimed, but commercial exploitation could feasibly take place there.

The sea-bed is divided as follows. The continental shelf is that part of the continental margin which is adjacent to the coast; it may be no more than 100m. deep, or as much as 300m. deep. Beyond the shelf, but still part of the margin, is the continental slope. Beyond this is the rise from the oceanic abyss. The abyss mostly lies at a depth of 300 metres, or more, below sea-level. The width of the continental shelf varies greatly; to the west of Europe it is wide — e.g., it extends to 320k. west of Cornwall — yet it is little more than 1k. wide off parts of the western coast of South America. The term 'sea' is used for those parts of the seas that lie adjacent to coasts, such as the North Sea or the Red Sea. The terms 'ocean' is used for the great expanse of the seas; there are five oceans; the Pacific, the Atlantic, the Indian, the Arctic, and the Antarctic. Much of the continental shelf has already been divided up amongst nation-states; the question is what should be done with the rest of the ocean sea-bed.

Professor Denman discusses the 'Sea-bed Resource', considering the economic potential of all sea-bed, not only that under the deep oceans.[6] The superjacent waters allow passage for ships; they provide a habitat for seaweed, such as kelp, for pelagic fish, such as herring, for demersal fish such as plaice, and for shellfish such as lobsters; moreover, sea water can be desalinated, and salt extracted. Waves can be used to generate electricity. The sea-bed is a source of minerals, sand and gravel from coastal areas, oil from the continental shelf, and manganese, nickel, cobalt, and copper, from the oceasn sea-bed. The sea-bed provides a basis for structures, such as harbours and marinas, oil drilling platforms, industrial plants, and housing. The seas are used also for submarine cables.

The 'Free for All' model means that governments do nothing about the ocean sea-bed. A real-life example shows the likely outcome from this model. An American company made a claim on a section of the ocean floor intending to bring up the manganese nodules lying there. It abandoned this scheme when it learnt that the US government would not recognise its claim. No company will invest large amounts of money unless it is sure that its government, or some other government, will protect its investment. The utilisation of the ocean sea-beds, of Antarctica, and of Outer Space, will all require large amounts of investment. Companies might, in theory, build up their own private armies to protect their investment, as the British East India Company did, but the 20th century state is jealous of its power, and would not let companies do this. This model would mean non-use of resources.

The 'Common Heritage of Mankind' approach has been held up as the ideal model. It is the basis of the United Nations Law of the Sea Convention (UNCLOS III), which had been introduced, and signed by a majority of the UN member states, by 1983. Only a few had ratified it. Many of the Western nations, including the USA and the UK, were reluctant to sign, let alone ratify, this Convention.[7] UNCLOS III envisages the creation of an international authority, the 'International Seabed Authority', which would have exclusive powers to grant access to the resources of the deep oceans. The ISA would have an operational arm known as the 'Enterprise', to engage in mining and other commercial activities on its behalf. The Enterprise would compete with national corporations and private sector companies. The Authority would control the ocean sea-bed, and would be the sole source of licences to exploit it. A company which wanted to mine a site would have to pay substantial fees and royalties to the ISA, and also offer the Authority half of the site, which the Authority could mine for itself. The company would have to supply the Authority with the technological know-how with which to exploit this site. This scheme would not interfere with the right of passage for ships, nor with fishing.

The proposal to treat the ocean sea-beds as the Common Heritage of Mankind was put to the UN in 1967, but the idea had been promoted before this, by the movement for world federalism. This concept underlies the 1979 Moon Treaty, which calls on nation-states to establish a joint management system 'to govern the exploitation of the natural resources of the Moon as such exploitation is about to become feasible'. It has been suggested that this principle should apply also to the Geo-Stationary Orbit for communications satellites, which is becoming congested, and to the exploitation of Antarctica. The model could be applied to the tropical rain-forests.[8] This could be an answer to the problem of the Remnant Commons, but it would be opposed by national governments. The Common Heritage approach aims at protecting the environment, while encouraging development in the less-developed countries. Revenues raised from use of natural resources would be used to finance this development.

UNCLOS III acknowledged that nations are claiming more of the seas than they traditionally did. It introduced the 'Exclusive Economic Zone'; this can extend up to 200 miles from the coasts, and the state can control fisheries within this zone, as well as the sea-bed. If the sea-bed is still on the Continental Shelf, sovereign rights can

The Remaining Commons

extend beyond this, but operators exploiting sea-bed minerals would make a payment to the ISA.

Professor Denman criticises the Convention on the grounds that: the ISA would be an international public monopoly, which would slow down development through inefficiency and bureaucracy; the Enterprise would present unfair competition to companies, who would be expected to hand over their new technology to the ISA for nothing; the ISA might interfere with the relevant mineral markets, as new supplies would reduce prices received by the existing suppliers, most of whom are relatively poor nations. He argues that it is unjust that companies which have incurred high costs, and run great risks, should be expected to relinquish much of their profit. He also points out that, as many nations have not signed the Convention the ISA could not truthfully claim to be acting for the benefit of 'all mankind'.[9] The system probably would deter private enterprise, for the residual rewards would hardly be worth the risk and effort involved. Accurate charts are essential to use of the sea-bed. The charting of the sea-bed is carried out by only a few of the nations, all of them developed ones; most nations do no charting. Few of the Western nations are likely to agree to the Convention proposed; their companies and government bodies are being called on to do the exploration, create the new technology, train the needed personnel, and risk lives and money to develop the ocean sea-bed, and then hand over much of their profit to nations who have contributed nothing. The Common Heritage approach would be open to the same objections if applied to Antarctica and Outer Space.

The Business as Usual model represents what is happening at present, and what has happened in the past. States have divided up the Remnant Commons into exclusive private property, while extending national jurisdiction into the Last Commons, subsequently making private property of these commons too. This was the process whereby the Americas, parts of Africa, and Australia and New Zealand, were occupied by Europeans. Much the same happened when Central Asia was occupied by the Russians and Han Chinese.

This model accepts private property in land, as opposed to the collective ownership of land usual amongst tribal peoples, which has an echo in the Common Heritage of Mankind approach. Business as

Usual is 'corporatist' (i.e., it includes a substantial amount of government intervention) and nationalistic, tending to provoke conflict between nations. It is not based firmly upon free market principles, which presuppose more respect for the freedom of the individual. The relevant unit is the state which creates and protects private property rights in land, in exchange for the loyalty of the beneficiaries. The state favours the interests of existing property-owners. The state is mercantilist, deterring imports by tariffs, encouraging exports by subsidies, interfering with trade and industry, providing benefits to its supporters, and taxing everyone else heavily. The state interferes with property rights — e.g., by planning controls — yet lets property owners escape full responsibility for their actions, by allowing limited liability for companies.

In the 20th century, socialist measures have reversed the movement towards private property; in some countries, Marxist governments have taken the land from existing owners, and treated it as the property of the state. In the UK, some private property, although not land as such, has been nationalised. But state control of property leads to inefficiency, and the trend towards private property has now been resumed. The collapse of Marxist governments will allow the restoration of private property. Privatisation in the UK has been copied elsewhere. Even so, the state is now so extensive that, in every country, much land is owned by specific government bodies. In the USA, the Federal government still owns large amounts of unoccupied land. Private property rights in land are always subject to the power of the state, which can acquire property by compulsory purchase.

Business as usual was the method used by the English and other European settlers in what is now the USA. They found a large region with a relatively small Amerindian population, who made use of the land as it was needed. The colonial process of carving up the land into private ownership might have taken place on the criterion of effective occupation, wherever land was unoccupied, but it did not. The land was deemed to be the property of the king, who distributed it to his friends or financiers. The American Revolution could have introduced occupation as the basis of ownership, seeing that this is what Locke recommended. Instead, the government of the USA took over the land-granting privilege, and treated unoccupied land as belonging to the state, so that persons who wanted it had to buy it. The claims to land of the indigenous peoples were largely ignored. The system was not ideal for the settlers either. A person could clear land, live on it and cultivate it for several years, and then suddenly find that someone else had acquired title to the land by purchase or grant from the government. The purchaser got the land cheaply, and could enjoy the improvements made by the original settler. He might hold the land for speculative gain, rather than using it himself. Even so, the USA developed the most successful economy that has ever been known. Thus Business as Usual is associated with economic success, and must be rated relatively efficient. Critics would argue that it is less satisfactory in terms of equity and ecology.

This model can include a free market variation. This has been observed only fleetingly in reality, but it would be superior to the existing practice in terms of equity. If the state intervened less in the economy, and levied lower taxes, especially on earned income, persons without property would have a better chance of acquiring some, and they would enjoy a higher standard of living. The essence of a free market system is that people pay for what they get. On this principle, property owners should pay for the property protection services of the state (i.e., for national defence and for law and order). The UK and the USA were close to being free market economies during the 19th century, but in neither country were the essential services of the state financed in this way. This model would mean that nation-states extended their territory out from the continental shelf into the rest of the continental margin, and then into the abyss. Trenches in the ocean floor would be used to demarcate national boundaries. Coastal nations would gain an immense amount of territory; the seas and oceans cover 71% (361m.sq.k.) of the Earth's surface, as opposed to only 29% (149m.sq.k.) for the land. Landlocked states might well be aggrieved, especially those such as Bolivia, which would have had a sea-coast, but for historical bad luck. The UK, which has a relatively large amount of continental shelf of Europe, would get a substantial section of the Atlantic floor, although Eire would do even better by comparison with its existing land area.

Business as Usual is unsatisfactory in terms of efficiency and equity. Also, it makes two political assumptions which are both unrealistic. First, it assumes that the nation-state is the natural unit of government, whereas history shows that the nation-state is relatively modern; tribes, city-states and empires existed previously, and lasted for long periods of time. Second, it assumes that existing nation-states are natural units. This can be challenged, by reference to states in Africa or Asia, or to the situation in Northern Ireland. Governments might like everyone to accept the legitimacy of existing nation-states, but not everyone does. When a nation-state lays claim to some part of the Last Commons, its claim may be disputed. Within a country, the central government may find that its control of natural resources in a region is challenged by the minority nationality who live there.

'Land and Liberty': the Foundation for the Right Solution The three obvious models all fail in one or more of the criteria; equity, efficiency, and ecology. Yet there are models which would be satisfactory on all three criteria. The basic model here is 'Land and Liberty', but it could give rise to several variations.

The essential idea is that what a person creates, using his or her talent and effort, belongs to that person. Conversely, what no-one has made, cannot belong to anyone. No person made the land, using 'land' in its comprehensive definition (i.e., all natural resources) and therefore no-one can own the land. This does not mean that the land should be nationalised; the state did not make the land either. What it does mean is that no person should be able to appropriate the 'economic rent' of the land (i.e., the rent which is paid by the user, not for assets or other services provided by the land-owner, but purely for the 'privilege' of gaining access to the land). Economists have misused the term 'economic rent', pretending that the return to a person's inherent talent is also a form of economic rent; in truth, it is a quasi-rent. The term 'pure rent' is less ambiguous. Pure rent is a payment for the use of unimproved land, a payment with nothing in return. The land-owner who lets someone cultivate a piece of derelict land is charging pure rent, for he provides no services in exchange. The term 'ground rent' is used in ordinary parlance, to mean a payment purely for land. A tax can be defined as a payment with nothing in return, so pure rent is similar to a tax, but, unlike a tax, it

The Remaining Commons

is taken by private individuals. It is a quasi-tax. The Land Value Tax is the best way to prevent private individuals from appropriating pure rent; it can replace other taxes, thus removing the burden of government from people whose income comes from their own endeavour. The LVT does not hinder the working of a market economy; it enables it to work more effectively. People can enjoy the full value of their own efforts, without paying any tax. People who want to hold land have to pay the LVT, irrespective of the use they make of it. They have an incentive either to use land efficiently, or to relinquish it. Buildings and other improvements would still be bought and sold, as the LVT does not fall upon these items, but only upon the land itself. In practice, the LVT should not take the whole of the annual value of the unimproved land (i.e., the annual value of the pure rent); if it took most, but not all, of the value, there would still be a market price for land, and a market in land, which would allow transactions in land without interference from the state. Prices would be very low, compared with what they are now. The selling price of land, in a free market, is always a given multiple of the net pure rent (i.e., pure rent after allowing for taxes and any management expenses) that can be obtained from that land. Land and Liberty is equitable; it respects the freedom of the individual, and lets each person keep what he or she produces. It is efficient; every individual has a strong incentive to create and produce, and there is no fiscal hindrance to the operation of the market economy. The government would take the pure rent on land, using it to pay for essential services, such as defence, and law and order and perhaps some others. The government would estimate annual land values, and determine the right tax rate. If the land market was able to operate freely, price discrepancies and price fluctuations would soon show whether the estimates and the tax rate were correct.

The LVT is usually envisaged as a tax upon Occupied Land, but it could be applied equally well to the Remnant Commons within a country, and to the Last Commons. However, if extended to the Last Commons, this model would share a weakness with the Business as Usual model, viz., that the right of the nation-state to control particular areas of land, or sea-bed, may be challenged.

This model could work as follows. The state, having claimed the continental shelf as its territory, would chart the sea-bed accurately.

It would then divide up the sea-bed into sectors, and announce that it was selling leases for each sector in turn, at say, at one-year intervals. Each sector would be sub-divided, and the state would sell individual sections, preferably by open auction to the highest bidder. Navigation would still be free, but otherwise a section should include the complete sea-bed resource (i.e., the superjacent waters as well as the sea-bed). The state would announce what ground rent had to be paid for the first twenty years, and warn that all leases would be renegotiated at the end of that time. The highest bidder for a section would be free to use it as he wished, or sell it to some one else. Provided that he paid his ground rent each year, he should not be asked to pay any other taxes — e.g., corporation tax. At the outset, there would be a general lack of knowledge. Relative to the pure rent, some buyers would find themselves paying too much ground rent, and others too little. The price of existing leases would reflect whether the ground rents were unduly high or low. Investors would have a strong incentive to learn, for both risks and rewards would be high, and, over time, the market in leases would approach an efficient market, provided that there was competition amongst initial bidders, and in the secondary market. This method allocates resources to those who believe that they can use them efficiently, and it penalises those who are wrong in their belief. A lease of twenty years gives time for investors to benefit from their development activities, and offers the government a second chance to set ground rents, if these were too low originally. If the government wanted to evict a lease-holder when his time was up (i.e., without giving him the chance to renew the lease) it would have to compensate him for the residual value of any usable fixed capital, but if he left derelict structures behind, it would charge him for removal. The same method could be applied if the state took over part of the ocean sea-bed, and also if it took territory in Antarctica or the Moon.

A variation is that nation-states collect the ground rent, keep part of it, and hand the rest over to an international body. This would accord with the Common Heritage of Mankind approach. As compared with the UNCLOS III proposals, it is more comprehensive, for it could apply to the ground rent from the continental shelf as well as to the ocean sea-bed. This variation recognises that there is no good reason why a particular nation-state should enjoy all the ground rent from its adjacent sea-beds. However, nation-states with substantial sea-beds would be reluctant to hand over large sums of money to a UN subsidiary. They might point out that many of the UN member states are controlled by corrupt or tyrannical governments, which would use the money either to buy arms or to enrich themselves. They might argue that countries which have done nothing to find, explore or develop these resources have no moral claim to them.

A compromise would be for nation-states to put part of the ground rent into a special international fund, with trustees appointed by themselves. The trustees would be 'Four Just Men', probably more than four, and including women; they would be appointed on their personal merits and experience. This 'World Welfare Fund' would have designated uses for these funds, such as disaster relief, the purchase of land for nature reserves, or the financing of scholarships. Funds could be used for research and development of general benefit, in areas such as earthquake prediction, control of pollution, conservation of the environment, alternative technology, utilisation of space, or protection of the Earth from disasters such as global warming or asteroid strikes. Countries reluctant to contribute to the international fund might devote part of their ground rent to similar types of activity or research, setting up designated funds at the national level. This would allow decentralisation, and make use of the research strengths of different countries.

The LVT, with revenues paid into an international fund, would be a good way of managing the ocean sea-beds, even if individual states were not prepared to introduce the LVT in the areas of the continental shelf that they are currently claiming. Professor Denman suggests that the International Seabed Authority should be set up as the supreme allocating agency for interests in the ocean sea-bed. It would grant secure interests in the ocean sea-bed, and register all titles, in exchange for payment equivalent to the pure rent. Interests would be sold to the highest bidder. The fund thus raised could be used to assist Third World countries to engage in development of the ocean sea-beds for themselves.[10]

There are other ideas which could be included in one or other of these models. The English laws on common land could be adapted to cover the sea-bed. Just as different people have particular common rights, so people might have particular rights over the sea-bed resource of a section (i.e., as opposed to all the rights). As with the basic model, they could buy leases for these rights, paying ground rent to the state each year, and having the right to sell the leases. There could be clearly designated fishing rights; this would control fishing more effectively than the present quota system, which is open to abuse, may reflect political bias, and is also wasteful — e.g., fish surplus to quota have to be thrown back into the sea, by which time most of them are dead. But fishery consortia which owned long-term leases on a fisheries would be strongly motivated to conserve fish stocks, and their membership would be small enough to co-operate effectively. The right to dump waste at sea would also be for sale, with the ground rent higher, the more noxious the waste. This would reflect the economic principle that costs 'external' to the producer, such as pollution, can be controlled best by 'internalising' them (i.e., imposing specific taxes, or other payments, upon the producer). Fishing consortia would not bid for areas where a lot of dumping took place, so that the government would lose revenue if it charged too low a ground rent for dumping. Rights to extract minerals, or to build structures at sea, would also be for sale; here, too, dumping would discourage bidders. Persons who owned leases on clean sections of sea-bed would be entitled to take legal action if waste drifted onto their sections. Skill and experience would be needed to demarcate specific rights properly, and set ground rents correctly. Potential bidders would be analysing the situation, so that, if ground rents for particular rights were set too low (or too high), secondary market lease prices would be relatively high (or low). This scheme is better than selling off the sea-bed resource as a whole. Only a very large consortium would have both the funds to buy a complete section, and the resources to make full use of it. In contrast, small fishing consortia would bid for fishery rights, and small firms bid for construction rights. This variation would be favourable to economic competition, and thus promote economic efficiency. If countries took different approaches, they might learn from each other.

Existing practice varies amongst countries; thus, in the U.K., the government grants leases in the sea-bed of the territorial sea, but not in the continental shelf outside this, where it grants only licences. In the USA, the Federal government grants leases for oil exploration in the sea-bed in the continental shelf also. The holder of a lease has more complete property rights than has the holder of a licence — e.g. a lease can be sold. In the USA, leases are sold to the highest bidder; in the UK, so far, licences have been awarded on a discretionary basis. The British government gave away the pure rent, and then tried to remedy this by imposing not only royalties on oil extracted, but also special taxes. Yet in Norway it is possible to hold the sea-bed as private property, although only in water up to two meters in depth.

The LVT could solve the problem of the Remnant Commons too; thus, in the Arctic, ground rent could be paid over to the indigenous peoples such as the Inuit (Eskimo); the case here is not that they own these resources, but that no-one does, and that they are entitled to compensation for the disruption that extraction of resources inflicts on their environment and on their social structure. A similar approach could be adopted in the Amazon. Tribal peoples in the USA have used royalty payments for oil found in tribal lands to improve their standard of living. In Canada, the money might reduce the need for welfare payments, which seem to have had a demoralising effect on the social structure of the tribal peoples.

There are more futuristic scenarios too. In view of the evils that have arisen from the conventional political and economic systems of the past, it might be worth giving less conventional systems a chance to show what they can achieve. There are ways of organising political life other than the nation-state; and, in a market economy, ways of organising economic production other than the limited liability company. There are also; partnerships; co-operatives; friendly societies; trusts; and charities. These might offer an ecologically better way to develop the Last Commons. If Antarctica should be opened up to development, an Antarctic Trust, analogous to the National Trust in Britain, could be set up to control those parts of Antarctica, and the Antarctic Ocean, which would be set aside as conservation areas. This Trust could ensure that no whaling took place, and might offer exotic holidays to the robust tourist. An ecologically sound feature of the LVT is that conservation areas can be completely exempted from tax. It is already possible to build cities on the seabed. Existing nation-states might let some of these sea-cities be run as co-operatives. Some ocean-cities could become independent states. The UK, which controls so much relatively shallow sea-bed, a total area equal to about twice the area of the dry land, might offer a site for a new 'Lyonesse' in exchange for the appropriate amount of LVT. Some ocean-cities might be run on free-market, minimal state lines, as in the 'Utopia' that Robert Nozick advocates; others could be run on the principles of traditional anarchism, or the more modern 'anarcho-capitalism', which keeps private property and the market system, but does away with the state. Some of these communities would offer free immigration for any persons desiring to go there, a life-line to the many people who find it hard to live in their own countries because of the tyranny of their governments. There are said to be some ten million refugees in Africa alone. A similar approach might be adopted in Antarctica. If these models worked on Earth, they might be used on the Moon too, or in the 'Space Cities' that have been proposed. After that, the Solar System is the limit.

NOTES

1 Selected Press Reports on Antarctica; 'Australians to ban polar oil drilling', *The Daily Telegraph*, Monday, August 20th, 1990; 'Airfield "threat to Antarctic"', *The Guardian*, May 7, 1990. The latter reports that the UK is building an airfield at its Rothera Antarctic research station; this is so that scientists will be able to travel there more easily, but critics say it would be an ideal base for mineral prospecting. The British government supports the Antarctic Mineral Convention, which would allow prospecting.
2 R. Bainton, *Here I Stand; The Classic Biography of Martin Luther* (Berkhamstead, Herts.: Lion Publishing, 1978), pp. 268-270, 280-281.
3 N. Keyfitz, 'The Growing Human Population', *Scientific American*, September 1989, pp. 70-77.
4 'Papal policy, poverty and Aids'; a letter to the *British Medical Journal*, from R. E. J. Ryder; *BMJ*; August 4, 1990, pp. 291-292. The writer noted that Mother Theresa's Sisters taught natural birth control methods to low-income women in Calcutta; for 1978, only 34 pregnancies occurred in nearly 20,000 women, a failure rate, at 0.2 pregnancies per 100 women users per year, no worse than that of the contraceptive pill; women are taught how to observe signs of ovulation,

so that they can avoid sexual activity on the necessary one or two days per cycle.

5 Henry George, *The Science of Political Economy* (1897; New York: Robert Schalkenbach Foundation, 1962), p. 153.
6 D. R. Denman, *Markets under the Sea?* (London, Institute of Economic Affairs, 1984. Hobart Paperback, 17), pp. 7-11.
7 Denman, *op. cit.*, pp. 30-38.
8 *World Federalism Today* (The Netherlands), World Association for World Federation, 1988.
9 Denman, *op. cit.*, pp. 38; 56-59.
10 D. R. Denman, 'Land Value Taxation in Deep Water', *Land and Liberty*, Nov./Dec. 1984, pp. 103-107; 115.

7
The Tragedy of the *Unmanaged* Commons: population and the disguises of Providence

GARRETT HARDIN

THE COMPLEX of concerns we blanket with the name 'the population problem' has been with us for almost two hundred years. Any 'problem' that persists that long without resolution should lead us to suspect subconscious resistances. In this instance a major resistance is, I think, centered around the concept of Providence. We would do well to look into the origin and variations of this concept.

The word 'Providence' was much used in the eighteenth century, but it is seldom heard now. Nonetheless, the idea behind the word still plays a role in shaping people's thoughts. There seems to be an almost irreducible hunger for this supportive idea. Psychoanalytically speaking, this hunger is no mystery: each of us starts life as a helpless little being to whom all the essentials must be supplied. It is natural and necessary that an infant should expect to be provided for. As we develop we outgrow some of these expectations; but under stress, or when puzzled, we may relapse into an infantile attitude of expecting Providence (under whatever name) to take care of us.

The Latin word *providere* means to see ahead, hence to provide for. As the word 'God' became somewhat unfashionable in the eighteenth century, 'Providence' became its surrogate. The psychoanalytic weight of the two words is much the same. This century was later labeled 'the Enlightenment' by those who approved the change.

In the same century another substitution was made, as Robert Nisbet tells us.[1] Turgot, one of the seminal minds of the time, made the personal transition in less than a year. In July of 1750, in a public address at the Sorbonne, Turgot praised the idea of Providence as one of Christianity's great gifts to the world. But by December of the same year he had decided that the idea of progress (which also has ancient roots) was far more deserving of admiration. As Nisbet says: 'with respect to the idea of progress, Turgot, without abandoning the structure or framework of his first address at the Sorbonne, secularized it.'

Progress — a secularized version of Providence — soon came to mean principally *technological* progress. A new faith developed: 'Technology will solve our problems.' This is surely a providential idea. The emotional appeal is the same; the hunger is the same. As the acknowledged historian of progress, J. B. Bury, says: 'it was just the theory of an active Providence that the theory of Progress was to replace; and it was not till men felt independent of Providence that they could organise a theory of Progress.'[2] We note that in 1751, after he had abandoned Providence for Progress, Turgot renounced his ecclesiastical ambitions.

At the end of the same decade, in *The Theory of Moral Sentiments*, Adam Smith gave memorable form to another providential idea:

> The rich ..., though they mean only their own conveniency, though the sole end which they propose be the gratification of their own vain and insatiable desires, ... divide with the poor the produce of all their improvements. They are led by an invisible hand to make nearly the same distribution of the necessaries of life which would have been made had the earth been divided into equal portions among all its inhabitants; and thus, without intending it, without knowing it, advance the interests of society ...[3]

Adam Smith's 'invisible hand' is, of course, a figure of speech. Note his clever salesmanship in tying the argument to what would, two centuries later, be called the 'trickle-down' theory of distribution, thus easing the pain of accepting what looks at first like wholly selfish behaviour. The selfish entrepreneur, though he intends only his own good (said Smith), nevertheless acts for the benefit of all society. Such is the faith of *laissez-faire;* it is surely a providential idea. Seventeen years later Adam Smith developed it more fully in his classic text, *The Wealth of Nations*.

Other men added rhetorical embellishments. Ten years before

Smith's classic work, La Riviere asserted that laissez-faire produced *l'ordre naturel*. Then, as now, the word 'natural' enjoyed prestige. In 1810 David Ricardo, in *The High Price of Bullion*, claimed that 'Where there is free competition, the interests of the individual and that of the community are *never* at variance.'[4] I have italicized the word 'never' to call attention to several points. First, italics suggest the authority Ricardo was trying to bestow on the idea. Second, the claim of an invariable correlation of individual and community interests is one that was easily accepted by economists, though it was, as we shall see, denied by many serious students of population, beginning with Malthus. Lastly, for many economists laissez-faire became something of a religious belief, a ready substitute for 'Providence'.

Pursuing the history of ideas to their earliest origins one finds the germ of laissez-faire in the writings of Chuang Tzu of the fourth century B.C.: 'Good order results spontaneously when things are left alone.'[5] Of course few in eighteenth century Europe were aware of what had been thought in China two millennia earlier. Following the idea of 'spontaneous order' all the way to the present we find that the Nobel economist F. A. Hayek, in a book published in 1988, echoes Chuang Tzu, matching the unqualified praise of Ricardo: 'Order generated without design can far outstrip plans men consciously contrive.'[6]

Few biologists would argue with that assertion: but what is explicitly said hardly justifies that which the author no doubt hopes the reader will infer, namely that human beings can *never* improve on nature. Even if human-generated order is usually a poor match for nature's designs it does not follow that economic libertarians are wise in holding that humanity should renounce all foresight, all planning and all intervention in the order of nature.

The Utterly Dismal Theorem

The congruence of self-interest and community interest implied by laissez-faire was a comforting one to the people of the late eighteenth century. Into this complacent world burst Malthus with his assertion that, when population is involved, laissez-faire reproduction does not automatically produce a pleasant world. Unhindered reproduction, he said, causes the population to increase 'geometrically' ('exponentially,' we say now), while the means of subsistence increases only arithmetically. Reproduction can easily outrun food production.

Malthus was right in the first assertion: in the absence of 'environmental resistance' exponential reproduction is the innate result of all healthy living. We can hardly imagine a different biology. But Malthus' belief that subsistence increases arithmetically has no basis in fact. There is no general law that predicts the rate at which the human species improves the technology with which the environment is exploited. Later commentators suggested that Malthus was dimly aware of the principle of 'diminishing returns.' Malthus denied this explanation. The dispute need not detain us here.

It is manifestly clear that Malthus's theory does not lead to the attainment of happiness through laissez-faire reproduction. This conclusion has been expressed unequivocally in our time by another economist, Kenneth Boulding. He first describes Malthus's 'famous dismal theorem of economics' which he summarizes in these words:

> ... if the only check on the growth of population is starvation and misery, then no matter how favorable the environment or how advanced the technology the population will grow until it is miserable and starves. The theorem, indeed, has a worse corollary which has been described as the utterly dismal theorem. This is the proposition that if the only check on the growth of population is starvation and misery, then any technological improvement will have the ultimate effect of increasing the sum of human misery, as it permits a larger population to live in precisely the same state of misery and starvation as before ...[7]

In spite of its pessimistic cast the *Essay* of Malthus was given a favourable reception when it first appeared. But its hard-headed approach to human problems was better suited to the century of the Enlightenment than it was to the succeeding Romantic century. A determined and continuing search was made for 'softer' mechanisms than the 'misery and vice' that Malthus proposed as the great controllers of population size. In 1832 (two years before the death of Malthus) one Thomas Rowe Edmonds put forward an interesting theory:

> Amongst the great body of the people at the present moment, sexual intercourse is the only gratification; and thus, by a most unfortunate

concurrence of adverse circumstances, population goes on augmenting at a period when it ought to be restrained... When [the working class] are better fed they will have other enjoyments at command than sexual intercourse, and their numbers, therefore, will not increase in the same proportion as at present.[8]

Society should make the poor rich, advised Edmonds, so that they will have better things to do with their free time than entertain one another as animals do. This recommendation was no doubt favourably received by many Victorians, who — publicly at any rate — deprecated sexual intercourse. The substitution theory even surfaced more than a century later when it was suggested that television sets be put in every village in India, so that villagers would discover that other recreations are more enjoyable than 'doin' what comes naturally.' Many villages in the Third World now have television sets, but the predicted effect on human fertility has failed to make its appearance.

Ten years after Edmonds' ill-starred proposal Thomas Doubleday put forward another:

It is a fact, admitted by all gardeners as well as botanists, that if a tree, plant, or flower, be placed in mould, either naturally or artificially made too rich for it, a plethoric state is produced, and fruitfulness ceases... There cannot be a doubt that, with the animal creation... fecundity is totally checked by the plethoric state... the doe, or female rabbit, and... the sow will *not* conceive if fed to a certain height of fatness... leanness is indispensable to conception...[9]

Is it true that fertility is inversely correlated with the quality of the diet? Doubleday's thesis of 1842 became a priori suspect when Darwin published his theory of evolution in 1859. Natural selection has the automatic effect of making good (though unconscious) economizers of all species. It makes Darwinian sense for individuals to convert an increase in food into an increase in progeny; a species that became more fertile under starvation conditions would imperil its survival.

Empirical facts corroborate the evolutionary predictions. In reviewing these it will help to make the distinction that has become standard in demography: *fecundity* is the potentiality for having children, while *fertility* measures the actual production of children. As far as the fecundity of human beings is concerned the effect of nutrition is beyond controversy. Rose Frisch, a leader in this field of research, has summarized the findings in this way: 'Good nutrition leads to greater weight, more body fat in the female, leading to regular menstruation and higher fecundity, [thus] leading to greater fertility.'[10]

The explanation of Doubleday's facts is easily given. The excessive fat of penned-up rabbits and pigs is an artefact of domestication: their relatives in the wild would never achieve such gross fatness, thanks in large part to the regimen of involuntary exercise imposed on them by predators. Natural selection has not had to deal with Doubleday's kind of 'plethoric state.'

From the earliest days students of population have tried to induce desired political changes from scientific facts. Edmonds, for instance, saw the hand of Providence at work: 'To better the condition of the labouring classes, that is, to place more food and comforts before them, however paradoxical it may appear, is the wisest mode to check redundancy.'[11] When Providence works this way it is easy for human beings to cooperate with her. But Frisch's findings point to the opposite conclusion, a fact that disturbs her (and no doubt many others). Of Rose Frisch it has been reported that: 'She expresses concern that her findings on the fat-fertility relationship might be used as 'scientific' documentation of the negative value of sending surplus food to the underfed populations of the world ... She believes "a greater effort is needed to provide contraceptive methods together with adequate nutrition."'[12]

The providential bias in population theories has been strong from the earliest days. Going back to 1847 we find that the anonymous translator of the works of a Genevan economist, Sismondi, opined that: 'Sanitary improvements, and whatever tends to lengthen life, are the most effectual means of restraining a too great increase of population.'[13] By the end of the nineteenth century the tender-hearted view of population dynamics had a firm hold on such influential people as those in the Bloomsbury set. Geoffrey Searle has given a telling description of their position:

> Socialists, predisposed to believe that the solution to all difficulties lay in a radical improvement of the social environment, also noted that there was an inverse relationship between fertility and income. From this they deduced that higher wages and better living conditions *automatically*

brought about a reduction in the birth rate. This was the conclusion reached by the Webbs [Sidney and Beatrice] in *Industrial Democracy* [1897], which includes a discussion of differential fertility within the working class. Many other socialists followed the Webbs' lead. Thus, Mrs. Pember Reeves wrote in 1913: '... for those who deplore large families in the case of poor people, it must be a comfort to remember a fact which experience shows us, that as poverty decreases, and as the standard of comfort rises, so does the size of the family diminish. Should we be able to conquer the problem of poverty, we should automatically solve the problem of the excessively large family.'[14]

The imputing of the miseries of overpopulation to the actions of injustice was made more explicit in 1952 in the writings of the Brazilian nutritionist, Josué de Castro. In *The Geography of Hunger* he wrote: 'Hunger has been chiefly created by the inhuman exploitation of colonial riches, by the latifundia and one-crop culture which lay waste the colony, so that the exploiting country can take too cheaply the raw materials its properous industrial economy requires.'[15]

Sadly, Castro reports that 'A large part of the world is not yet convinced of the necessity of doing away with hunger once for all,' which is unfortunate because: 'when all the world's parts are indissolubly linked into one living whole, it is no longer possible to let one region rot and starve without infecting the rest, and threatening the whole world with death.'[16] One can empathize with Castro's intention — namely, to mobilize the indifferent to eradicate hunger from the world — without accepting his hypothesis that hunger is infectious in the same way that microbial diseases are infectious. If hunger spreads from the poor to the rich it is either because the rich are too stupid to manage their own affairs, or because they become infected by the idea of sharing-without-limit. Ideas, even malfunctional ones, *are* infectious.

All of the many causes proposed for overpopulation suffer from the same logical weakness: they assume that correlation equals causation. But correlation can be read in either direction. Mrs. Reeves' assertion that 'as poverty decreases, the size of the family diminishes,' implies that wealth is the *cause* of diminished fertility. Why did she not say, 'as the size of the family diminishes, wealth increases'? In truth, most couples, rich or poor, know that adding another child to their family will, in all probability, diminish their

The Tragedy of the Unmanaged Commons

wealth and well-being. So the hypothesis that fertility *causes* poverty is not an ungrounded speculation. Closer to the truth is the hypothesis that the causal relation of poverty and fertility is a circular one, an increase in either tending to increase the other: a true vicious circle.

Long ago logicians labeled the error of deducing cause from sequence as the *post hoc ergo propter hoc* fallacy. ('After this, therefore because of this.') It's a pity that many scholars continue to fall into this trap. One who did not was Joseph Townsend, an English minister. Commenting on his travels in Spain in 1791 he wrote: 'In a fully peopled country, to say, that no one shall suffer want is absurd. Could you supply their wants, you would soon double their numbers.'[17] Note that this was said eight years before Malthus' *Essay* was published. Was this insight a new discovery of Townsend's? Undoubtedly it was not. It is highly probable that ordinary folk understood this population principle for millennia, but it was not often voiced precisely because 'everybody knew it.' Then after Malthus it seemed too heartless and pessimistic a thought to state in public. The assertion of more providential principles was a surer path to public favor.

Anti-Malthusian hypotheses are legion. The diminution of fertility was, at various times, asserted to follow from: amusements alternative to sex; rich food; excess protein; better sanitation; industrialization; modernization (whatever that is); land reform; social justice; lessening of infant mortality; education; or — according to one's political bias — the adoption of communism or capitalism. The pattern is clear: since the most plausible proposals for controlling population are 'unacceptable,' whoever has the temerity to admit that population might be a problem promptly sees a chance to advance the reform of his choice by asserting that *his* reform is the best way to control population. Providence is in the saddle again.

The less doctrinaire commentators sometimes say that simple wealth is all that is needed to bring down fertility. This raises a question of definition, which is implicit in most of the entries on the reformers' lists. What is wealth, really? Both income and wealth per capita are greater in European countries than they are in the 'Third World' countries. By conventional measures, wealth and fertility are inversely related. But it has been remarked that, in Europe at least, 'a housing shortage is the best contraceptive.' Can a shortage be a true form of wealth? A young couple reduced to sharing the inadequate apartment of parents cannot agree that this shortage is wealth. As concerns fertility and population matters, the Gross National Product is a gross and inaccurate measure of real wealth. Statistics are tricky.

In the middle of the twentieth century, there appeared a population hypothesis so minimally specified as to be almost mystical in nature, namely the *Benign Demographic Transition*. The initial adjective has here been added to the usual form of the name for reasons that will be made clear presently.

The Benign Demographic Transition

Ignoring short-term fluctuations, the population of Europe was nearly stable for many centuries, with both fertility and mortality at high levels (the rate of each being about 40 per thousand population per year). In the last few centuries both fertility and mortality have fallen, with mortality falling first. The result has been an increase in population. After a delay of some time, fertility also fell. It is reasonable to assume that, sooner or later in a world of limits, the fertility rate must once again equal the mortality rate, but this time at a low level for both. This situation seems to have been reached in some of the Central European countries (Hungary and West Germany, for instance). The *change* from [High Fertility & High Mortality] to [Low Fertility & Low Mortality] is called the *demographic transition*. It was first identified in France in 1934 under the name 'révolution démographique.'[18] The anglicization of the name came a decade later.

The term 'demographic transition' has come to be more than mere description. Implicitly it is a theory about the way human populations automatically adjust to improved circumstances. It is assumed that the transition will eventually be complete (low fertility = low mortality) and stable, even though there has not been time to validate the latter point. It is also assumed that the forces that keep fertility low will (providentially!) not be painful to contemplate or experience. The fact that pain was not emphasized in the transition experience in European history is no doubt a consequence of two factors: the slowness of the transition (it took place over some two or three centuries); and the fact that most histories were written by the comfortable people who suffered the least from the transition. It was easy for demographers immersed in a European culture to assume that European history was the model for the history of all cultures, sooner or later. The demographic transition was seen as a historical imperative. Such a gratuitous assumption has been condemned by the philospher Karl Popper as *historicism*.[19] The demographic transition theory is a *post hoc* fallacy universalized and projected into the future.

If the world has limits — which is the only reasonable assumption — terrestrial population growth must eventually come to an end as the aggregate fertility rate once more becomes equal to the aggregate mortality rate. For both to be high, or both low, would equally well bring the transition to a close, but transitionists assume that both will be low: that is the reason for calling the theory they support the *Benign* Demographic Transition Theory. As used in argumentation the theory implied that making people rich and comfortable would remove the threat of overpopulation.

By 1969 a widely used population textbook called transition theory 'one of the best documented generalizations in the social sciences.'[20] Only a few years later the demographer Michael Teitelbaum expressed serious doubts: 'its explanatory power has come into increasing scientific doubt at the very time that it is achieving its greatest acceptance by nonscientists.'[21] In 1985 Teitelbaum and Winter spelled out a more forceful criticism: 'It is doubtful whether this theory was ever truly a theory at all (i.e., a set of hypotheses with predictive force) ...'[22]

The literature undercutting the Benign Demographic Transition theory grows ever larger. Etienne van de Walle concludes that 'central Africa is one vast contradiction of the theory: mortality has fallen, and fertility has risen, for two generations, with no end in sight.'[23] Ester Boserup predicts that 'Population increase will be rapid in Africa for many decades ...'[24] Demographers and other professional students of population have learned their lesson, but still the Benign Demographic Transition theory guides the work of those engaged in professional *telephilanthropy* — philanthropy targeted on people who are distant in space or ethnic characteristics.

There are two reasons for the continued fashionability of the Benign Demographic Transition theory. First, it is a providential theory and hence eminently acceptable. Second, it justifies the jobs of those who are employed by telephilanthropic foundations. The persistence of hunger and poverty in distant lands after millions of dollars have been poured into them discourages domestic donors; an optimistic reference to the Benign Demographic transition can often quiet doubts and loosen purse-strings.

As transition theory declined in prestige there developed a realization that perhaps the basic theory of human population dynamics was not providential after all. Perhaps the details of human behavoir needed to be studied more carefully? Fortunately the basis of this study was laid early in the nineteenth century, though it was noticed by virtually no one, probably because the resultant ' theory of the commons' is the very opposite of a providential theory.

The Tragedy of the Commons

The Reverend Thomas Robert Malthus sought an explanation of his dismal theorem in the comparison of his two ratios (one of which we no longer defend). A better approach was taken by another man of the cloth in 1833, the year before Malthus died. This man was the Oxford mathematician and economist William Forster Lloyd. He showed how the properties of a distribution system, interacting with human nature, can produce unwanted effects.

In a manner that would develop into a habit in science a century later, Lloyd began by setting up a 'model':

> Why are the cattle on a common so puny and stunted? Why is the common itself so bare-worn, and cropped so differently from the adjoining inclosures? ... The difference depends on the difference of the way in which an increase of stock in the two cases affects the circumstances of the author of the increase. If a person puts more cattle into his own field, the amount of the subsistence which they consume is all deducted from that which was at the command, of his original stock; and if, before, there was no more than a sufficiency of pasture, he reaps no benefit from the additional cattle, what is gained in one way being lost in another. But if he puts more cattle on a common, the food which they consume forms a deduction which is shared between all the cattle, as well that of others as

his own, in proportion to their number, and only a small part of it is taken from his own cattle.[25]

A careful reading shows that Lloyd had a clear conception of *carrying capacity* and the unfortunate consequences of exceeding it.[26] Short-run self-interest drives a herdsman in a common to add animals to his herd beyond the carrying capacity of the domain because the profit from so doing accrues to him alone, while the attendant costs caused by overpopulation are commonized over the entire community of herdsmen.

In a common pasture that is managed by no powers other than those of herdsmen acting individually, the exploiters are caught in a 'Double C — Double P Game' (CC—PP Game): *Commonize the Costs while Privatizing the Profits*.[27] Unhappily, in the long run all the herdsmen lose in an unmanaged common; but — so long as they cling to this system — they cannot escape ruin. Ruin that is both foreseen *and* inevitable is the very essence of Greek tragedy: recall, if you will, *Oedipus Rex*.

The idea of the tragedy of the commons has ancient but modest roots. Antiquarians like to quote Aristotle: 'That which is common to the greatest number has the least care bestowed upon it. Everyone thinks chiefly of his own, hardly at all of the common interest.'[28] Aristotle's statement is undoubtedly a precursor of the theory of the commons, but it is not rich enough in meaning to generate the formal theory. The closest Aristotle's aphorism comes to mathematics is a vague hint of less and more. But what Lloyd said, though he used no mathematical symbols, has led to explicit mathematical equations.[29]

The primary interest of the Oxford economist was not in malnourished cows but in human overpopulation. 'Marriage is a present good,' he said, 'but in a community of goods, where the children are maintained at public tables, or where each family takes according to its necessities out of the common stock, these difficulties [impinging on the parents] are removed from the individual. They spread themselves, and overflow the whole surface of society, and press equally on every part.'[30] What Lloyd assumes in this model is a distribution system resembling the one Karl Marx praised 42 years later: '*From each according to his ability, to each according to his needs.*'[31] Marx, ignorant of Lloyd's work, naively promoted his motto as a formula for felicity.

It is puzzling that Lloyd should have so emphasized the dangers of commonizing the costs of child-rearing, for in his day and his community these costs were almost entirely privatized. Since Lloyd's time the commonization of the costs of child-rearing has gone much further and Lloyd's strictures are much more appropriate. Guilt-mongers of our time delight in blaming parents for the overpopulation of a nation: such has been the message of Zero Population Growth, Inc., an American organization operating principally on college campuses. ZPG literature never refers to Lloyd's work. This is a pity, for he pointed out long ago that 'the simple fact of a country being overpopulous ... is not, of itself, sufficient evidence that the fault lies in the people themselves, or a proof of the absence of a prudential disposition. The fault may rest, not with them as individuals, but with *the constitution of the society, of which they form part.*'[32]

Not blame but *mechanism* was Lloyd's quarry as he puzzled over the persistence of human suffering. How was his work received in his day? Apparently it had little impact. The reasons were partly personal.[33] He suffered the handicap of being a member of a sickly family. In five years he gave only a very few lectures at Oxford and then, with private means, retired to Prestwood, Great Missenden, where he lived 'in apparent obscurity' until his death from a stroke at age fifty-eight.

In 1953 the United Nations published a large and useful summary of population doctrines and beliefs under the title *The Determinants and Consequences of Population Trends*. Out of a total of 330,000 words only 43 are devoted to Lloyd, and these occur at the end of a long footnote. Worse, in summarizing Lloyd's contribution to the theory of population this scholarly work gets his position 180 degrees wrong. (Since the book is the work of a committee we don't know whom to blame.) It's no wonder that the resurrection of Lloyd's work in 1968 came as a surprise.[34]

Laissez-Faire and Equality

Production, trade, distribution: what limits to freedom shall we impose on these interrelated functions? The laissez-faire position is that there should be complete freedom for the first two, while the third must be constrained by the rights of private property. Setting aside the vexed question of property, what about the first two functions? Looking at the world as it is, Walter Lippmann once wrote some revealing words (to which italics have here been added):

> The pure doctrine of non-intervention in production and trade has never in fact been practiced anywhere. Even Adam Smith, let alone John Stuart Mill, recognized exceptions to the rule. One could go further, I believe, and argue plausibly that most men have shown in their behaviour that *they wished to impose free capitalism on others and to escape it themselves.* Employers have believed in it for their employees, and have appealed to it against factory laws and unionism. But they have not hesitated to call upon the state for protection against foreign competitors. Manufacturers who had to ship goods have not hesitated much about regulating the railroads ...
> There is no reason to think that business men under capitalism have had any consistent conviction of laissez-faire. Their employees have certainly not had it. They have voted for tariffs when they were told their jobs depended upon them. They have voted to close the labor market by restricting immigration. They have voted for labor laws and they have organized unions. Like their employers they have believed in *laissez-faire for others.*[35]

The paradox can be put in the following terms. However passionately theoreticians may cling to symmetry and reciprocity in elaborating their theories of production and trade, those who are actual practitioners of economic living can be just as passionate in defending asymmetry and non-reciprocity in their daily lives. The merits of the case, as concerns production and trade, will not be argued here: our present task is to take up the distribution function.

The *thrust* of rhetorical pronouncements identified as 'idealistic' is symmetrical and reciprocal. Traditional religions, atheistical egalitarianism, and liberation theology all glorify equality in distribution. But intentions do not necessarily lead to accomplishment. Distributing a community's wealth in the light of Marx's ideal (*From each* ...) first produces inequality, and then (ultimately) widespread poverty. For two reasons:

First, human abilities are the product of the interaction of innate abilities and training. People are unequal at birth, and education exaggerates their inequality. Consequently productivity varies fantastically from one individual to another.

Second, what should be the grounds for allocating wealth? Idealists tell us that distribution should be according to a person's 'need.' But who determines 'need'? If agents of the state do so, freedom goes out as restraint and resentment come in. Revolution may be just around the corner. On the other hand, when each individual is the sole judge of his own need, the door is opened to greed. Adam Smith spoke of the 'insatiable desires' of the rich, but the desires of the poor can also be difficult to control. Rich or poor, people vary in their susceptibility to satiation. A political decision to satisfy variable 'needs' would end up giving greater rewards to the insatiable. Is that the 'fairness' that idealists seek?

'From each according to his ability, to each according to his needs' defines a highly asymmetrical, non-reciprocal system of distribution. *You* must contribute to the common pot according to *your* ability, while *I* demand the right to take out of the pot according to *my* needs, *as I reckon them.* 'Need creates right,' say I. But with every *I* saying this, in a world of shortages there can be no spontaneously generated stability. (If there were no shortages there would be no problem of course: but that does not describe our world.)

We need to look at the commons from another point of view, namely its relation to responsibility. Unfortunately, most of the statements that include the word 'responsibility' are vacuous rhetoric. Typically, a politician who proclaims his responsibility thereby claims power; he will oppose attempts to make him operationally responsible for his errors. To serve the needs of society, responsibility needs to be defined in the following way: *An agent is fully responsible when he pays all the costs of the benefits he receives.*

Is a distribution by the formula of the commons a responsible distribution? The formula for the system of the commons may be written as CC—PP: *Commonize the Costs against everyone, but Privatize the Profits – to me.* The first term of each dyad represents the actor, which is C in the first dyad and P in the second. Since the actors are different — C versus P — commonizing does not meet our operational definition of responsibility.

Irresponsibility opens the door to malfunction and uncontrollable costs. Applications of the theory of the commons extend far beyond common pastures, far beyond overpopulation among human beings. For instance, the theory extends to the capture, by speculators, of gains in the value of real estate as a result of community development. This diversion of community wealth was vigorously condemned by Henry George. Robert Andelson has explained the deep equivalence of George's ideas and commons theory.[36] The theory extends to the dysfunctional multiplication of water projects made possible by the federal commonization called 'subsidies.'[37] The theory is applicable to all insurance schemes, which commonize the losses of a few among all those who subscribe to a system; though insurance is a defensible way of dealing with exceptional losses, it inevitably encourages carelessness and dishonesty. The theory of the commons also applies to the many variants of socialized medicine, as Howard Hiatt first made clear.[38] In the medical case the waste is due less to the abuse of the commonized system by hypochondriacs than it is to its exploitation by liability lawyers whose forensic creativity pushes physicians into the practice of 'defensive medicine,' that is, the employment of expensive medical procedures that defend doctors against lawyers, producing a waste of resources that defrauds the general public. Like Proteus of the Greek myth, the irresponsible commons take on ever new forms in a society in which all too many people fail to keep in the forefronts of their minds the economists' anti-Providential assertion that 'There's no such thing as a free lunch.'

In the pure case, commonizing leads to ruin. But the modern state operates as a 'mixed economy,' and so ruin is less common than simple waste. Moreover, under conditions of true plenty the unmanaged commons is not only tolerable, it may also be the most economical way of exploiting the environment. When an American frontiersman shot a dozen passenger pigeons for his dinner he harmed no one. Restricting such activities of the pioneers would have been wasteful of human time and effort.

Criticisms of the Commons Theory

After the resurrection and elaboration of Lloyd's theory of the commons several papers were published arguing that even with shortages a commonized resource need not necessarily come to a bad end. Some of the criticisms are just and call for a clarification of the idea of 'commons.' Arthur F. McEvoy (1987) spoke of 'the commons myth,' maintaining that it:

> ... misrepresents the way common lands were used in the archetypical case (i.e. England before the privatization of landed property). English farmers met twice a year at manor court to plan production for the coming months. On those occasions they certainly would have exchanged information about the state of their lands and sanctioned those who took more than their fair share from the common pool. Likewise, Italian, Chinese, and other immigrant fishing communities in late nineteenth-century California kept very tight control over the allocation and harvest of their resources so as to produce what we would now call an optimum yield for their group. As the *San Francisco Chronicle* put it in 1907, 'if any Italian thinks it is possible to catch crabs for the market without joining the association, let him try it.'[39]

McEvoy's criticism has merit, but the merit must be evaluated in the light of a remark made by the philosopher Alfred North Whitehead: 'All propositions are erroneous unless they are construed in reference to a background which we experience without any conscious analysis.'[40] Clearly, the background of the resources discussed by Lloyd (and later by myself) was one of *non*-management of the commons under conditions of scarcity. In contrast, the English farmers and Italian fishermen cited by McEvoy were *managing* access to the resources they were exploiting. The title of my 1968 paper should have been 'The Tragedy of the *Unmanaged* Commons.' The commons discussed by McEvoy were managed by forces that are variously called 'community pressure' or 'shame.' When pressures are given the legislated form of laws the result is sometimes called 'socialism.'

By long tradition, the open ocean — far beyond the reach of national sovereignties — is an unmanaged common. That is why the stocks of most oceanic fisheries are now accelerating toward exhaustion. Oceanic fisheries haven't a chance of survival so long as their exploitation is guided by the rubric, 'freedom of the seas' (*read*, 'laissez-faire' once more). An apparent exception is the Alaska fur-seal resource which has prospered for nearly a century, but that is because the commons of its breeding grounds in the Pribilof Islands are in fact managed jointly by only two exploiters, Russia and the United States.

A more serious case is that of air pollution which is out of control because the absorptive capacities of the atmosphere are treated as unmanaged commons. As people have become concerned with the proven damage of acid rain and the possible disaster of an atmospheric greenhouse, nations have moved closer to converting the global atmosphere from an unmanaged common to a managed one. (The political roadblocks to this reform are, of course, formidable.)

We should speak of the 'commons model,' rather than the 'commons myth.' Both Lloyd and I investigated the logical properties of this model (though this use of the word 'model' did not develop until the twentieth century). Whether any particular case is a materialization of that model is a historical question — and of only secondary importance. What human ecologists are most concerned with are the commons of our time that are truly unmanaged (or poorly managed). After these have been identified the next question is, How can we bring about the successful management of the remaining, deteriorating commons?

In a strict sense, it is not the commons that need managing, but the people who exploit them. Managing people requires a deep knowledge of human nature — but what is the nature of human beings? McEvoy is not satisfied with the answers he infers from the literature. He says that the 'shortcoming of the tragic myth of the commons is its strangely unidimensional picture of *human* nature. The farmers on Hardin's pasture do not seem to talk to one another. As individuals, they are alienated, rational, utility-maximizing automatons and little else. The sum total of their social life is the grim, Hobbesian struggle of each against all and all together against the pasture in which they are trapped.' This is a serious misapprehension of the evidence, as can be shown by abandoning the hypothetical model to examine some relevant empirical evidence.

The Hutterites of northwestern North America have adapted their behaviour to the providential motto of Karl Marx. (Whether they even know about Marx is not important.) Each Hutterite gives such labor as he or she feels is reasonable to the community, and takes out of the common stores what he/she feels is needful. Hutterites are admirable and successful farmers, and they have discovered something about human nature and its bearing on the limitations of the commons that should interest everyone. John Baden and Richard Stroup describe the problem:

There is a saying commonly heard among the Hutterites: 'All colonies (especially "other" colonies) have their drones.' Further, it is recognized that the number of 'drones' increases more than proportionately with an increase in colony size. Given that: (1) all goods are public goods, (2) individual economic incentives are minimal, and (3) material differentials are outlawed, a rational, maximizing person would operate to maximize his pleasure, including leisure. Included in such self-seeking activities are trips into town or to a neighboring ranch to 'check on' or 'pick up' something allegedly relevant to his assigned task.[41]

Keeping in mind McEvoy's roster of the shortcomings of exploiters of the commons we must judge that the Hutterites are, on the testimony of Baden and Stroup, rational and utility-maximizing. But, to use McEvoy's term, are Hutterites *alienated* from their community? Far from it. Many independent accounts make it crystal clear that the Hutterites lead a richly communal life, far from a 'grim, Hobbesian struggle of each against all.' Though the word 'struggle' seems too violent and too colorful, some sort of competition does seem to be going on. No English word is entirely adequate to describe the low-key jostling of wills in a Hutterite community; the word 'competition' will have to do. The Oxford English Dictionary defines 'compete' as 'to strive after (something) in company or together.' It must be said that 'togetherness' is a specialty of Hutterites: as the community increases in size there's many a competition between 'gold-bricks' or 'goof-offs' to see who can get the cushy assignments on the community's work-roster. No bloodletting, no alienation: just quiet 'jockeying for position,' to use an image from harness-racing.

What is the result of this very human behavior? The Hutterites have learned that they can make the Marxian system of distribution work only within rather narrow limits: from (approximately) 60 to 150 persons in the colony. The lower limit is explained by the economist's favourite 'economies of scale.' The upper limit is explained by 'human nature,' more mysterious but just as undeniable a reality as economies of scale.

What aspect of human nature is involved in the control of a *nominally* unmanaged commons? Words are treacherous, but close observation of well-functioning groups exploiting a common resource — herdsmen, fishermen, Hutterite farmers, or whomever —

The Tragedy of the Unmanaged Commons

leads to the strong feeling that it is old-fashioned *shame* that keeps would-be defectors in line. For this to work the size of the decision-making group must be small, apparently less than 150. Let us call this the *Hutterite Limit*.

The observations needed to test the Hutterite limit have usually escaped recording. Traditional anthropology has not been sufficiently numerate to establish the effects of scale. Nevertheless some confirmations of the Hutterite limit have been recorded,[42] with no clear-cut disconfirmations. A study of population control in modern China showed the importance of close observation in discerning the effective social arrangements. The first observation indicated a group of two thousand people as the unit of control in Beijing. More careful observation showed that the actual unit within which control was exerted varied between 50 and 150 people.[43] Conclusion: the Hutterite limit was observed.

Intuitively, the scale effect makes sense. It is a matter of common observation that the effectiveness of shame depends very much on face-to-face confrontations. It is easy for a small group to impose a feeling of shame on its errant members; in a large group, the feeling doesn't transmit well. It looks as though self-seeking is something of a biological constant, while shame is diluted by numbers. That is why formal, explicit government is more necessary in large groups than small. Idealists who feel repelled by explicit government — and such idealists are numerous in our society — should be advised to work for reductions in the size of the operational groups.

Implicitly referring to groups of trans-Hutterite size, James Madison aptly made the connection between human nature and the necessity of government:

> Ambition must be made to counteract ambition. The interest of the man must be connected with the constitutional rights of the place. It may be a reflection on human nature, that such devices should be necessary to control the abuses of Government. But what is Government itself, but the greatest of all reflections on human nature? If men were angels, no Government would be necessary.[44]

Wise as it is, the last sentence cries out for correction: 'If *all* men (and women) were angels, no Government would be necessary.' Observations of unmanaged commons ('no Government') show that when the Hutterite limit is transgressed non-conforming behavior (which may begin with a minority of one) is infective. The larger the group, the more rapid the infection. Destructive behavior that begins with a minority soon becomes the behavior of the majority.

This makes sense. The non-conformer benefits from his actions in a community in which the majority conform to a self-denying ideal. As such a minority visibly prospers, another factor in human nature enters in: *envy*. One by one, hitherto self-denying conformers, envious of the prosperity of non-conformers, join the ranks of the less-than-angels. Positive feedback sets in. The ideal withers away. The process is sensitive to scale; only by keeping the size of the group small can shame triumph over envy.

That this needs saying is evidence of the power of taboo. In the 1960s the 'Free Speech' movement in Berkeley effectively ended the taboo on many four-letter English words, *but not on the four-letter word 'envy.'* As Helmut Schoeck's scholarly study shows, envy is still one of the most powerfully tabooed words of our society.[45] Much that should be discussed under the subject of 'envy' is often automatically converted into the uncompromising assertion of 'rights.'

Psychological denial not only lays a taboo on existent words, it can also slow the coinage of new ones that affront ruling attitudes. 'Optimism' was coined in 1737; 'pessimism' came along 57 years later. 'Shortage' was coined in 1868; 'longage' arrived 107 years later. Optimists who believe in Providence are energized by the word 'shortage' to look harder for more resources, which they are sure must be out there, someplace. To admit that there is a 'longage' of people or demands is to give up the belief in a providential plethora of resources. It is no wonder that 'longage' is not yet an accepted part of the popular vocabulary.

The world of terrestrial resources is strictly limited, but not seriously so if we can learn to curb human demands. Given temperate demands, our world is vast —

> And has more than enough — for no more than enough.
> There is a shortage of nothing, save will and wisdom;
> But there is a longage of people.[46]

Every asserted 'shortage' of supply can equally aptly be described as a 'longage' of demand. Those who trumpet 'shortages' are likely to fight vigorously for 'rights.' (Remember '... to each according to his needs.') This position bespeaks an admirable egalitarian sentiment, but how does the natural environment fare in such a rhetorical environment? If 'needs' include the need to reproduce at will, the drive toward equality of per capita distribution will finally exhaust the environment. In an unmanaged — or weakly managed — common, 'shortage' implies 'rights' implies *ruin*.

But if we admit that envy is a natural and powerful part of human nature, a part that needs to be curbed, we will speak less often of shortages of supplies and begin to think about longages of people and longages of human desires. When we see longage as the central problem there is a possibility that we may find ways of controlling the proportions of the various populations and the dimensions of their demands, thus making it possible for at least a modicum of the world's environmental riches to be passed on to our grandchildren. The rhetoric we speak reveals the models with which our minds do their work. The rhetoric we live by determines our effects upon the world.

NOTES

1. Robert Nisbet, *History of the Idea of Progress* (New York: Basic Books, 1980), pp. 181-182.
2. J.B. Bury, *The Idea of Progress* (1932; New York: Dover, 1955), p. 73.
3. Adam Smith, *The Theory of Moral Sentiments* (1759; Indianapolis, Indiana: Liberty Classics, 1976), p. 304.
4. W. Stark, *The History of Economics in its Relation to Social Development* (New York: Oxford University Press, 1944), p. 24.
5. Ronald Hamowy, *The Scottish Enlightenment and the Theory of Spontaneous Order* (Carbondale, Illinois: Southern Illinois University Press, 1987), p. 6.
6. Friedrich August Hayek, *The Fatal Conceit* (Chicago: University of Chicago Press, 1988), p. 8.
7. Kenneth E. Boulding, *The Image* (Ann Arbor, Michigan: University of Michigan Press, 1956), p. 117.
8. Garrett Hardin, *Population, Evolution and Birth Control* (2nd edition; San Francisco: W.H. Freeman, 1969), p. 34.

9   *Ibid*, p. 36.
10 Rose E. Frisch, 'Demographic implications of the biological determinants of female fecundity', *Social Biology*, 22 (1975), p. 22.
11 E. P. Hutchinson, *The Population Debate* (Boston: Houghton Mifflin, 1967), p. 345. (The passage is quoted from a work of Edmonds, 1828).
12 News report, *Technology Review*, 78, 4 (1976), p. 24.
13 D. E. C. Eversley, *Social Theories of Fertility and the Malthusian Debate* (Oxford: Clarendon Press, 1959), p. 201.
14 J. DuPaquier, A. Fauve-Chamoux, and E. Grebenik, eds., *Malthus Past and Present* (New York: Academic Press, 1983), p. 345.
15 Josué de Castro, *The Geography of Hunger* (Boston: Little Brown, 1952).
16 *Ibid*, pp. 21 and 24.
17 E. P. Hutchinson, *loc. cit.*, p. 131.
18 Etienne van de Walle [Book review], *Population and Development Review*, 13 (1987), pp. 547-550.
19 Karl R. Popper, *The Poverty of Historicism* (London: Routledge & Kegan Paul, 1957).
20 William Petersen, *Population* (2nd edition; New York: Macmillan, 1969), p. 11.
21 Michael S. Teitelbaum, 'Relevance of demographic transition theory for developing countries', *Science*, 188 (1975), p. 420.
22 Michael S. Teitelbaum and Jay M. Winter, *The Fear of Population Decline* (Orlando, Florida: Academic Press, 1985), p. 14.
23 *Vide* 8, *supra*.
24 Ester Boserup, 'Economic and demographic interrelationships in sub-Saharan Africa', *Population and Development Review*, 11 (1985), p. 395.
25 William Forster Lloyd, *Two Lectures on the Checks to Population* (1833; facsimile edition; New York: Augustus M. Kelley, 1968), pp. 30-31.
26 Garrett Hardin, 'Sentiment, guilt, and reason in the management of wild herds', *Cato Journal*, 2 (1982), pp. 823-833.
27 Garrett Hardin, *Filters Against Folly* (New York: Viking, 1985), chapter 10.
28 Aristotle, *Politics* (New York: Viking, 1971), p. 27 (Book 2, chapter 3).
29 Garrett Hardin and John Baden, eds., *Managing the Commons* (San Francisco: W. H. Freeman, 1977). See chapters by H. V. Muhsam, 'An algebraic theory of the commons' and Daniel Fife, 'Killing the goose'.
30 Lloyd, *op. cit.*, p. 21.
31 Karl Marx, 'Critique of the Gotha program' in R. C. Tucker, *The Marx-Engels Reader* (New York: Norton, 1972), p. 388.
32 Lloyd, *op. cit.*, pp. 22-23.
33 Richard M. Romano, 'William Forster Lloyd — a non-Ricardian?, *History of Political Economy*, 9, 3 (1977), pp. 412-441.

34 Garrett Hardin, 'The tragedy of the commons', *Science*, 162 (1968), pp. 1243-1248.
35 Walter Lippman, *The Method of Freedom* (New York: Macmillan, 1934), pp. 25-26.
36 Robert V. Andelson, 'Commons Without Tragedy', this volume, chapter 2.
37 Marc Reisner, *Cadillac Desert* (New York: Viking, 1986).
38 Howard H. Hiatt, 'Protecting the medical commons: who is responsible?', *New England Journal of Medicine*, 293 (1975), pp. 235-241.
39 Arthur F. McEvoy, 'Toward an interactive theory of nature and culture: Ecology, production, and cognition in the California fishing industry', *Environmental Review*, 11 (1987), p. 299.
40 Alfred North Whitehead, *Essays in Science and Philosophy* (New York: Philosophical Library, 1948), pp. 85-86.
41 John Baden and Richard Stroup, 'Choice, faith, and politics: the political economy of Hutterite communes', *Public Choice*, 12 (1972), pp. 1-11.
42 Nathan Keyfitz, *Population and Biology*, (Liege: Ordina Editions, 1986), p. 150.
43 Ruth & Victor W. Sidel, 'Medicine in China: individual and society', *Hastings Center Studies*, 2, 3 (1974), pp. 23-36.
44 James Madison (1788), in *The Federalist*, Number 50 (New York: Scribner, 1893), p. 360.
45 Helmut Schoeck, *Envy* (New York: Harcourt, Brace & World, 1969).
46 Garrett Hardin, 'Carrying Capacity' in *Stalking the Wild Taboo* (Los Altos, California: William Kaufmann, 1976), pp. 260-261.

About the Contributors

Robert V. Andelson (Ph.D., University of Southern California), professor of philosophy and a member of the Graduate School faculty at Auburn University, is author of *Imputed Rights: An Essay in Christian Social Theory* (1971), editor and co-author of *Critics of Henry George* (1979), and joint-author (with J. M. Dawsey) of *From Wasteland to Promised Land: Liberation Theology for a Post-Marxist World* (in press). An ordained Congregationalist minister, his articles in ethics and social philosophy have appeared in scholarly periodicals over several decades. He served on the editorial board of *The Personalist* for the last five years of its existence, and continues to serve on that of *The American Journal of Economics and Sociology*.

Roy Douglas (Ph.D., University of Edinburgh), reader emeritus in the department of general studies, University of Surrey, began his professional career in the field of biology, but his books have made him a recognized authority on modern political history. They include *Law for Technologists* (1964), *The History of the British Liberal Party, 1895-1970* (1971), *Land, People and Politics: The Land Question in the United Kingdom, 1878-1952* (1976), *In the Year of Munich* (1977), *The Advent of War, 1939-40* (1978), *From War to Cold War, 1942-48* (1981), *New Alliances, 1940-41* (1982), *World Crisis and British Decline, 1929-56* (1986), and *World War, 1939-45: The Cartoonists' Vision* (1990). He is also author of a number of articles, essays, and book chapters on historical, philosophical and scientific subjects, and editor of *1939: A Retrospect Forty Years After* (1983). Dr. Douglas is, in addition, a barrister, and was on five occasions a Liberal candidate for Parliament.

Alexandra R. Hardie (Ph.D., University of Exeter), lecturer in economics at Exeter, is author of seven articles and book chapters, and co-author of two articles on economic policy.

Garrett Hardin (Ph.D., Stanford University), professor emeritus of human ecology, University of California at Santa Barbara, is generally recognized as one of the seminal thinkers of our time. His books include *Nature and Man's Fate* (1959), *Exploring New Ethics for Survival* (1972), *Naked Emperors: Essays of a Taboo-Stalker* (1982), and *Filters Against Folly: How to Survive Despite Economists, Ecologists, and the Merely Eloquent* (1985). His most widely-reprinted articles are 'The Tragedy of the Commons' (1968) and 'Living on a Lifeboat' (1974).

Fred Harrison (B.A., Oxford University; M.Sc., University of London), founder and director of the Centre for Incentive Taxation, was for more than twenty years an investigative reporter for well-known London weeklies. He is author of *The Power in the Land* (1983), *Brady and Hindley: The Genesis of the Moors Murders* (1986), of chapters in three other books, and of monographs and articles on subjects ranging from politics to environmental and urban issues. Since 1978 he has served as editor of the international bi-monthly journal, *Land and Liberty*.

David Richards (M.A., Oxford University), was from 1983 to 1985 convenor of the Land Policy Working Group of the United Kingdom Green Party. He is senior researcher with the Economics and Social Science Research Association, London. He supervised a major portion of the research for *Costing the Earth* (1989), to which he contributed a chapter, as he also has to other books.

T. Nicolaus Tideman (Ph.D., University of Chicago), professor of economics at Virginia Polytechnic Institute and State University, has been a research associate at the Kennedy School of Government, Harvard University; a member of the senior staff of the President's Council of Economic Advisers; and a member of the economics faculty at Harvard. He is editor or co-editor of two books, sole author of 28 and co-author of 21 journal articles and book chapters — all in economics, public choice, and related areas.

Index

Ackerman, Bruce, and 'liberalism' for land and wealth, 110
Adaptability, of humans to environment, 46
Africa: enclosure conflicts in, 138, 171; land tenure in, 103; future birth rates, 171. See also Desert; South Africa
Agriculture: effects of development of on population, enabling resource accumulation, 49; sustainable practices of damaged by Philippine resettlement policies, 73; decline of family farm in, 91-92; protectionism of harms all nations, 93-94; higher productivity of family farm in, 94; transformation from subsistence to commercial, 98
Aid programs, and contraception, 22-23, 167; tendency of to benefit large landowners and exacerbate poverty, 90
AIDS, as example of exponential growth rate, 47-48
Altruism, as marginal, not primary, motive of individual, 36
Amazon. See Brazil
Andelson, Robert V., on population control, 15-16
Anderson, Jay M., on industrial tax for commons use, 39
Antarctics: nations' claims to, 133; as new Last Commons, future Remnant Commons, 133; Mineral Convention, 160
Aristotle, on tragedy of the commons, 173
Asia, examples of enclosure conflicts in, 137
Atmosphere, as unmanaged, polluted commons, 178-79

Baal, land tenure in, 83
Baden, John, on population growth rate, 31; and Richard Stroup, on Hutterites and ideal community size relative to goods distribution, 179-80
Benefits, locationally or socially produced, allocation of, 2. See also Goods
Benign Demographic Transition. See Demographic transition
Bennett, Jon and Susan George, on shift from independent to dependent labour force, 104
Bloom, Bridget, on European Economic Community as boon to larger farms, 91

Boserup, Ester, on predicted higher African birth rates, 171
Boulding, Kenneth, on Malthus and corollary that technology increases human misery, 165
Boundaries, national, to be flexible, with rental prices for marginal changes in, 119
Brazil, environmental damage in linked to lack of access to land, 21-23; need for international efforts at land reform in, as Amazon damage harms entire world, 22; government of favours landowners, 22; land speculation in, especially Amazon area, 32; as example of internal migration to alleviate population pressure, 73; and enclosure, deforestation, of Amazon forest land, 137
Bury, J. R., on progress and providence, 163
Busey, James R., on tenets of economic thought compared with those of other spheres of life, 27-28
Business cycle, Malthus's embryonic ideas on, 61

Canada, and enclosure conflict with Mohawk Indians, 137
Capital accumulation, and productivity and wages, 78
Cash economy, change to a cause of farmer's poverty, 97-99
Castro, Josue de, in *The Geography of Hunger*, on poverty caused by colonial exploitation of resources, and worldwide effects of local hunger, 168
CC-PP Game (Commonize the Costs But Privatize the Profits), adverse effects of, 173
Child-rearing, costs of more commonized today, 174
China, and example of Hutterite limit, 181
Chuang Tru, fourth century B.C. laissez-fairist, 164
Citizen's dividend. See Land rent
Claims, on people and their labor products, in Locke, 115
Clarke, Colin W. and Daniel Fife, on ecologic irresponsibility, 41
Class, distinctions in result of unfair land access, 90

Index

Commodities, overproduction of for status demands, 92

Commons, theory of needed to help solve population, socioecologic, other problems, ix, 25, 177-78; rights of access to and laws on, 2, 133-35; effect of technology and population growth on, pollution and overuse of, and rules governing, 12; extended vs. enclosed, 14; as global resources not arrogated to individuals or nations, 21; history of management of, 36, 95-96, 173-74, 175-79; as a model of political-economic system of environmental utilization, 37; Hardin's theory of as Weberian ideal type or logical construct, 37; preservation of dependent on socialized rent, other economic reforms, 41; lessons from on demographic and ecologic behavior, 52; managed vs. unmanaged, 88, 95, 173, 177-79; best procedures for generating objectives, hypotheses, models, and assessments of solutions for, including cost-benefit appraisal, 143-48; theory of opposed to providence, 172; tragedy of, 173; logical properties of model of vs. myth of, 179; irresponsibility of prevalent formula of, as CC-PP Game, 176; more aspects of than overuse and overpopulation, 176-77

Kinds of:

Last: as part of global commons, 2; defined, 132; reduced pressures on through land value tax, 140, 143, 155-56; solutions to problems of, with goal of socioecologic balance, would help other commons, 143, 146; and need for incentives, financial and technological aid, 148; and Remnant, benefits to of land value tax, 155, 159

Remaining: defined, and suggestions for, 130-32; two kinds of (Last and Remnant), 132; and need for sound laws to avoid injustice, violence, and war, 139; three reasons for problems of, 139-41; and irrational (exponential population growth) and rational (citizen action) behavior concerning, 143; international effort, needed to save, 142

Remnant: part of global commons, claimed by nations, but not yet private proprety, 132; examples of conflict over, 136; and worldwide enclosures of, 136-39; land value tax on extracted resources of, 140, 155-57, 159

Models for management of, for land tenure systems related to environmental use, 148-57:

Business as Usual, inadequate, with erroneous assumption that nation-state is natural governmental unit, possible free

Commons — *continued*

market variations, 153-54

Common Heritage of Mankind, arguments for and against, 150-51; based on United Nations, 149-51

Free for All, as seen in sea-bed, 149

Land and Liberty, best of four alternative systems of environmental use, as it is equitable, efficient, ecologically wise, 155

Commonwealth, proposed ideal government which is economically fair and ecologically sound, 109; traditional claims that land of belongs to members of as inconsistent and conflict-provoking, 109; claims to land of should be based on rights of present and future individuals, not nations, 115. See Lock; Territory

Community, insurable risk of dissolution of as market determinant of value of community's territory, 119-20

Competition, among governments for citizens, 121-22

Condorcet, Marquis de, ideas of on freedom attacked by Malthus, 53

Conflict, inevitable result within nations over Remnant Commons and between nations over Last Commons, 136, 139; avoidance of with Last Commons land value tax, 154

Consensus, vital in change to Lockean proviso system, 126

Contraception, and Catholic church, 18; linked to foreign aid, 22-23; as vital complement to better nutrition, 167

Corporations, limited liability of for ecological damage, 152-53

Critical mass, affected by minute increments, 126

Customs, social, as human rules, including demographic, balancing quality of life and species survival, 48-49; as aid to humans' adaptation to nature, 58

Danger, Zone of: human disequilibrium with environment because of exponential growth rate, 52

Darwinian survival: dependent on quality of land tenure system, 49-50; of better fed as species economizer, 166

Death, as logical fate of human species, in Malthus, 59

Decentralisation. See Government

Deforestation. See Africa; Brazil; Environment

Demand, rise in per capita exceeds population rise, causing land values rise, 91

Democracy, eradicated in Germany because of enclosures, 137

Demographic transition: Hardin on, 19; imported only partially by less developed nations, 93; hypothesis and criticism of, 170-73;

Demographic transition — *continued*
reasons for popularity of, 173
Demography, and pressure on environment, ix; subjectivity of, 44; benign and malign views of, 45; crisis in caused not by industrial revolution but ensuing changes in land tenure systems, 50; Malthus's ideas as foundation of science of, 61; cultural context of, 63. See Demographic transition; Population
Denman, Donald, and Sea-bed Resource, 149
Desert, result of human environmental abuse, 38, 84, 104
Development, compact vs. sprawl, viii. See also Land
Distribution: trickle-down theory of, 163; Lloyd's system of similar to Marx's, 173; limited by private property rights, 174-75; according to need as asymmetrical, non-reciprocal, and cause of inequality, poverty, 175-76
Dorfman, Robert, on rent as unearned income paid for use of nonproducible resources, 86. See also Land rent
Doubleday, Thomas. See Plethoric state
Duggar, Benjamin Minge, Lecture program at Auburn U., with Hardin as lecturer, vii

Earth, carrying capacity of: finite, though extendable by technology, 29; consequences of exceeding, 173
Ecology: distortions of by government policies, 5-6; other possible remedies for problems of, 24; damage to as rationale for international approach to demographic problems of, 44; damaged by division between landed and landless people, 58; pricing of services of, 123; damage to during conflicts, 137-38; as intergenerational equity, 147n; and concern for unmanaged or poorly managed commons, 179
Economies of scale, and human nature, 180
Economists, neoclassical, on rent as excess earning over amount needed to retain present production use, 86
Economy, growth of relative to population size and living standards, 1; mixed, as remedy to inevitable ruin under unmanaged commons, 177
Edel, Matthew, on how shared land rent avoids Malthusian trap of low output growth with high population growth, 102
Edmonds, Thomas Rowe. See Plethoric state
Ehrlich, Paul, and *New World, New Mind*, 12; and *The Population Bomb* and *The Population Explosion*, with human species' fate as enslavement or death, 70
Emigration, freedom of in commonwealth model, 116
Enclosure movement: tragic effects of, 35; and

Enclosure movement — *continued*
resulting overuse of remaining commons, 36; laws on ecologically good but socially unjust, 41; coincident with Industrial Revolution, 61; in England, dividing Remnant Commons, 98, 136-37. See also Commons
Entropy, and natural resources, 146
Environment: demographic and ecologic factors in destruction of, ix, 6, 8, 21-23, 30-31, 38, 131; resistance to policy changes on, 9; and libertarians, 22; salvation of dependent on population control, 31, 183; George's concern for, 34, 62-63; benefits to from cheaper land, compact cities, 40; four models of utilization of, 40; humans' traditional self-limiting demands on, 45; present policies toward treat symptoms, not causes, 105; primary problem of due to unfair access to land, 105. See also Commons
Envy, as taboo concept and word, with desires based on misinterpreted as rights, 182-83
Equality, social, among humans anathema to Malthus, 53
Equilibrium, in society under commonwealth model, 110
Essay on the Principle of Population. See Malthus
Ethiopia, and exploitive land tenure system, 104
Eugenics, inverted operation of, 19, 35n
European Economic Community, and larger benefits of to larger farms, 91-92; conflicts in over fishing rights, 139

Family, size: and government intervention, 1; cultural and economic aspects of, 18-19
Famine, Sudanese, due to overuse of marginal land, 104
Fecundity: as potentiality for having children, 166
Fee Simple, as freehold ownership in private property, 135
Fertility, as measure of actual production of children, 166. See also Population
Fife, Daniel and Colin W. Clark, on ecologic irresponsibility, 41
Food, increase in not limited arithmetically, 165
Force, invalid territorial justification, as it can readily be supplanted by new force, 111
France, shrinking farm size in due to subdivision, 63
Free market, in true form would release underused land to those who need it, 63
French Revolution, and vision of just society compared with Malthus's vision, 67
Frisch, Rose, on dilemma when aid to poor nations raises fertility as well as nutritional levels, 167

Gaffney, Mason, on quest for unearned land increments, 91

Gaia, Lovelock's theory of as dynamic whole combining all of earth's organic, inorganic, and atmospheric components, 45

Genetic stream, as a commons, 35n

George, Henry: as theorist of underlying institutional causes of poverty, in which denial of individual's birthright to land by private owners unleashes economic behavior at odds with balanced society, to be solved by land distribution through payment of economic rent rather than land seizure and subdivision (economic model linking ecologic issues with Ricardo's spatial concept of rent, including population dispersal, production process, and income distribution), and test of theory needed, vii, ix, 62-65; 78; and *Progress and Poverty*, 3, 27; libertarian economics, social philosophy of supported by Andelson, 15; erroneously thought to favour land nationalisation, 33; on ecology, in *Social Problems*, 33n, and ethical implications of earth's limits, 96; and Malthus, criticism of, and illumination of problems unresolved by, 46, 62, 75; and free market reform, 75; perspective of more important now, with Marxism's failure, 75; on poverty and population, 81, n30; on fair, impartial rules, 145; relationship between his ideas and those on commons, 177; See also Land

George, Susan. See Bennett

Germany, enclosure conflicts in and loss of democracy, 137

Giradet, Herbert, on ecologic effects of big estates, 84; on biblical Joseph's famine prediction, which enabled Pharaoh to gain power by buying cheap land, 100

Godwin, William, ideas of on rights attacked by Malthus, 53

Goods: individual valued more than social, 35; public, need for voluntary payment for during transition to commonwealth, 125. See also Benefits

Government: damage by policies of on demography, ecology, 1, 5-6; and special interest groups, 22-23; as impediment to human desires, 22-23; and reciprocity in freedom, 31; as clearinghouse for territorial distribution, 121; control of property by inefficient, 152; and decentralisation and human nature, 93, 181. See also Commonwealth; Nations

Green Revolution: as short-term, inadequate solution to poverty, actually increasing it as food becomes export good, 100-101

Guyana, as nation with rich resources, poor institutions and people, 72

Hardie, Alex, on commons and international law, 14

Hardin, Garrett, Dugger lecturer, Auburn U., vii; and *The Tragedy of the Commons*, vii, 10-11, 35, 39-40, and rebuttals, 36-37, 177-79; views similar to George's obscured by semantic differences in use of word "commons", vii, 33; heuristic device of, vii, viii; correspondence from, vii, viii; on tendency of humans to overuse commons, 10-11, 35, 172-83; and tragedy of unmanaged commons, 25, 79, 183; as neo-Malthusian on ecology, 33; on genetic stream as a kind of commons, 35n; "Ethical implications of Carrying Capacity", 38; on taxation, in *Stalking the Wild Taboo*, 39; apparent endorsement of land value tax, 39-40. See also Commons; Demographic transition; Hutterite; Lloyd; Population

Harrison, Fred: on theories of Malthus and George 4; on primary poverty, land systems, and population, 17-18

Hayek, F. A., and laissez-faire, 164

Henley Centre for Forecasting, on use of pollution fees for social benefits, 89

Hiatt, Howard, and waste in medical costs because of commonized malpractice insurance fees, 177

High Price of Bullion, The. See Ricardo

History, as territorial justification, hides original claim by force, 112. See also Territory

Homeostasis, of human society within changing environment vital for social evolution and natural resources preservation, 48

Humanity: destruction of, 6; nature of perhaps incompatible with more complex technology, 12; survival of vs. individual right to reproduce, 30, 183; and coercion, 44; normal, abnormal development of, interacting with environment, 46-47; survival of threatened by inequality of individual access to land, 52; knowledge of interaction with nature, vital in solving problems, 146; unequal abilities of lead to unequal production production, needs, and demands of, 175; management of needed to curb earth's exploitation, 179. See also Commons; Population; Society

Hunger, not socially caused until 19th century, 49

Hutterite, limit (irresponsible social behaviour increases and individual sense of shame decreases as group size increases), 179-82; society as example of adaptive human behavior, 179-81

Immigration: exclusive of, 117; unlimited, as part of alternative political structure, 160

Immiseration, Malthus's law of, 57, 61, 74

Improvements. See Land value tax

Income, inequality of assumed by Malthus as normal, 57; tax of consonant with Lockean-proviso commonwealth if citizens agree to so pay for public goods, 116; guaranteed, through proportional territorial shares, 121

Individual: reproductive rights of, 30; restrictions on freedom of, 116; and idea of providence, in which interests of accord with those of community, 164

Individualism, Jeffersonian, dependent on socialization of rent, 41; and Marxism, as encouraging land abuse, 96

Individual Democracy. See Webb

Industrial Revolution, enhancer of human ability to use nature, 50

Inquiry into the Nature and Progress of Rent. See Malthus

Institutions: effects of on national wealth, more important to living standards than natural resources, 27; structure of causes poverty, death, 46

Insurance: as commonizer of losses of a few among many, 177; against natural resource use later proven excessive, 121

International Monetary Fund, riots due to its policies, 104

International Seabed Authority: powers and organization of, 150; as resource allocation model, 157

Irresponsibility, and resultant abuses, high costs, 176-77

Japan: land values and economic injustice in, 92-93; and its land tax effect on better education, demographics, productivity, life quality, 102-3; development of contrasted with Java's, 102-3

Java, forced labour and development in, 102-03

Jefferson, Thomas: on abuse of abundant land, 95; individualism of dependent on rent socialization, 41

Kagami, Nobumitsu, on Japan's unfair society, 93

Kenya, ecologic crisis in due to land maldistribution, not population rise, 71

Keynes, John Maynard, in accord with Malthus on unemployment and demand-side character of business cycles, 81, n21

Knowledge, investment in as public good, 125

Kuwait-Iraqi war, over natural resources neither created, 14

Labour: in conflict with employers after loss of commons land, 67-68; at mercy of landlord in Latin America, 94; for wages instead of tenancy, 95; products of belong to laborer, provided land used does not exceed citizen's proportion, 116, 175; and capital,

Labour — *continued*
product of as rental value from current and past use, 119

Laissez-faire, includes rules, 145-46; as type of providence, 163; flawed in practice, 174-75. See also LaRiviere; Libertarians

Lancaster, Kelvin, on income distribution as function of sale of factor services, 87

Land:
commons vs. private ownership: problems of include use of resources worldwide, human poverty, 23-25; community restrictions on use of, 25; common rights in, not nationalization of, 33; transition to private ownership, 46; communal access central to a society in harmony with nature, including stable population growth, 51; maldistribution of rights as poverty cause, 58, 62, 110; property rights in land erroneously considered by some as akin to natural rights, 60, require close scrutiny, because of environmental threats, 76, inequitable, ecologically destructive, 84, include a bundle of rights and restrictions, 85; effects of US enclosure on poor, 96; relations between rich and poor nations, 97; land as negotiable asset, 98, cumulative subdivision of, a poverty cause, 99; as 'positional good', 100; foreign ownership of in Africa, 104; use of, not perpetual ownership of, as solution to problems of poverty, war, environment, 110; finiteness of makes all claims to perpetual possession inconsistent with Lockean proviso, 114; surface and natural resource rights to differ, 114; inefficient use of and concern over Remaining Commons, 140-42; disadvantages of state ownership of, 152

laws: on occupied or private land, 133-36; English common, as alternative model of use of, 157-58

margin: government pressure on, 5; cultivation of affected by population rise, 32; intra-marginal, greater use of as poverty solution, 68; concept of marginal (rentless) denied by Malthus, 68-69; sub-marginal, overuse of and ecologic damage by farming or wrong development, 91; super-marginal, and underuse of due to speculation, 91

monopoly of: fundamental cause of poverty, 28; as factor in population rise, and remedy through land value tax, 74; and power, 90

reform: need for in Brazil, with world pressure to halt damage from Amazon forest destruction, 22; unsuccessful when based on subdivision, 63; examples of inappropriate, 94-95

Index 193

Land — *continued*
  rent, economic, of (also termed ground rent or pure rent): shaping New World destiny, viii; Ricardo's contribution of spatial dimension of, 54; full capture of enables removal of taxes from labour and capital, 65; alternative concerning application of, 77; environmental, population crisis if appropriated privately, instead of captured by government for equal benefit of all, 77; as profit or income (actual or imputed) accruing to land, as payment for resource quality, 86-87; citizen's dividend as fair distribution of, 87; of land as part of global commons, 88; private appropriation of root of Africa's problems, 104-5; of all world territory to be equitably divided between all humans and future generations of humans, 117; defined, and comparison with a true tax, 154-55; belongs to no individual, since land is not the creation of any individual, 154; selling price as multiple of, 155; to be shared between nation-state and international body, 156; speculation in land curbed by capture of, 176-77
  tenure systems: evolved as humans' sustenance modes changed to survive in changing changing environment, competing with other species, 49-50; as human rules to harmonize group relations and ensure ecologic viability, 49; history of as tribal-based or private owner-based, 50-51; private owner-based and exclusionary power, 50; misalignment of with production system and ecology, 52-53; of common rights as population stabilization mechanism vs. private rights, as population conflict mechanism, 58; Malthus's recognition of bad effect of in colonies but failure to admit that Britain's enclosures had same effect at home, 58; as root of population problem caused not by pressure on the environment but unequal access to resources, 74; centrifugal effect of, causing urban sprawl, under private rights sytem, 74; Roman system of cause of current problems, 84; centrifugal and centripetal effects of, 91; damaging effect of by developed nations on less developed nations, 94; as universal tools of the powerful, 95-96; effect of on socio-economic structures, 97-98; reform of only solution to poverty, 100; of USA developed based on privilege, not equity, 152-53
  value tax: similar ideas on of Malthus and George, 3; exemption of improvements on land (which are rightful products of labor and capital, to be bought and sold)

Land — *continued*
  from, 25, 155; proposed by Malthus to solve Irish poverty, 29; failure to adopt and resultant ecologic damage, 32; as ecology preserver in George's fur seal example, 33n, as virtually self-regulating, efficient and uncorrupt, 38-39; secures the advantages of both commons and enclosures, 41; by rectifying distribution, liberates production, 40; neutralises landlord's monopoly power, 62; as fiscal device to bridge institutional divide, 65; centripetal effect of, attracting people to underused urban sites, 73-74; in Japan, 92-93; withering away of since feudal era, 98; India's failure to impose benefits large landowners who receive goods, services at little or no cost, 101; need for individual to estimate amount used, to compensate others if used excessively, 127; as equitable, efficient solution for unused or underused land (Remaining Commons), 142; as incentive to efficient land use, 155; upon less than total land value, for market effectiveness, 155; best way to assure payment of rent to society (which created land value) rather than to individual (who did not), 155; ecologic advantages of, 159.
  See also Commons, Territory

Landowner: power of to exclude people whose lives depend on land access, 60; depressing influence of on economy when their purchases do not equal rising production, 61; distinction between landless and, 97; transformed responsibilities of in Europe at end of feudal era, 98

LaRiviere, and l'ordre naturel promoted by laissez-faire, 164

Latifundia, as large estates with nonuse or underuse of land, 22-23, 94

Latin America: as example of exponential, ecologically unsustainable population growth due to institutional failure, 58; land tenure history of, 94-95. See also Redclift

Law: statutory augmented by administrative, 38; and corruption, 38; statute, English, 135; German common, replaced by Roman, 137; importance of, including enforcement, in land tenure systems, 147

Leases: auction of resources proposed, 114-15, 156; advantage of over sales of resources, 158

Libertarians, and environment, 15, 22, 30-31, 110, 112-13, 160. See also Laissez-faire

Life: normal and abnormal models of development of and interaction with environmental sustenance, 46-47

Lippmann, Walter, on lack of true laissez-faire in production, 175

Living standards. See Quality of life

Lloyd, William Forster: theory of population

Lloyd, William Forster — *continued*
  growth and distribution, exemplified by overgrazed commons, neglected by scholars, 172-74; suggestion that society, not individual, is to blame for such disequilibrium, 174
Locke, John: ideas on assumed rights of nations, 14; reduced conflict in world run according to proviso of, 109, 124; justification of territorial claims based on 'proviso' of, 113; problems in Lockean proviso world, 125-26; advised wise but unheeded land tenure alternative, 152
Longage, of people and their desires, and need to recognize in providing fair access to environmental goods, 183
Lovelock, James. See Gaia
Luther, Martin, and enclosures in Germany, 137

Madison, James, on need for government to counteract individual ambitions, 181
Malthus, Thomas: *Essay on the Principles of Population*, 2, 53, 165; and George's refutation of, including revisions by Malthus, 3, 28, 110; fallacious mathematics methodology of, 28; as founder of demography, 45; ideological biases of, 46; on unfavourable ratio between food and population, 52, 172; *Inquiry into the Nature and Progress of Rent*, and influence on Ricardo, 53; on land rent as surplus income, as due to population and labour force increase, lowering wages, 54-56; vice, misery, and moral restraint as populations checks, 56; aware of tenure system effect on land supply and population growth rates, 57; fears that land reform would increase population and provoke economic crisis, 63; damaging influence on demography, as he saw nature as limited, human poverty as inevitable, 66; theories of linked to defense of landlords against egalitarian theories which might deprive them of their land, 67; and Malthusian trap, 77; as discoverer of proximate, not basic, poverty cause, 78; and subsistence crises, 93; denial by of correlated interests of community and individual, 164; hypotheses opposed to those of, 169
Manifest destiny, as euphemism for territory claimed by might, 111
Mansholt Plan, to remedy effects of European land subdivision, 63
Market forces: and ecologic preservation, 31-32; freed by land value tax to be cooperative, voluntary exchange, 40
Marx, Karl: collapse of influence of, ix, 152; socialist philosophy of response to unequal land access, 75; on army of surplus workers, 80, n4; and distribution system, 173

Maximization, as rational human behaviour, 35, 37; sometimes ecologically destructive, 41
McEvoy, Arthur F., critic of commons 'myth', 177, 179
Medicine, socialized, as commonization, exploited by liability lawyers, 177
Migration, within a nation, to ease overpopulation, 73
Mill, John Stuart: rejection of Malthus's mathematics by, 28; on tax of future land value increments, 29; *On Liberty*, 30
Mineral rights, varying national laws on, 135
Mohawk Indians, and conflict with Canada over enclosures, 137
Monopoly. See Land monopoly
Moral dilemma, of poverty amidst plenty, 65, 68
Morality, relative to time, 38
More, Sir Thomas, and land, population in Utopia, 99
Mortality. See Demographic transition
Mosaic law, to curb concentrated land ownership, 100
Myrdal, Gunnar, on effects of instituting property rights and monetization in colonies, 97-98; on reform of land tenure as primary need, preceding all other reforms, 102

Nations: poor, and population problems, trends, living standards of, 4, 18-19; effects of renouncing absolute sovereignty by, 14; need of to recognize Lockean proviso, proportionate sharing of land value rents, including paying those with subproportionate shares, 128. See Territory
Need, as basis of wealth allocation leads to greed, 176
Neo-Lockean justification, of national claims to land, 109
Nisbet, Robert, on Turgot and progress, 162
Non-profit organizations, as best depositories for excess land value rent from citizens on voluntary basis, prior to institutional change, 127-28
Nozick, Robert, and relationship between his ideas on libertarian communities and Tideman's, 110; on utopia, 160
Nutrition, effect of on fecundity, 167

Oceans: as unmanaged commons accelerating towards exhaustion, 2, 178; worldwide conflicts over resources division of, 138
Ornstein, Robert. See Ehrlich
Oxfam. See Whittemore
Ozanne, Julian, on population pressure on Kenyan economy, 70

Parenting opportunities, as limited resource subject to, rules, allocation, 123-24

Index

Parking meter, Hardin's example of fee, varied by time used, as commons change, like land tax varied by value, 40

Pastoralism, effects of humans' transition to from hunting, and gathering, 49

Peace, advantages for when territorial claims are based on proportionality of Lockean proviso, 109, 115, 125, 128

Pearce, David, on pollution fees to offset other taxes, 89

Peasants, war with German landlords over enclosures, 137

Penn, William, on land rent tax for community needs, viii

Pensions, effects of as safeguard against poverty, 139

Philanthropy, guided by dubious demographic ideas, 171-72. See also Demographic transition

Philippines: unfair land tenure in forces internal migration to alleviate population pressures, 73, 94

Philosophy, moral, as guide for evaluation of commons models proposed to solve socioecologic problems, 146

Pitt the Younger, and reversal of his support for poor after reading Malthus, 67

Plethoric state, theory of population decrease, 165-69

Pliny the Elder, on latifundia, 83

Pollution: effect of on earth's self-regulating system, 7; attempts to curb, difficulty of showing damage by, 7; financial transfers to offset incomes foregone from not polluting, 8, 9; individual vs. government responsibility for, 36; fees to curb, proposed by Hardin, like George's tax, 39; internal vs. external consequences of, effect on commonwealth's land values, 122-23; need for better data, technology, and self-discipline concerning, 142-43; as significant use of Remaining Commons, 142; other ways to curb, 143. See also Pearce

Poor Law, England's first the result of land enclosures, 98

Popper, Sir Karl, on need for freedom in search for truth, 146; condemnation by, as historicism, of ideas like demographic transition, 171

Population:
control: effectiveness and ethics of, 2-3, 15-16, 20-21, 63; individual and institutional, 16, 75, 160, n4; vital to avoid environmental doom, 29-30, 183; Malthus's checks of vice, misery, moral restraint, 56-57; unnecessary in just society, George demonstrates, 63; conflicting ideas on, 166-67; parenting opportunities as limited resource, subject to allocation and rules, 123-34

Population — *continued*
excess: concept of implies poverty or resource depletion as fate, 69-70, 110, 123; illogic in theories of, 168-69

growth rate: exponential in last 200 years, creating socioecologic instability and conflict, 1-12, 15, 17-18, 45, 48, 59, 72-74, 123, 136, 139, 162, 164-69; varied by national wealth, quality of life (including financial value of children), sexual equality, 18-19, 99

maldistribution: chief problem of Africa, Latin America, 103-5

problems: caused by landlessness, resultant low wages, 28, 77-79, 85, 90, 105; by poverty, not fertility, 85; by poorer nations importing culture, health measures of richer, 93; a possible concern under Lockean proviso, 123; rise in conflict, 136, 139; relative to growth of food supply, 164-65

size: relative to economic growth and living standards, 1-6; UN data, 2; less important than stability and sustainability, 50; Population Crisis Committee data, 50; worldwide, as basis for each individual's proportional land resources claim, 109, 117; forecasts, 139; link to poverty, 168

theories: (Malthus) to postulate impossibility of achieving better living standards for all, 53; to confute charge that land tenure system causes poverty, 69; on marginal land of unmanaged commons, 95; (Ricardo) effect of spatial basis of rent on, 74; (providence) 167-69; (fallacious) 166-69. See also Demographic transition; Demography; Longage; Malthus; Reproduction

Positional economy, goods of as status symbols leading to waste of natural resources, 92

Poverty: caused by institutional maladjustment of unjust land tenure systems, including spread of Roman law and rise of cash economy, not population rise, 27, 77-78, 81, n30, 83-84, 95-104, 110, 140-41; wider meaning of in environmental terms, 28; rights of poor people usually subordinate to rights of property, 64; of poor nations builds wealth of rich nations, 105

Principles of Political Economy and Taxation. See Ricardo

Private enterprise and private philanthropy as two systems of use of environment, 40

Production: increase in from capital accumulation has no effect on population pressure on wages, 56; lags in when labourer gets no return of rent on his land, according to Malthus, 59-60; higher and cheaper on family farm, 94; alternative ways of organizing, 159; and trade, unlimited freedom proposed for, 174-75;

Progress and Poverty. See George
Property rights: need for periodic reexamination of exclusionary power of private land tenure as social justice concepts alter, 38, 51; subordinate to equal interests of every member of society, 64; transformation of for stable society, 76, 82, n36; inequitable and environmentally destructive, 84; private, as best for progress and productivity, questioned, 84; traditionally based on might and history, ideally based on equal claims of all humans, present and future, 109; for preservation of environment, 131; laws on and differences in alternative modes of, 134-46; private, not dependent on outright resource ownership, 147; recognition of required by trade, 147; not equitable in property or created by persona, 154. See also Land tenure; Rothbard
Protectionism. See Trade
Providence: definition, examples of ideas on, 162; benign demographic transition and, 170-72; idea of threatened by longage of people or their demands, 182-83

Quality of life, improved, 4; and environmental degradation, 28. See also Living standards
Quasi-rent, as return to person's inherent talent, 154

Rationing, of nonproducibles within a nation and between nations, 88-89
Reader, John, confusing historic with global commons, 37
Reagan, Ronald, and failed antipoverty policies because of failure to deal with cause, 68
Recession, and land speculation, viii. See also Business cycle; Land
Redclift, Michael, on landlessness and forced labor in Latin America, 94; on conflicts between peasant farmers and rentiers, 97; critical of Brandt Report, which fails to show poverty caused by unequal access to natural resources, 100
Reeves, Mrs. Pember, on quality of life rise link to population fall, 168
Rent. See Land rent
Reproduction: exponential rate of normal, in absence of environmental resistance, 16, 165; unlimited individual right to vs. right to burden society with children which parents can't or won't support, 30; right of, at will, in conflict with right to equal per capita distribution of earth's resources, 183. See also Fertility; Hardin; Lloyd; Population; Society
Resources, natural: human destruction of, 5, 70; and national monopoly of, 13; and global vs. national rights to, 14; preservation

Resources — *continued*
of, and global community, 25; humanity's survival dependent on ability to synchronize needs and desires with availability of, 49; wasted in 'positional economy', 94; ownership of by poor nations enables bargaining with richer nations, 97; best allocation of lease auctions, 114-15, 156; and factors of technology, timing, 120-21; assessment of more difficult than of earth's surface, 120-21; users of to pay into fund for future generations, 121; national conflicts over, 136; and sea-beds, 133; need for better use of because of rising populations, 140-42; sufficient, though limited, if demands can be curbed responsibly, 182-83
Responsibility, in relation to commons and society, 176. See also Hutterite
Revenue: three factors of sufficiency of, 121; chief source should be excess of land rents in developed areas over undeveloped areas, 122. See also Land rent; Land value tax
Rhetoric, effects of, in thought and action, on world, 183
Ricardo, David: *Principles of Political Economy and Taxation,* rent theory of and Malthus's attempt at integration with demographic theory, 53-54; on differences with Malthus, 53-56; and *The High Price of Bullion,* 164. See also Land; Population
Richards, David: on changing legal concepts of land and on other parts of global commons, 23
Roman Law, as cause of socioecologic crisis, 83-85; examples of, 134-35
Rothbard, Murray, on ownership based on transformation of any previously unowned thing, 112-13

Sampson, Antony, and *The Midas Touch,* on cycle of poverty and environmental destruction, 105
Schoeck, Helmut, on envy as taboo concept and word, 182
Scotland, enclosure conflicts in, 137
Sea-bed, current national policies on, and implications, 132-33; as model for best use of Last Commons, 148-49
Searle, Geoffrey, on British socialists' views that higher quality of life lowers birth rate, 167-68
Self-interest: failure of appeal to, 11; and individual excess; short- and long-term effects of, 173
Shame, as individual awareness of irresponsibility towards commons which decreases as population increases, 180-81
Sismondi, J. C. L. S. de, translator of on higher quality of life resulting in lower birth rate, 167

Smith, Adam: and land rent tax, viii; on redistribution of land to landless, 65-66; and poverty alleviation, had his view prevailed, 67; and 'invisible hand' as economic providence, in *The Theory of Moral Sentiments*, and *The Wealth of Nations*, 163

Socialism: failure of, ix, 75, 152; Hardin's use of term, 38; as system of use of environment, 40

Society: polarized in terms of wealth distribution, 59, 84; and responsibility to provide sustainable environment for individual, through equal land access, 64; interdependence of its goals of ecology, efficiency, and equity, 147; planned vs. unplanned, 164. See also Humanity

South Africa, apartheid in and inequitable land tenure, 103

Speculation. See Land

Spence, Thomas, jailed for land value tax advocacy, 82, n36

Spinoza, Baruch, and land rent tax, viii

Stability, as vital land tenure principle, 50

Subsistence: crises of predicted by Malthus, 93; insecurity of in poorer nations causes population rise, 93

Substitution theory, of population decrease, 166

Sudan, land ownership recent and exploitive in, 104

Summary View of the Principle of Population A, as Malthus's mature revision of his ideas, 53

Sustainability, as vital land tenure principle, 45, 48, 50, 147

Swinbank, Alan, on farmers who compete to buy land rather than to lower production costs, 91-92

Tax: poll, English, as absurd fiscal policy, 81-82, n33; of rental income, 86; reduction as efficient distribution of land rent, 87; can include others besides that on land rent, if citizens so decide, 110; on labour, capital, likely cut as commonwealths compete for citizens, 121; as way to combat pollution, 143; reform as aid to free market variation of Business As Usual model, 153; as a payment with nothing in return, 154-55

Technology: effects of on population growth, 3; effects of on pollution, on living standards, 9; simpler as well as more advanced needed, 143; and relationship to progress, 163; and increased ability to alter environment, 165

Teen mothers, and costs to taxpayer, 30n

Teitelbaum, Michael, and criticism of benign demographic transition as unscientific, 171

Telephilanthropy, as aid targeted on people distant in space or ethnic characteristics,

Telephilanthropy — *continued*
171. See also Philanthropy

Television, increased viewing of theorized as birth curb, 166

Temple, Archbishop, on self-interest and justice, 36

Tenure, of property, security of more important than ownership 147

Territory:
claims to: of nations traditionally justified by power, not conducive to peace, should be justified by proportional claims of individual citizens, 111, 115, 125; portability of, 116-17; number of claimants as equitability factor, 117; evaluation of, 117; clearinghouse of to compensate subproportionate claimants, 121; equal sharing of as proposed norm, on which good citizens can act before institutional change, 127

limits to: Lockean proviso as guide to what individual can claim, 114; use of (as flow of services) satisfies Lockean proviso without exhausting land, 114; increasingly extended over adjacent seas by nations, 138

rental value: based on fertility, location, other factors, 117-18; and exclusion value, due to current and historic use, 118-20; approximation of, especially between nations, at boundary, 119

resources: use of as basis for claim on, as long as claims consistent with Lockean proviso, 113. See also Commons; Land

Thatcher, Margaret, and failure of antipoverty programs because of failure to deal with basic cause, 68

Theory of Moral Sentiments, The. See Smith

Tideman, Nicolaus, and nation-state's moral authority, 13

Tiebout, Charles, and relationship of his voluntary communities based on neo-Lockean proviso, 111

Time, as critical factor in search for commons solution, 143

Todaro, Michael: on problems of rural migration to cities, 92; on landlords and power, 94, 98-99

Torbel, commons in Switzerland, 36

Torrey, Archer, on history of biblical land laws, 83

Townsend, Joseph, on link between rising wealth and rising population, 169

Trade: and Malthus's opposition to free, 67; international favours developed nations over undeveloped, 93-94; as better than war in providing resources 147; tariffs, union curbs and privileges, as curbs on, 175

Tragedy of the Commons, The. See Hardin

Turgot. See Nisbet

United Nations: population forecasts by and implications of if George and Ricardo are ignored, 74; and Brandt Report, 100; Food and Agriculture Organization World Conference on Agrarian Reform and Rural Development, 101; and report on Determinants and Consequences of Population Trends, 174
US Bureau of Land Management, and land abuse, 95
USA, development of as example of Business As Usual, 152-53
USSR, whale catches by as commons abuse, 35-36; and land tenure in, 96
Utopia, and other models of commons use, 99, 160

Value, subjective and economic, 120
Veblen, Thorstein, on speculators, 91
Voluntarism, importance of in implementing commonwealth proposal, 127

Wade, Nicholas, on Sahel desertification caused by Western aid policies, 38
Wages: higher when land rent is taxed and labour is not, viii; as determined by labour on rent-free margin, 54; fund theory and Ricardo's use of, 56; fall in when population rises without access to land, 56
Walle, Etienne van de, on Africa as example contradicting benign demographic transition, 171
War, of benefit to few, harm to many, 147
Water, increased national claims to in oceans, 14-15; as abused commons in excessive

Water — *continued*
irrigation
Wealth of Nations, The. See Smith
Wealth: allocation of, 87, 176; and ability to increase through ownership of national and international lands, 101; rise in as link to lower fertility questioned, 169
Webb, Sidney and Beatrice, in *Industrial Democracy*, on working class, wealth, and population rate, 168
Welfare: less need for under land rent tax system, viii; undeserved if individual reproduces beyond ability to care for children, 63-64
Weston, David, on car as status symbol, 93
Whales, decimation of by selfishness of USSR, 35-36
Whitehead, Alfred North, on need to place propositions in correct context, 177
Whittemore, Claire, and Oxfam publication, *Land for People*, 101
Wilderness, ecologic value of and effect on land rent, 122
Wolf, Martin, on fair distribution of land entitlements, 88
World Bank: and poverty data by similar groups used to justify population control, 72; on rural hunger, 100; wrong policies of, 104
World federalism, and Moon Treaty of as forerunner to Law of the Sea Convention, 150

Zero Population Growth, Inc., as organization which blames overpopulation on individual instead of institutions, 174